Champion of Sail

R W Leyland (1842–1921)

Champion of Sail

R W Leyland and his
Shipping Line

DAVID WALKER

DEDICATION

To Adèle Sharples who started me on the road to my discoveries and to Nicholas David Leyland Walker who entered the world just as the final draft was about to be written.

Note. All illustrations not otherwise credited are from the author's collection.

First published in 1986 by Conway Maritime Press Ltd, 24 Bride Lane, Fleet Street, London EC4Y 8DR

ISBN 0 85177 402 4

Designed by Dave Mills
Typesetting and page make-up by C R Barber & Partners (Highlands) Ltd
Printed and bound by R J Acford, Chichester

Contents

Preface

My interest in R W Leyland's shipping activities started at an early age. My grandmother, his daughter, recalled many stories from her youth and in her flat was a large oil painting of the shipowner, which although not a beautiful work of art, was inspiring. The part that Leyland played in Liverpool shipping circles, and the impact his ships had internationally, I did not fully appreciate until much later. In about 1973 I discovered several volumes of private letters written by Leyland, together with partnership deeds and company reports, which led to much further research. At about the same time I heard that the *Wavertree* was being restored in New York. In spite of the many difficulties, all those involved in her restoration at the South Street Seaport Museum have done a wonderful job. It is perhaps ironic to note that much of R W Leyland's ambition to become a sailing ship owner was born during the time he spent in the region of Buenos Aires and surprisingly, it was here that the *Wavertree* was found about a hundred years later.

Over the last twelve years, my enquiries have taken me to many places and I have had some very interesting conversations with different people. There are several people, however, who deserve special mention. Mr Neville Langley has been a generous benefactor, retrieving many details and making discoveries in the United States. My thanks to the staff at the National Maritime Museum, Greenwich, London and my grateful appreciation to Mr Alex Hurst and Mr Richard Cookson for the use of some of their material. Permission to quote from Basil Lubbock's *The Last of the Windjammers* Vol II was kindly granted by Messrs Brown, Son and & Ferguson, Ltd, Glasgow, and Binford & Mort Publishing gave permission to reproduce two photographs (p162) from *Pacific Graveyard* by J A Gibbs. Mr Michael Stammers, Curator of the Merseyside Maritime Museum, has not only provided the introduction but he has inspired me to keep going, and the completion of this work owes a great deal to him. My thanks, also, to Mrs Harriet Brooke and Mrs Susan Adams for typing the manuscript and to my wife, for being patient while the work was being written.

David Walker

Yalding, Kent
September 1985

A photograph of King's Dock taken in the early 1890s from Queen's Dock. In the foreground next to the old cast-iron swing-bridge is a 'wenner packet' steamer, and in the background many deep-sea square-rigged vessels, behind which are the Wapping warehouses with a clock on the end wall.

MERSEYSIDE MARITIME MUSEUM

Introduction

Commercial sailing ships and the men who owned and sailed them have vanished with the passage of time. But their fascination remains: the adventure, the hardship, and above all the beauty and romance of the sailing ship era have a potent allure for modern man. This was powerfully demonstrated on the Mersey in August 1984 when no less than a million people lined its shore to witness the departure of the sail training ships in the Tall Ships Race. More than half a century after the last square-rigger was struck from the Liverpool register and nostalgia had had its way it is far too easy to forget that these beautiful and sometimes deadly ships were run for profit and not for sentiment, and this is as true for the Leyland fleet as any other. When they made losses they were sold.

By the latter half of the nineteenth century Liverpool was the second port of the kingdom after London. In fact it was first for exports and it still controlled the great transatlantic passenger trade. The dock authority had invested vast sums in building docks to accommodate the ever growing number of vessels using the port. Almost six miles of docks lined the north bank of the Mersey with another three running inland from the south bank at Birkenhead. A growing proportion of these docks were devoted to the liner trades – regular steamer services carrying freight to and from all the continents of the world – lines like the Pacific Steam Navigation Company to South America (locally known as the Birkenhead Navy), the Blue Funnel line to the Far East and Australia, the Bibby Line to Burma, the Clan Line to India and East Africa, Elder Dempster to West Africa, and many more.

In the 1860s not a few of these lines had relied on sail, especially on the long haul routes. But the development of economical compound steam engines, the establishment of the worldwide network of coal depots for refuelling and the opening of the Suez Canal paved the way for the steam cargo liner to take over the regular and high freight rate trades from the sailing ship. They could offer a quicker and more regular service at comparable cost. But the sailing ship did not disappear. There were increasing quantities of low cost bulk cargoes, like grain from the West Coast of the USA, Argentina and Australia to Europe to feed the Continent's growing industrial population, and coal from South Wales. Sailing ships grew larger and were built in iron and later steel and were equipped with stronger spars and more labour saving appliances such as capstans and steam donkey engines to make them highly competitive in these kinds of bulk trade. Leyland ships were among the biggest and the finest of this last generation of bulk carrying sailing ships. Many of these vessels discharged at Liverpool but there were problems. With the pressure on dock facilities they were increasingly confined to the older smaller docks, eg The Salthouse, Albert, Canning, Queen's and King's docks of the south docks area. The congestion was worse there and the rate of discharge slower. The other problem was that there were fewer and fewer outward cargoes on offer, apart from salt which usually paid a low return and was slow to load from Mersey barges (flats). Nevertheless Liverpool was very much a sailing ship centre. The Exchange or 'Change as it was known locally, was an active market for fixing freights for sailing ships. The local banks were happy to finance investment in sail, and there was a substantial body of local sailing ship owners. For instance, in 1889 the Liverpool Sailing Ship Owners Mutual Indemnity Association had 1,740,014 tons of shipping in its membership. R W Leyland as a leading owner was on its committee. Most of these ships traded voyage by voyage – tramping – and rarely saw their home port.

The end of the next decade saw the beginning of the end of this vast local fleet. The prolonged depression of rates plus competition from cheaper flags, notably the Scandinavians, caused many local sailing ship owners to sell or lay up their vessels. Some got out of shipowning or concentrated on ship brokerage, and others, including Leyland, were able to gather enough resources to make the extra investment to buy steamers. By the outbreak of the First World War the once great Liverpool sailing ship fleet had been reduced to a very small flotilla of ageing vessels and in the war itself many of these fell victim to German submarines. It was the end of the Liverpool sailing ship and her owners. Since then a lot has been written about these last windjammers but much of this work has been concentrated on the ships and not the people involved in their management. David Walker's indefatigable research into his own family of shipowners greatly helps to fill the gap in our knowledge of the last of the Liverpool sailing ship owners.

Michael Stammers,
Curator of the Merseyside Maritime Museum

Lime Street, Liverpool. St George's Hall is on the left of the picture with the Walker Art Gallery and the Court House in the background. These opulent buildings reflect the wealth of the United Kingdom's second port.

MERSEYSIDE MARITIME MUSEUM

Bird's eye view of Liverpool, as seen from a balloon. This picture first appeared in a supplement to the *Graphic* on 22 August 1885. In the left background is St George's Hall and Lime Street. Note the immense area of docks and warehouses on the waterfront. Twenty years later St George's dock in the middle foreground was filled in to make way for the new headquarters buildings of the Mersey Docks and Harbour Board, the Cunard Steam Ship Company and the Royal Liver Insurance Company. Just to the right of this is the area of Albert Dock which has been restored and developed to form the Merseyside Maritime Museum.

NATIONAL MARITIME MUSEUM

Part One

The Company

Old-style dock work. A cargo of sugar is unloaded and weighed.
MERSEYSIDE MARITIME MUSEUM

CHAPTER ONE

Early Years

In the early 1860s Ralph Watts Leyland made an extended tour of the Mediterranean for the benefit of his health and stayed in Constantinople for some time. A little later he went to South America for three years where he worked on the Pampas and in Buenos Aires. It was during this time in South America that he learnt a great deal about shipping and many of the business contacts he made during this period were useful to him in his later shipping company.

In about 1867 Leyland, having returned from South America and with no particular occupation in mind, joined a friend in a marine insurance business in Liverpool. It is not known who this person was that helped Leyland out in his early business career or whether R W Leyland was a partner in the firm. Certainly, one of the people with whom he had close contact at this time was Alexander Cassels of the shipping firm W H Ross & Company of Liverpool, but no further details of his business are known. However, in 1869 Cassels was appointed as an underwriter to a marine insurance company and R W Leyland, with his younger brother George Richardson Leyland, took over the broker business in his own name and opened an account with the Bank of Liverpool the same year. The two brothers rented a small office in the basement of Exchange Buildings in Liverpool and for a few years carried on the work of insurance brokers.

The Leyland brothers were reasonably successful and by the late 1870s they regularly insured about a hundred sailing ships and these were insured two or three times a year on various voyages. Early in 1880 Leyland tried to expand his business and at the beginning of the year they

Canning Dock and Customs House, Liverpool.
NATIONAL MARITIME MUSEUM

were asked to take over the Liverpool Mutual Marine Insurance Association. He wished to extend his business to Newcastle and through Mr Dickie, a broker in Glasgow, he felt he could build up contacts for many thousands of pounds of insurance on steamers. He proposed a new venture with Mr Dickie in which together they would charge a 5 per cent brokerage to principals of steamship companies and split the proceeds equally. Leyland wrote to Mr Dickie:

> Our object in going together being that we would introduce you to the offices and urge our friends to give you the speciality for Glasgow, and work it as far as we could into your hands, – while you, by your personal interviews with principals, would explain to them the terms of the Glasgow underwriters business, the nature of payments, settlement of losses and probable premiums according to voyages.

However, this enterprise never materialised and the gentleman withdrew his contact with the Leyland brothers, since he felt there would be great difficulty in finding underwriters for East Coast steamers.

Nevertheless, Leyland was not to be deterred and in May 1880 he wrote to Mr W Bromham in Hull trying to force him to use his contacts with shipping companies. He believed it would be cheaper for the underwriters and principals of shipping companies in the long term if they joined his association.

All this seems to have produced results, for Leyland later revealed that they were dealing with two sets of Glasgow underwriters in addition to their regular business at Lloyds. They had also put out contacts for a new clerk for their association at a salary of £80–£100 a year, and had decided that they were not going to go into the underwriting business in their own name. It must

One of the older ships the firm purchased was the *British India*, an iron ship with a registered net tonnage of 1199 tons built in 1868 by Laird Brothers, Birkenhead. This scene of their shipyard was produced at about the same time.
MERSEYSIDE MARITIME MUSEUM

have been about this time that they realised that competition was becoming so great in the insurance broking world that it would be wise for them to turn their full attention to shipping. Marine insurance had in fact been undergoing some serious changes because in former days it was confined to Lloyd's and private firms, to whom the brokers were useful. However, with the appearance of large public companies which began to take up the business it made it even more difficult for the middlemen, the brokers, to carry on. In order to turn their attention to something more profitable, the Leyland brothers persuaded Arthur J Preston a senior partner in the firm of Preston and Peachy in London, to join them in Liverpool. Leyland recorded in his letters: 'We have made arrangements with him by which he leaves his firm, and comes down to us in Liverpool, as manager of our insurance business.' With this expansion in their business they moved from one office within Exchange Buildings to 19/20 Exchange Buildings which was at the heart of the shipping community, and they were thus able to turn their attentions to their shipping business.

First Ventures in Shipowning

The Leyland brothers had been involved in shipping for several years through the ownership of some shares in vessels held by other companies. They had confined themselves to an interest in sailing ships, mainly iron vessels, as with their insurance, since neither of them had any knowledge of steamers and R W Leyland had picked up a great deal of knowledge about sailing vessels in his earlier days abroad. However, they started their own business in shipping by purchasing several old sailing vessels from other companies, and one nineteenth century Liverpool book refers to the *Pride of Wales* as the first ship that the two brothers owned in 1874. There is no indication of their ownership of this vessel in any surviving records but it may well be that they held a few shares in this ship which was managed by Alexander Ramage & Company of Liverpool. In a sales ledger of the shipbroking firm C W Kellock & Company there is a reference to the sale of the *Pride of Wales* to Ramage for £7400 on 10 December 1873.

However, on 16 October 1875 C W Kellock & Company purchased the *Doxford* for £8000 on behalf of R W Leyland & Company. This was the first vessel bought and also managed by the Leyland brothers. She was an iron barque of 682 tons net with an overall length of 178ft, built by W Doxford & Sons, Sunderland in 1868. Until Leyland bought her she was owned by Horatio Nelson Hughes whose office was at 5 Chapel Street, Liverpool. The change of ownership of the vessel was registered on 30 October 1875, with R W Leyland purchasing all 64 shares. Hughes kept an indirect ownership of part of the vessel through a mortgage of £1000 to R W Leyland but this was not registered until nearly three years later. A short time after the purchase of the vessel Leyland sold four shares to a Liverpool shipowner, John Murray Gladstone, who thereafter supplied the sails for subsequent Leyland vessels. He was a relation by marriage of Leyland and was a very close business contact with the two brothers. Ten shares were sold to their cousin Joseph Angelis Dominic Watts and a further twelve shares to a Manchester merchant, Adam Skelly Orr. A little later, Leyland sold two shares to his brother G R Leyland but these were the only two shares that were registered in his partner's name. Thomas Henry Withers was appointed master of the *Doxford* and so that he had some interest in the ship the company asked him to purchase four shares. He was able to do this partly by securing a loan from Gladstone. The effect of the sale of these shares meant that R W Leyland retained 34 shares and thus was the registered managing owner of the vessel, even though part of the shares he held in this vessel were subject to a mortgage with the previous owner.

For the next four years the two brothers continued in their marine insurance business and it was not until August 1879 that they bought their second vessel from J M Gladstone. This seems a long period of time when one looks at their rapid purchase of new ships in the middle 1880s. The *Doxford* appears to have been a successful vessel with which to start their shipping company, but the delay in purchasing their second ship seems to indicate that it was not until about 1878 that they decided to turn their attentions fully to their shipping business rather than to marine insurance. The *San Luis* was a three-masted barque like the *Doxford*, with a slightly lower gross tonnage of 600 tons, and built in 1864 by T Royden & Sons, Liverpool. R W Leyland purchased 22 of the 64 shares on 19 August 1879 and by a letter of the same date he was registered as the managing owner of the vessel. His brother-in-law, John Thompson, had held eight shares in this vessel for the previous seven years and presumably it was through him that the business transaction was secured. Leyland sold several shares almost immediately to various people, including his brother G R Leyland and E E Talbot, an insurance broker in Rumford Street, Liverpool who also had purchased two shares in the earlier Leyland vessel *Doxford* by this date. This left Leyland with only 13 shares; yet despite this minority interest he was managing owner of the vessel. By spreading the ownership of the vessel he was able to acquire more ships under his management, with the shares being held by close business contacts or members of the family.

Another clear example of this control of a vessel by owning only a few shares in it can be seen in the case of their third ship, the *Nelson*. This was a three-masted, full-rigged ship of a considerably larger tonnage, 1248 tons. She had been built in 1862 and owned by a well-known Liverpool merchant, James Beazley, and had been registered with the British Shipowners Company Limited, Liverpool of which Mr Beazley was managing owner. On 11 May 1880 this company sold R W Leyland 48 shares in the vessel and thus Leyland was registered as the managing owner of the ship. However, over the next four months Leyland sold 22 of these shares to a variety of people, retaining only 26 shares, but these were sufficient to let him retain the managing interest of the ship. Eight shares were sold to John Piggott, a Liverpool merchant, and two shares were sold to two brothers by the name of Hopps. His cousin Mr Watts of Grassendale Park also purchased four shares in this vessel, to add to those which he already held in the *Doxford*. Once again Mr Talbot purchased two shares. Later in the year, in October 1880, G R Leyland was able to acquire the remaining shares which the British Shipowners Company still possessed. George Barker, a Liverpool brewer and a relation of Leyland, also purchased some shares from him a year later.

The Leylands purchased the *Nelson* for £7500 and again the shipbrokers C W Kellock & Company were responsible for the sale. The vessel was berthed in the Salthouse Dock, Liverpool. Edward Watkins was appointed master and with his appointment to the command of the vessel he was expected to purchase 6/64ths of the vessel, to ensure that as master he had some financial interest in the ship under his command. This was a considerable sum of money for Captain Watkins and he had some difficulty in finding it. Leyland wrote to Captain Watkins' solicitors:

> We could have had half a dozen commanders for the vessel who were to put down a £1000 each for the shares and the command but we preferred Watkins as he was mate in one of our vessels previously. We have made up our ownery – including Captain Watkins for six 64ths – and the last of the money must be paid on Monday. We cannot pretend to advance money ourselves for these shares as we have quite enough to do to find money for our own shares. If Watkins cannot pay the money on Monday he forfeits his 10% deposit and of course his agreement as to command with us falls to the ground.

Some agreement must have been made with Watkins for he did not purchase three shares in the ship until sixteen months later in September 1881, and the rest of the shares he purchased in September 1882.

Sometimes the purchase of shares in the vessel could involve an additional business agreement. For instance, he wrote to F Nodin, a well known Liverpool shipowner: 'In consideration of your taking $\frac{1}{8}$th interest in the *Nelson* with us, we undertake that all freighting or chartering during our management should be done through you, for which you are to receive $1\frac{1}{4}$% brokerage.' However, this agreement only caused complications later as Nodin thought that the Leyland brothers were going to put all their freighting or chartering through them for all their ships.

The *Nelson* sailed to Galle in one hundred days and from there she went to Calcutta and Leyland wrote to one shareholder: 'We look for a happy return on this vessel.'

Their shipping business had started to go reasonably well although the value of the *Doxford* was 'not so high at present as when we bought her, although we expect in a year or two the value will have risen nearly to what we originally paid. I should think on 27 June last [1880] the vessel would have been worth £6500.' However, the *Nelson* was valued at £10,600 and this was much more than they had paid for her. Leyland wrote to a shareholder: 'You might reasonably take a percentage off both of these as shares of ships are not relatively as valuable as the whole ship.' Even so the return on capital outlay in ships under their management was fairly worthwhile and the encouragement of shareholders made them look further afield to expand their shipping empire.

Although R W Leyland & Company managed and largely owned some other smaller vessels such as the *Thomas Hamlin*, 688 tons, which they had purchased in July 1880, they started to turn their attention to acquiring larger vessels from other companies. For instance in February 1881 Leyland wrote to his sister Mary saying that they had just purchased the iron ship *Gitana* of 1367 tons for £10,400. She had been built twenty years earlier but: 'We think there is a good prospect of making money out of her.' He encouraged John and Mary Thompson to take one share each for 'it is not a very large outlay and I think you may reasonably reckon on 20 per cent per annum out of it.'

At the same time as Leyland was encouraging people to buy shares of vessels in his ownership he also requested the Bank of Liverpool to extend the overdraft on their company to £10,000 if required, so that they could further extend their business. As security for this sum they offered their working capital in the business which was valued at £15,000 and the profit upon that. They also offered as security their 2/5ths interest in the estate of their late father, Mr Ralph Leyland, which probably amounted to £14,000 at this date.

With this security the bank agreed, and Leyland purchased another ship, the *British India*, built in 1864 by Laird Brothers, Birkenhead. He purchased 48 shares from the British Shipowners Company Limited of Liverpool and again sold a number of these shares shortly after, mainly to people such as George Barker and John Piggott, who had already invested in his ships, and for the first time to one of his other brothers, Henry Leyland. The rest of the shares in the British Shipowners Company were sold to Leyland later in the year and in total he retained 30 shares, so once again he was the managing owner. As with several previous ships his partner G R Leyland only became involved in the ownership of the vessels at a later date.

First New Ship Ordered

They were now the proud owners of six sailing vessels, and in late summer 1881 they ordered their first ship – a vessel of a much larger size. This was the *Grassendale*, named after the village in which the family had a number of houses. In December 1881 he wrote to a potential shareholder:

> It so happens that we are building a fine new iron ship of about 1760 tons to be launched early next month. Contract

The *King Cenric*, a wooden ship that the Leylands owned for a few years before selling her to a Norwegian company in 1889. She was one of the older vessels with which the firm started in shipping.
NORSK SJØFARTSMUSEUM

> price £12 15s per ton. We have made this into a Limited Liability Company consisting of about 230 shares of £100. We can let you have a few of these shares if you care to have them. This is probably a better investment for you than a ship held in the ordinary manner as all liability on your part ceases on the payment up of the number of shares you care to take. The price of shares is advancing and we could not replace this vessel under considerable advance in price, and we look forward to receiving very good dividends from her. We insure the ship fully and cover all contingencies and in no case are you liable for more than the amount paid up. The vessel is to be called the *Grassendale*. Colonel Harrison and his sister Miss Harrison have each taken shares and also Captain Manning and Mrs Latham and Emma Parker. This being a limited company it is better suited as an investment for people not in business and ladies. We intend to make all our new ships for the future into Limited Liability Companies.

When she was launched in January 1882, the *Grassendale* was the first iron sailing ship to be built by R Williamson at their new yard in Workington. This vessel was 266ft long, had one deck, and was rigged as a three-masted ship. She was registered in Liverpool as the Sailing Ship Grassendale Company on 1 March 1882 with R W Leyland as managing owner.

The business continued to go well even though they had to increase their overdraft once more with the Bank of Liverpool by a further £2500. In justifying this Leyland wrote: 'During the next four months we shall collect nearly £27,000 on freights of five incoming vessels that we manage and are largely owned by ourselves. The vessels are chartered – cargoes on board – and homeward bound.' As security they handed the bank stamped policies of insurance on the freight of the ships *Nelson* and *Gitana*.

The new ship required greater management than vessels held in the ordinary manner and there are a number of letters answering queries from shareholders. She was insured for £2000 more than they paid for her and she was also insured against capture and seizure. He revealed that members of the family held 22 shares in the ship whilst he and his brother held 26 and 22 shares respectively; so the family between them owned nearly a third of the vessel. He explained the company's policy on freights and cargo when he wrote:

> Every ship stands on its own merits, according to the port it is in – the season of the year – and the market rate of freight offering. It would be utterly impossible for us to give one ship a preference over another, we are entirely dependent on the freight market. Our great aim is to do the best for each ship, as the circumstances and opportunities offer.

Loss of the *Nelson*

The *Nelson*, which Leyland had purchased in 1880, was only to survive another 2½ years under the new management. After her journey to Galle and Calcutta she returned to Dundee, arriving in May 1881. She left South Shields for Valparaiso in June arriving in Caldera in September 1881. From here she went to Portland, Oregon and returned to England in August 1882. On 14 October 1882 she left South Shields for Valparaiso but only a few days later, on 25 October, she was abandoned in a sinking condition. The cargo of coal had shifted and the ship was on her beam ends. Two days later the ship was noticed abandoned and a steamer went to assist her but it was not until 3 November that it was reported in the *Lloyd's Weekly Summary* that the crew had been saved. The vessel eventually sank off Schouwen and over the next few days various pieces, including part of a white painted boat marked *Nelson* in blue letters, and from a sloop two painted rosettes decorated with a red flag marked with white letters, R W L + C, were washed ashore on the coast of Leesland (Zeeland).

A three-masted barque, in not dissimilar markings to a Leyland vessel, attracting some attention when ready to leave the Canning half tide dock in about 1895.
MERSEYSIDE MARITIME MUSEUM

More Orders and Purchases

Although the Leylands were presumably upset by the loss of this older unit of their fleet, they continued to purchase both old and new vessels. Shortly after the launch of the *Grassendale* they contracted with Williamson of Workington to build another ship, the *Aigburth*, of similar size to the *Grassendale*. They arranged to pay for her in three instalments, namely, at exchange of contracts on 1 June 1882, on launching which was expected in July, and on completion which was expected in August. The launching of this vessel was in fact delayed until October 1882. As well as these bills, they had outstanding two bills for the ship *Grassendale*.

Leylands had also placed another order with the same yard in 1883 for the steel ship *Garston*. This was the only steel vessel that they ordered until the giant three-masted ships *Speke* and *Ditton* in 1891. Leyland wrote to one shareholder concerning the *Garston*: 'The vessel is steel plated and will be an enormous carrier – therefore a profitable ship.'

One of the older ships which they bought at this time was the *Twilight*, an iron barque of 631 tons built by R Napier & Sons, Glasgow in 1855. In the 1880s she was owned by E Bates & Sons, and Edward Percy Bates looked after the management of the Liverpool office. He subsequently became an MP and in 1886 was made a baronet. From 1870 they began adding steamers to their fleet but they continued to acquire sailing ships until 1884. Their private letter books are deposited at the National Maritime Museum, Greenwich, London, and from these we are able to learn some details of the sale of the ship *Twilight* to Leyland. On 19 July 1882 Gilbert Bates wrote to his brother Ted; 'We shall sell her if we can find a purchaser. She is too small in these days.' A few days later on 24 July he observed, 'Have had no reasonable offer for *Twilight* – Kellock says £2500 now or £4 per ton.' The next day he noted that the ship was discharging. On 26 July he reported:

> *Twilight* – have sold as she stands to W and R Leyland [sic] for £3000 and deposit paid – I did this without Kellock's help but nevertheless told them to send in a contract – all cash in thirty days or their acceptance at six months and not more than half with 5% interest added. *Twilight* is 28 years old, has wooden bulwarks and stanchions and is, I think, well sold at £5 per ton.

The firm was well pleased with this sale and Leyland does not seem to have acquired a bargain here.

CHAPTER TWO

Golden Years

In 1883 the Leylands increased the size of their overdraft facility with the Bank of Liverpool to £15,000 in order to expand their business. They did this because they feared that not all the shares would have been paid for by the completion date for their new ship the *Cressington*, then in the course of construction at Southampton. This ship was launched on 22 November 1883 and was the first vessel of over 2000 tons to be built for the firm. She was also the first ship to be built for them by the well known shipbuilders Oswald, Mordaunt & Company of Southampton. Leyland had tried to persuade Mr Hardy Williamson to reduce his prices as they forecast a drop in demand for new ships but he had refused. T R Oswald, however, had offered £1 a ton less on his new ships and this was a considerable saving on these huge carriers. The shares were taken up fairly quickly and in one letter he listed the number of lawyers and people of influence in Liverpool who had bought shares in this ship. He wrote, 'The Head Manager of the Bank of Liverpool is a shareholder in this vessel, and the bulk of the rest of the shareholders are people with money – merchants, brokers etc.' The Leyland brothers were speculating fairly heavily and with some justification he could write 'We are always hard up – advancing for the ships.'

The *Cressington*

The *Cressington* after completion at the Woolston yard

An oil painting of the *Grassendale*, probably the one built in 1885 to replace the ship of the same name which had gone missing. Note the fact that unlike many Leyland ships of this period she lacked black and white painted ports. Most of the sailing ships built for the company were named after suburbs of Liverpool.
COURTESY MICHAEL STAMMERS

The *Aigburth*, the second vessel built for the company is seen here in about 1900 with part of her main topmast missing. She began her career with an accident on launching when she got stuck on a bank at the end of the ways. No damage was noticed but she had to be put into dry dock at Liverpool for inspection.
COURTESY J H REID

went round to load a cargo of railway iron, bricks, coal and coke at Cardiff for San Francisco. She had barely started her eventful career when she ran into trouble. In May 1884 in the High Court of Justice of the Admiralty Division a case of salvage was brought by the owner of a tug called *Mount Etna* against the owners of the *Cressington*. This concerned the amount of damage to the *Cressington*, the tug *Mount Etna* and another vessel. Apparently in the early evening of 12 January 1884 the *Cressington* with a crew of 36 hands was proceeding down the Cardiff drain in tow of the steam tug *Mount Etna*. In the course of being towed from the Cardiff docks into the Bristol Channel, the *Cressington* was in collision with another vessel, the *Firdene*, and was driven ashore off Penarth Head near Cardiff, where she lay upon a hard stone bottom in a position of extreme danger.

After the collision and before the *Cressington* went ashore, the *Mount Etna* got hold of a rope from the port quarter of the *Cressington* but could get no strain upon her before the *Cressington* grounded. After that the *Mount Etna*, with the assistance of two other tugs, got the *Cressington* afloat and towed her into dock. In the judgment on the cost of salvage it was pointed out that the tug was under a duty towards the vessel of which she was in charge and that she was responsible for not putting the vessel into a false position with an independent vessel. It was felt that the tug was entitled to the cost of some salvage but not on the same scale as if no collision had occurred. It was held that the tug had done no more than what she had been employed to do and that there would always be some danger in towing. The sum of £200 was deemed sufficient for the salvage.

The *Cressington*, after an eventful start to her career, served the company for 17 years before being sold to another Liverpool shipowner. Later she served under Italian owners before flying the Norwegian flag as the *Songvand* (seen here). In June 1917 she was sunk by submarines off the Scilly Isles on a passage from Cardiff to Santon.
NORSK SJØFARTSMUSEUM

The owners of the *Cressington* made representations to the underwriters for the cost of repairs but this was not the last of this incident. In July 1884 Leyland wrote a very long letter to the Vicar of Drayton about a comment the vicar's wife had made 'That all the money ought in honesty be returned back to the underwriters.' It seemed that Leyland had turned the incident into good effect. He wrote:

> It implies that I as manager of the Cressington Company am doing a dishonest action in arranging to make an apparent profit out of the accident of the ship at the expense of the underwriters.
>
> Now this is absolutely and entirely untrue and Mrs Howell is quite wrong in her premises. Nothing has been done without the full sanction and knowledge of the underwriters. I have not acted without authority from my co-owners and the full sanction of our underwriters. If by any small amount of skill and knowledge of shipping matters, we as managers have been able to turn the compromise with underwriters to good account – it is with the knowledge of underwriters, and they are quite satisfied it should be so. Suppose instead of the 50% being sufficient to cover the cost of repairs – that it had been insufficient! Do you suppose the underwriters would have given us any more? Certainly not.
>
> With the authority of my co-owners – and the sanction of underwriters, a compromise was arranged and it was reckoned by underwriters that this 50% was to include all repairs to ship – and to give compensation to the new vessel being damaged at commencement of voyage.
>
> Is our time, trouble and anxiety, and labour of travelling to and from and mentally calculating and arranging at Cardiff, to count for nothing? There was just the chance of much greater damage developing when the ship came to be opened out in the wrecked state in which she lay – this chance was taken by shareholders in general meeting assembled – on the strength of our opinion. Is all this to go for nothing? Risk, time, experience etc. etc.!
>
> Then too the ship carries more iron in her than necessary through repairs – thus displacing so much weight carrying power for cargo – and so much loss of freight per annum. It is trifling certainly – nevertheless it is against the ship. Then again the fact of having been ashore, and her back broken, necessitating heavy repairs, will always be against the vessel – more especially if we want to sell – though for all trading merchantable and insurable purposes the ship is as good as ever.
>
> There are dozens of pros and cons – impossible to write, or answer, unless suggested by question. Of course if you lived here and attended meetings you would hear all the questions thrashed out, and be able to satisfy yourself on every point. I want Mrs Howell to understand that this return to shareholders is perfectly right and that it is with the knowledge of underwriters in principle – though of course they have not exact figures, that is not their business. The underwriters claim the 50% from owners of *Firdene* which did all the damage, and will get as much as their state can yield. I do not like the word honest or dishonest being introduced – it is not applicable. My aim has always been to make 'a good name better than width'.

More New Ships

Leyland had ordered one more sailing ship from Williamson at a price of £9 per ton, which was commenced in October 1884 and launched in September 1885. This was a replacement for the *Grassendale*, which had disappeared the previous year after leaving New York for Shanghai with petroleum. They also purchased a new ship from the Palmers Shipbuilding Company, Jarrow which they named *Otterspool*. However, the rest of the Leyland sailing vessels were built by Oswald, Mordaunt & Company, Southampton.

Innovatory Ideas

With the construction of the *Cressington* a new phase in the history of R W Leyland & Company can be traced. In Thomas Oswald, Leyland found a man with similar daring and initiative to combat the problems of competition for sailing ships. Together they ushered in a whole new era of sailing ships by constructing even larger carriers, and the *Cressington*, the first of these, was the largest sailing ship to have been built at the Southampton yard. Between 1883 and 1887 Leyland contracted for 10 vessels from Oswald, Mordaunt & Company, creating his own distinctive style in both their size and construction. For instance, they averaged about 277ft in length and were constructed with a bold sweeping sheer and long bow overhang. Each ship was named after a district of Liverpool and they were painted with white lower masts, black topmasts and topgallant masts, white yards, bowsprit, boom and gaff. The hull was grey with red boot topping, and a row of painted ports on a white

The *Otterspool*, built in 1884 by Palmers Company of Newcastle, seen here in San Francisco.
COURTESY J H REID

band below the black painted bulwarks, the poop was white.

Although it may be argued that there was no call for sailing ships, in the opinion of Leyland and several Liverpool shipowners there would always be a number of routes open to sailing ships. With perishable cargoes being squeezed out of the sailing vessels' capacity, there were still commodities like grain, coal, nitrate and guano that offered a reasonable freightage to the square-rigger. Shipowners at the time questioned him as to the wisdom of his ventures. The following story, told by R W Leyland's son, is quite feasible but the year would have been 1885, not 1888. (From *Sea Breezes*, vol 14, July–Dec 1952, October issue, p266 onwards.)

> One day about the year 1888 my father was on Change and a friend (in spite of being a rival owner) came to him and said 'Leyland, I hear you have got 5 ships building down at Woolston just now, aren't you going it a bit?' My father said he felt quite justified and pointed out that the new ships were really good ships and big carriers with what should be a reasonable turn of speed etc. etc., in fact the usual talk of a proud owner. His friend chaffed him and remarked 'Why don't you make it a round half dozen, I bet you a fiver you don't'. My father said 'Done' walked over to the telegraph office in the news room and sent off a telegram to the builders ordering a sixth ship to be laid down forthwith. He then collected the £5 bet and took his friend off to celebrate and that was that – one way of building up a fleet.

Investment and Management

Undoubtedly Leyland was speculating heavily. However his good management is reflected in the price that he paid for his ships (which he said 'were about the lowest prices which were paid for new ships') and that even in depressed times people were prepared to purchase shares in companies under his management. His speculation is apparent from a letter in September 1884 when he contracted for the first of the 6 vessels of those 12 months, the *Allerton*. Having agreed the price of just under £17,000 for this ship he writes of a contract for another ship:

> This [contract] we would have to submit to certain friends before we could close, as really the difficulty of getting up ownery in ships is very great just at present. We only suggest this as Mr Mordaunt said he is offering a bargain – we are not want of a ship except at 12 months ahead delivery.

Bearing these two points in mind it is astonishing to believe that they ordered before the end of 1885, five more vessels.

If one compares Leyland's shipping activities with the general pattern of shipping in the 1880s, he purchased new ships during a low period in the trade cycle. Between 1881 and 1883 shipping was one of the main areas for the formation of joint stock companies and almost in consequence of this spurt, a depression followed until 1887. At the end of 1884 this feeling of depression, provoked by a fall in prices and shrinking profit margins, left the shipping industry almost prostrate, with shipyards empty and docks crowded with idle vessels. The mid 1880s was one of the worst periods for overseas markets in the late nineteenth century and it was not until 1887 that there was a growing demand for cargo space. Yet Leyland chose these years to build his new ships. It may well have been shrewd business on Leyland's part to buy vessels cheap, realising that the depression would not last long and once more his vessels would be able to reap handsome profits. Even so it was a remarkable risk to take.

In a letter of March 1886 the two brothers wrote that six of the vessels for which they had contracted within the previous 18 months were sailing. Asking for an advance of money to meet these bills, they pointed out to the manager of the Bank of Liverpool that 'Even at present low freights, these large vessels are paying very well' and that they would probably pay the whole sum off (about £14,000) 'at the end of the voyage.' Leyland clearly believed that even in depressed times he could find profitable work for his ships.

In acquiring new ships for his fleet more time had to be given to the administration of their office. There are many letters to shareholders such as this one where the person was backing out of their business. Leyland wrote:

> As an investment I know there is nothing better. The *Nelson* and *Grassendale* have shown you how the money comes back in case of loss – the rest of the ships I think show fair results and I think all round your shipping investments with us have done very well. Let us keep your name in these boats – the cheapest ever built and equal to the best.

When he was purchasing a new horse he even took the opportunity to ask the dealer whether he would take a few shares in the vessel under construction.

> Would you like to invest a little money in one of the finest sailing ships in England – at the cheapest price ever sold. At the present rates of freight (which are bad) the vessel pays from 10–20%. It is a thoroughly good investment. The sailing ships of this type always pay well and I would advise you to take a few shares if you can. The vessel is to be launched tomorrow and we have only a few shares left.

The Leyland brothers earned their money in various ways. Their insurance business which was in the charge of A J Preston covered their vessels for more than the accidents and mishaps that could be insured by underwriters, except at enormous cost. It was customary for owners to bind themselves into mutual societies, of which this business was one such club. Each owner paid in, according to the number of ships owned and club members were entitled to draw from the common funds to meet costs of accidents not covered by insurance in the ordinary marine policy. As well as this they carried on a fairly large merchant business. As managers of these vessels in the different companies, the brothers earned a 1 per cent commission on each new ship that was formed into a company and also a commission on the ships' cargoes. Even so, profits were small and at this stage shrinking: in 1882 the profits were £2826, in 1883 £2470 and in 1884 £1561.

Organisation of Voyages

The regularity of steamships enabled them to make extra voyages each year whereas a sailing ship often took only one charter, such as the new season's wheat. It required considerable skill on the part of the shipowner to convert a possible loss into a profit, and therefore there was a great attention to detail, with the owners knowing all possible trades that a ship might be called upon to work, as well as the cost of loading different cargoes in different ports. Ralph Leyland junior summed this up in an article in *Sea Breezes* (vol 14, July–Dec 1962, October issue) when he wrote: 'Management in those days was naturally very different to what it is today and probably not nearly so arduous. On the other hand much more attention to detail was probably paid by the directors and managers.' In European waters it was relatively easy for the managing owners to check on, and supervise, the close detail of the shipping of a cargo, but in foreign ports they had to depend upon the reliability and honesty of their masters and on their local agents. It was essential therefore to plan out a ship's voyages to prevent idling in expensive ports and to prevent it being kept waiting or having to make voyages in ballast. The object seemed to be to spend the maximum time carrying inexpensively loaded cargoes to cheap discharging ports at a high rate of freight; therefore these ships could not afford to lose money by handling cargoes at a loss. Although the owners might have fixed the charter for a ship, it was essential that the master, who handled the ship's disbursements and some of its freights, was reliable.

Some idea of the costs of a round voyage in the middle years of the 1880s can be determined from the letters of R W Leyland. For instance, in July 1886 he wrote to the manager of the Bank of Liverpool concerning their ship *Halewood.* The outward freight to Melbourne from the United Kingdom was £2950 and the cross freight from Newcastle to San Francisco was about £1350. At this date the ship was about to load in San Francisco for the United Kingdom or Continent a freight of 35s or 40s per ton and this would have grossed £5700 at 35s or £6500 at 40s for the homeward passage. Therefore in round figures the gross freight was a little over £10,000. The ship's disbursements when the ship was in San Francisco, were about £4075 and there were other payments due. Therefore after expenses she would probably have made £3–4000 on this one round voyage.

Similarly, at about the same time, Leyland wrote to the Bank of Liverpool concerning an advance freight for the *Otterspool.* She was chartered to load cargo at Frederickstadt for Melbourne, a freight of £3 10s per standard of timber, and therefore the company expected to make about £3000 on her outward journey. She was also loaded with 400 tons of rails at 9s per ton freightage. At about the same time the *Woolton* was chartered to load a similar cargo at Frederickstadt for Melbourne at £3 8s 9d per standard of timber, and they expected to make about £3800 from her, with disbursements in the region of £800 which would have to be recovered from this amount. A little later on, when both ships were on their way to Australia with their loaded cargoes, it was

clear what costs were involved when G R Leyland wrote to the Bank of Liverpool, 'the amount of *Otterspool* freight to be collected will amount to £2891 and of *Woolton* freight to £3533 and the Melbourne disbursements in each case we do not anticipate will exceed £600, we hope less.'

There were all sorts of other management details that

A picture of the Liverpool Exchange where shipowners, brokers and others gathered daily at noon and at 4pm to discuss business. R W Leyland was one of the most colourful characters on the 'Change, he always wore a traditional morning coat and top hat.
MERSEYSIDE MARITIME MUSEUM

The *Toxteth* was built in 1887, with a Liverpool house. This was a bridge deck amidships; below was a saloon and accommodation for the master and officers. This was a somewhat unusual feature to have on a sailing vessel at this time; the *Toxteth* inaugurated the practice in the Leyland fleet.
NATIONAL MARITIME MUSEUM

needed to be worked out in Liverpool. Although presumably the design of the Leyland ships was agreed down in Southampton with the builders Oswald, Mordaunt & Company, Leyland insisted on having the sails for his ships made in Liverpool by J M Gladstone & Company. In one letter to the sail-makers Leyland wrote:

> We have casually glanced at the figures handed to us by yourselves this morning and we find to our astonishment that the number of yards of materials in the sails of *Allerton*, 2020 tons are vastly less than the number of yards in sails of the *Otterspool* 1800 tons – or in the *Aigburth* 1798 tons.
>
> Evidently there is something wrong, we must have it put right. Either the *Otterspool* and *Aigburth* sails are too big or the *Allerton* sails are too small and we must thoroughly go into the matter. In the meantime please suspend work in connection with *Allerton* sails – and negotiations with Messrs Oswald, Mordaunt & Company regarding the *Allerton* sails.

Law Suits

The company also spent a disproportionate amount of time and money on law suits connected with the different companies over various issues. These could take a variety of forms. For instance, in May 1885 a series of summons were heard against the Sailing Ship Cressington Company in the Liverpool City Police Court for having refused to pay wages to a number of seamen. Apparently while the *Cressington* was in San Francisco in December 1884 several men had deserted and the complainants with others joined the ship. Before leaving San Francisco and going on board the men were induced to sign certain papers. On nearing home their captain gave his respective account to each of the men to sign and they discovered that a sum of $50 had been deducted from their wages. It seems these were notes of advance payment for $50 to be paid to their boarding house masters, and the captain duly paid for them. The men, however, thought they signed these papers to show that they were on board this ship. Somewhat naturally the defence argued that if these men had been swindled by the boarding house keepers it was their own look out and not that of the company. In his judgment Mr Raffles said:

> I don't like the look of this case at all. The men have been done. I think the best way would be to give a verdict for half of the $50. I must say I think the Captain ought to have made more enquiry into the matter.

The case of an accident to the ship *Garston* resulted in six actions in various courts between February 1885 and October 1886. Apparently the Sailing Ship Garston Company had contracted with Hickie Bowman & Company to load a cargo of coal at Cardiff for shipment to Bombay. The vessel had been chartered in Hamburg in October 1884 and she then proceeded to Cardiff to load coal. The charter party stipulated that two-thirds of the freight should be paid within 10 days of the vessel leaving her final port, in this case Cardiff. As she was leaving Cardiff on the night of 22 December 1884 she came into collision with a steamer, was driven up on a bank, and had ultimately to be taken back and her cargo discharged. The collision with the steamer, the *Creadon*, was only a mile outside Cardiff and the *Garston* was so

The *Liverpool* in London, probably on her first visit there in 1889. Here she loaded a large cargo for her maiden voyage to Melbourne, and took one cabin and ten steerage passengers.
NATIONAL MARITIME MUSEUM

damaged that she had to put back for repairs and refit. Eventually she sailed for Bombay, arriving there in June 1885.

The first action was brought to recover £1687 6s 5d which was two-thirds of the freight. The question in dispute was whether the collision took place in or out of the port of Cardiff, so the main point of concern was where the boundary of the commercial as distinguished from the fiscal port of Cardiff lay. The plaintiff contended that the *Garston* was out of the commercial port of Cardiff when, after being struck on the port bow, she was driven ashore, and that this was a little distance from the mouth of the River Taff. However, his Lordship decided that the vessel was still within the limits of the port of Cardiff and that being so, the vessel had not sailed and therefore he would not allow the freight charges for the plaintiff. R W Leyland & Company resorted to the Court of Appeal where once again their appeal was turned down.

The Sailing Ship Garston Company, not wishing to be completely outdone, brought a further action against Hickie, Bowman & Company in February 1886 stating that in the accident a quantity of the coal had suffered from some pulverisation in the subsequent re-handling, and when sold fetched less than it ought to have done – hence the action of a claim of £139 for general averages and £81 for balance of freight. The defendants claimed that the general average was based on the York and Antwerp rules, whereby charges of average should be based upon the value of the property at the end of the voyage. They also counter claimed for £800 in respect of the damage to the cargo, which the plaintiffs replied had been accepted in the charter party.

In giving judgment for the plaintiffs and against the defendants on the counter claim, the judge remarked that the vessel appeared to have been a profitable one for the lawyers since there had already been five actions at this stage. In this action the defendants appealed against the judgment of the Court of Appeal but the earlier judgment was upheld, their lordships believing that the estimate of the value of the cargo should be at the port of destination, not shipment, and that perils of the sea also included dangers of navigation which therefore would include the dangers of collision with other ships not caused by the negligence of the carrying party.

Leyland also made a number of claims against other parties for a breach of their charters. Their most common cause of complaint was for demurrage, in other words compensation for the delay in loading or unloading one of their vessels. A typical case was that of the *King Cenric* which was chartered in October 1885 to Radford & Company, London and proceeded to the Birkenhead tips to take on a large cargo of coal destined for San Diego on the Californian coast. The vessel was loaded in the customary way, subject to the colliery guarantee, and the plaintiff alleged and gave evidence to show that the vessel ought to have been loaded in five days at the outside, but the defendants had delayed the vessel seven days over and above this limit and therefore demurrage at the rate of £25 per day was claimed. In their defence, Radford & Company said that the cause of the delay had been the fault of the colliery owners and the shippers were exempt from liability through a clause in the charter party. However, judgment was given in favour of the plaintiffs.

KEY TO GROUP PICTURE.

LIVERPOOL SHIPOWNERS' ASSOCIATION, 1890-91.

PUBLISHED BY **BARRAUDS, LIVERPOOL** AND **LONDON.**

1—William K. Jackson.
2—W. Roberts.
3—W. Houston.
4—L. H. Macintyre.
5—S. R. Chadwick.
6—W. De Wolf.
7—Henry Fernie.
8—Richard Wakeham.
9—Neil MacVicar.
10—W. B. Sproule.
11—Thomas B Sinclair.
12—James Hugh Potter.
13—Harold B. Steel.
14—James Gillison.
15—J. Sproat.
16—A. Williamson.
17—C. G. Dunn.
18—Claus Brodersen.
19—T. L. Robertson.
20—Wallace Sinclair.
21—Samuel G. Sinclair.
22—R. R. Lockett.
23—Edwin A. Beazley.
24—Gifford Nicholson.
25—J B. Cruikshank.
26—J. H. Beazley.
27—J D. Shallcross.
28—William Gracie.
29—Andrew Anderson.
30—L. Davies.
31—Joseph H. Worthington.
32—William Nicol.
33—William Just.
34—Sir James Poole, Knt., J.P.
35—A. Wood.
36—J. Macdonald.
37—Alexander L. Duncan.
38—T. H. Ismay, J.P.
39—Gilbert M. Steeves.
40—R. G. Bell.
41—T. R. Shallcross, J.P.
42—R. H. Dixon.
43—T. Vosper.
44—J. Houston.
45—M. C. Friend.
46—J. R. Haws.
47—R. Hughes Jones.
48—E. Roberts.
49—J. E. Anderson.
50—W. J. Doward.
51—R. K. Kelley.
52—William H. Lyne.
53—Milton Stuart.
54—W. B. Bowring.
55—John Japp.
56—John Edgar.
57—G. H Potter.
58—F. H. Vaughan.
59—J. T. De Wolf.
60—William Nicholson.
61—G. P. Wakeham.
62—Charles E. De Wolf.
63—J. Rankin.
64—J. G. Nicholson.
65—T. Rome.
66—A. Dahl.
67—S. R. Sandbach.
68—William Goffey.
69—James Goffey.
70—R. W. Leyland.
71—G. R. Leyland.
72—Walter Chambers.
73—James Mills.
74—Joseph Chadwick.
75—J. E. Tinne.
76—William Potter.
77—Edward F. Powell.
78—John Williamson.
79—Henry F. Fox.

Key to the Shipowners Association photograph (shown opposite). R W Leyland is no 70, G R Leyland no 71.
COURTESY WEIGHTMANS

They also brought cases for demurrage in foreign ports. The *Halewood* for instance under Captain Stap arrived at Antwerp in 1889 from San Francisco with a cargo of 55,745 sacks of wheat weighing 3515 tons. According to the charter party the ship was to be discharged in line with the custom of the port. The Antwerp Tribunal of

Commerce was called to decide on the number of sacks of wheat that should be discharged daily. The captain of the ship stated that there was no custom at Antwerp for the discharge of a ship like the *Halewood* and that the rate of discharge for the cargo should take into account the facilities offered by their appliances in the port and the fact that the discharge could also be affected at the same time from all four hatches of the ship. Stap stated that at other places he had discharged as much as 363 tons in a single day. At Hull the custom was 190 tons a day, at Liverpool from 300 to 400 tons and at Dublin 180 tons. He maintained that the proper quantity at Antwerp was 180 tons per working day.

However, the consignee argued that he was only bound to take delivery of 100 tons a day by the custom of the port and named several ships which had been discharged on that basis. It was agreed that the arguments of the captain were well founded in principle and it was only reasonable to suppose that the increased accommodation in the port of Antwerp should shorten the time formerly allowed for the discharge of a ship, and therefore it was suggested that the consignees should in their own interests, as well as that of the port, arrange with the representatives of shipowners to fix a new scale of lay days. However, as this had not been done and the case was being tested on the existing custom as described by the defender, and there were no other conditions stipulated to the charter party, then the judgment must be given against the claim for eight days demurrage.

On other occasions the managers were taken to court concerning the damage to cargoes carried in their ships. A typical case was the action brought against R W Leyland & Company for their ship *Gitana* in 1889 in the Admiralty Division of the High Court of Justice. The cargo of grain belonging to Messrs Spiller & Company of Cardiff was found to be damaged when it was discharged at Cardiff. A considerable part of the cargo had been damaged by salt water which had penetrated through a crack in the coaming of the hatchway. Messrs Spiller & Company maintained that the way in which the anchor had been stowed caused a hole through which water also reached and damaged a further portion of the cargo. However, the defendants believed that it could not have got down the main hatchway since the coamings had been caulked and pitched and were covered with three tarpaulins. They maintained that if salt water had got in it must have been through the straining of the ship in severe weather.

A remarkable photograph of the Liverpool Shipowners Association taken in 1891. This is the only photograph available of the two shipowners, R W and G R Leyland together, seen here at the height of their fame.
COURTESY WEIGHTMANS

DITTON
HOWARD COMPANY, CO
BR. SHIP DITTON. 2699 TONS NET REGISTER,

The original judgment had been given in favour of the plaintiffs and hence the defendants appealed, maintaining that the damage had been done due to straining and leaking resulting from heavy weather. Their appeal was not upheld, and they were forced to pay for the damage resulting from salt water going through the main hatchway and through the hole alleged to have been caused by the stowage of the anchor, but it was felt that any damage by another cause, such as the possibility of salt water damaging the cargo near the mast, must be excluded.

Damage caused by salt water was the reason for a further action brought against the company two years later in the same court; this time they were defending an amount claimed for damage to a wheat cargo in their ship *Cressington*. It was maintained that the captain of the ship had not taken sufficient steps to remedy the leakage and that the method used in dunnaging the ship in the between deck waterways was improper and that this increased the damage in the lower hold. In the judgment it was felt that the damage had been caused by an inflow of water during navigation and by the terms of the charter party – 'perils of the sea and accidents of navigation, even when occasioned by the negligence, default or error in judgment of pilot, master, mariner or other servants of the shipowners' – the shipping company was exempt. However, they were liable for the insufficient dunnage and the damage caused by this.

Office Administration

For the administration of the fleet the office in Liverpool employed comparatively few staff. Apart from the two brothers and A J Preston, who was mainly in charge of the insurance side of the business, there were probably about seven other staff whose total salaries amounted to a little over £700 in the middle years of the 1880s. The firm was particularly dependent upon two people, the cashier Talbot and the bookkeeper Alf J Turner. In 1886 the firm took on an apprentice, Sewallis Winter, at a salary of £100 spread over five years; later he was to become a junior partner of the firm. The Winters were cousins, and Sewallis was the son of Lieutenant-Colonel H B Winter of Norwich who was later a director of the Leyland Shipping Company Limited. Other members of the family, such as James Winter of Cromer, had shares in Leyland ships. The solicitors for the whole length of the partnership and also the company formation of the 1890s were Hill, Dickinson and Lightbound.

Financing New Construction

With their vast increase in shipping tonnage between 1884 and 1886 they had some difficulty arranging the finance for the purchase of *Leyland Brothers* and of the *Toxteth* just when the shipbuilding industry was coming out of recession. Due to the poor financial situation in the firm of Oswald, Mordaunt & Company they were unable to delay the payment of bills and they had to look elsewhere for finance. For instance, shortly after the registration of the *Leyland Brothers*, they transferred the shares into the name of a merchant, Christian Adolphus Lichtenburg, and secured their current account with him through this. It was not until February 1888 that they were discharged from this mortgage and they were then able to form the ship into the Sailing Ship Leyland Brothers Company Limited.

In the case of the *Toxteth*, which was launched on 12 March 1887 at Southampton, Leylands paid a quarter of the cost of the vessel and then sought help from the Bank of Liverpool to pay off the rest of the cost of the vessel as the bills became due on 10 April 1887. They wrote to the bank as follows:

> We request you will kindly take up these acceptances as they become due charging same to sailing ship *Toxteth* account of R W Leyland & Company. We have placed the sum of £— to the credit of the account and ask you to be good enough to temporarily supply the deficiency. We are selling shares in the vessel as fast as we can and we expect to place the whole of them very shortly. We undertake to pay into the account all purchase monies of the shares immediately we receive them for the purpose of entirely liquidating your advance, and at the same time we will hand you stamped policies for any amount you may wish. We also pledge to you as security to the Bank all insured shares of the said ship, and further we ourselves as a separate firm guarantee to you repayment of any advances you may make on account of the said ship. Vessel costs £21,800 and the amount of bills represents ¾ cash to pay builders up to launching settlement.

The bank agreed that their *Toxteth* overdraft remain open until 18 September. The ship was insured for £22,000 and they handed stamped policies to the bank for £10,000.

Flagship of the Fleet

By the year 1888, R W Leyland & Company were the managing owners of 21 sailing ships and they were considering all the different options open to them for further expansion of their fleet. In this year Leyland decided to build the flagship of his fleet, appropriately called the *Liverpool*. Of all the letters that have survived, those concerning the construction of the *Liverpool* with Russell & Company, Port Glasgow are perhaps the most interesting, for although this ship when built was the largest ship under the Red Ensign, they do show that Leyland intended to build the first five-masted sailing ship in the world. In his specifications for the *Liverpool* Leyland did mention the possibility of fitting an engine, but the vessel was completed without one. Without doubt he was considering the possibility of an auxiliary vessel, but like other shipowners he may have realised that the

This excellent photograph of one of the most infamous Leyland vessels, the *Ditton*, was taken in Oakland Creek, San Francisco. She was the largest three-masted sailing ship under the Red Ensign in the 1890's and is perhaps best remembered for her collisions in Newcastle, New South Wales in 1902.

advantages of an auxiliary were imaginary in square-rigged ships. For example, engines wasted space and added considerably to the capital and running costs of the vessel. Leyland firmly believed that the answer to powered competition was to increase the power of the sailing ships themselves and that probably an engine was too small and too weak to be of use in a vessel of this size. He held that a way to develop better sailing ships was to build larger vessels. To one shareholder at this date he wrote, 'Replying to your question about the paying capabilities of a large ship – we think the larger the better. It is the tendency of the age, both in steam and sail, and all our experience points in that direction.'

So Leyland dropped the idea of an auxiliary vessel and built the largest ship of its kind – square-rigged on all four masts – the *Liverpool*. While work was progressing with this ship in Port Glasgow, Leyland tried to agree a new contract with Russell & Company for an even larger vessel of 3430 tons minimum register to carry a larger deadweight tonnage proportionate to the *Liverpool* and it was for this vessel that he required five masts. She would have been square-rigged and many years earlier than the *Preussen*, the only five-masted fully square-rigged sailing ship ever built.

Partly due to the volume of work at Russell & Company and the fact they failed to agree upon a reasonable price Leyland did not build this vessel, but clearly he discussed with the builders the possibilities of building the first five-masted sailing ship in the world. As they could not agree this contract, Leyland once more turned his attentions to building three-masted sailing ships. A little later, in October 1889, he finally reached an agreement with Thomas Oswald, who had moved and set up a new company in Milford Haven, and signed contracts for the building of the *Ditton* and *Speke*, which were probably the two largest three-masted sailing ships ever built. Ralph Leyland junior was to comment many years later that the *Ditton* was 'reputed to be the tallest ship in the world.' These two ships were built of steel, whereas the *Liverpool* was constructed of iron. R W Leyland & Company had become the proud owners of the largest iron sailing ship firm in the United Kingdom, and they have been described as the main supporters of the late nineteenth century full-rigged ship.

It is interesting to note Leyland's preference for iron rather than steel sailing ships and possibly it may be argued that he was rather too conservative in this respect. The first steel vessel was the barque *Altcar* which had been built as long ago as 1864 and in subsequent years it was common to make certain fittings, even yards and masts, out of steel. About the year 1882 there were the first signs that iron was being ousted by steel in ship construction and in the next year Leyland had built the steel ship *Garston*, but for some reason he returned to construction in iron until the *Speke* and *Ditton* were built in 1891. Leyland had always preferred iron, and even in his marine insurance business he seems to have insured only iron sailing ships in the 1880s. It is impossible to determine the reason for this preference but it could have been that T R Oswald or the designer of his ships, who was possibly Hercules Linton (the designer of the *Cutty Sark*), recommended iron for ship construction. Certainly Oswald did not build his first steel ship, the *Benita*, until 1887.

They were undoubtedly traditional in their ship construction as Alan Villiers noted when he wrote: 'In fact, with one exception that was the only kind of ship they [Leylands] ever built – the standard three-masted ship, the most awkward, work making, man killing rig the big Cape Horner could have.' Possibly the four-masted barque would have been a better handler than these large full-rigged ships. By building to a standard design that had been worked out at Southampton, and by building in iron Leyland may have been able to acquire more ships at lower prices than other shipowners were able to for their ships.

A Move Towards Acquiring Steamships

Towards the end of the 1880s and in the early 1890s R W Leyland & Company were considering the introduction of steamers to their fleet. They had no experience in the management of steamships but in *Lloyd's Register* for 1888/1889, amongst the vessels listed, is the small steamship *Londos*. This ship had a registered tonnage of 209 tons and was built in 1860 by Richardson, Duck & Company at Stockton-on-Tees. It would be interesting to know how the firm came to own so small a steamship but it is perhaps no coincidence that J M Mordaunt was the previous owner.

Certainly by 1892 they were beginning to learn the necessary details for the management of steamships by purchasing shares in other steamship companies. However, in 1892 there was a depression in shipping and this was not the time to expand their business further. Leyland made this point at a meeting of the Liverpool Shipwrights Association at the very end of 1891 when he commented on the shipbuilding market. He considered the prospects for 1892 were poor and that the production of tonnage during the past few years had been: 'Beyond the ship carrying necessities of the world.' Times were beginning to change and competition was becoming even greater.

CHAPTER THREE

Difficult Years

Towards the end of 1892 R W Leyland went on an extended tour of India and Upper Burma and it was on his return from this trip in early 1893 that he found that all was not well in his shipping business, which had been left in the sole charge of his partner and brother, George Leyland. George Leyland had speculated both in his name and in the name of the firm and had accumulated enormous losses which eventually resulted in a breakdown in the partnership and caused a 'forced and hurried sale' of G R Leyland's share in the partnership. However, this period in the company's history is well documented, for Leyland deposited a number of letters in the hands of the trustees of his will in August 1895 and in these he conclusively proved his solvency at the time he travelled to India in November 1892.

The first indication Leyland had of his brother's speculation came in a letter that his brother sent to him when he was in Calcutta in December 1892. It read:

> I wrote you a long letter about 10 days ago but I did not mention to you about Frederick Leyland & Company, as I was not certain how things would go.
>
> Grey Hill and Walter Glynn approached me to go on the Board and after mature deliberation and going carefully into the figures, I decided it would be to the interest of the firm to do so. Not only on account of the fees which will be about £1000 per annum (which go to the firm) but also to learn a practical lesson in steam ship owning – also to add prestige to our firm when we bring out our own company and to get in touch with the monied people in London. This affair has gone through and I signed the first cheque for the new company yesterday for £40,000. We have not taken over the fleet yet as the money has to be collected. The shares are all taken up. Walter Glynn is to be Managing Director at a salary of £6000 per annum, he has retired from his own firm, and is to manage the whole business. Christopher Furness is Chairman, I think they want me to be Deputy, it will depend on the duties they expect me to perform.
>
> The Leyland family keep £200,000 in the fleet. I shall be the only Leyland however in the management.
>
> We have added Mr Speed and Mr Val Prinsep to the Board. I had to go to London about the matter on Wednesday. I inspected the *Cressington* and *Woolton* at the same time. I have taken £15,000 in shares which I shall retain or dispose of to friends and have arranged the money with Simpson, you take half or not of what remains as you like. It is the finest business affair I ever saw. I enclose a prospectus which gives all particulars. The results of the last 6 months show £180,000 profit after deducting £52,500 for depreciation, after paying debenture and preference Interest £10,000 sinking fund, and 15% dividend on ordinary these figures show £152,500 actual reserve.

Leyland wrote:

> On my return home at the beginning of 1893, I did not agree to take any of these shares. I signed no cheques on Bank of Liverpool, for the payment of shares, nor did I give any instructions or accept any responsibility at any time in any way.
>
> On Thursday November 16th 1893 the Bank of Liverpool sold the 1500 £10 shares for £5 11s 6d per share and have sent me debit note for loss, say £7091 7s 9d – on the old firm No 2 account.
>
> I annex copy of memo I made regarding this sale on the day.
>
> Copy of Memo of R W Leyland Thursday November 16th 1893 12.30pm
>
> Mr Simpson wrote note asking me to call upon him. Went at once. Found Mr Norman Hill with him discussing sale of 15,000 Frederick Leyland shares, which belonged to Mr George Leyland. Mr Hill said he thought his broker could obtain £5 11s 6d – of 750 shares of £10 each and strongly urged Mr Simpson should authorise this sale and with the proceeds (and a few hundred pounds more) that he should pay off the final call of £4500 on the 1500 shares and keep the 750 shares to see how things shaped in the future. Mr Simpson said he could sell the whole 1500 shares probably to the Frederick Leyland Company direct for £5 10s per share but thought Mr Norman Hill's suggestion a good one, and that the Bank would be disposed to hold the 750 shares for a time to see how matters went.
>
> It was then arranged that Mr Hill should at once see his stockbroker, and get the £5 11s 6d for the 750 shares.

The *Riversdale* was the last sailing vessel built for the company. She was launched in 1894 at the yard of William Hamilton & Co, Port Glasgow, and it is probable that she was offered to the Leyland Line at a cheap rate (price £17,200). She was sistership to the *Barfillan*, *Hyderbad* and *Blackbraes*.
NATIONAL MARITIME MUSEUM

At 3.30pm I went into the Bank about other business. Mr Simpson took me into his private office and informed me that he had gone into Frederick Leyland Company's office, and that he had told them the purpose of the above – that they had then offered him £5 11s 6d for the whole 1500 shares, together with some arrangement as to arrears of interest and that he had closed the transaction with them on these terms.

Post Nuptial Settlement Details

He also wrote a letter to the trustees of his will in August 1895. It read:

Having regard to the post nuptial settlement made by me upon my wife and children in the month of November 1892 and the circumstances which occurred in connection with the firm of R W Leyland & Company in the spring of 1893, I think it well to put on record why such settlement was then made and to declare and prove my absolute solvency and the solvency of my firm at the time I made the settlement.

My reasons for making the settlement were – in the first place, because I had made no settlement of any sort on my marriage, nor had I made any provision for my wife and children other than by will – and this thought had troubled me for some years past, as my children were born into the world.

In the second place I had been very ill in the summer and autumn of 1892, and was proceeding to India for the benefit of my health, in November 1892. I thought it would be well to make a settlement then without further delay.

At the time I made the settlement I deposited with Mr Norman Hill a sealed envelope describing what I possessed at that time, but this did not include the goodwill or value of the business of R W Leyland & Company.

I herewith enclose monthly balance sheets of my firm for the months of September to October and November 1892, also 'recapitulations' for those months drawn up by Messrs Talbot and Turner – cashier and bookkeeper in the office at the time.

Our largest creditor at that time and in fact the only one of any importance, was the Bank of Liverpool. My firm had been doing business with this bank, since about 1869, and our relations were of the most satisfactory nature. We had an overdraft account, called a No 2 account. To secure this we (my brother and myself) deposited securities in shipping shares, and in the estate of my late father to the extent of what then was considered to represent between £50,000 and £60,000.

We drew on this No 2 account for the disbursement of our limited liability companies ships – or other ships – and for the purpose of paying for our shipping shares etc.

I find that after deducting what the shipping companies, and other vessels, owed us, we owed to the Bank of Liverpool the following amounts on the following dates.

September 30th 1892 ......£25,422 4 shillings and 3 pence
October 1st 1892..........£24,787 4 shillings and 7 pence
November 30th 1892 ......£21,135 7 shillings and 8 pence

This sum was amply secured by the shipping shares, and interest in the late R Leyland's estate and the Bank was quite satisfied with the security. My firm's liabilities at the above dates (outside the Bank of Liverpool) were very small, and a few hundreds of pounds would have paid them. We had the prospect soon of making some thousands of pounds profits, which would have gone in the reduction of our debt to the Bank.

The profits alluded to were those accruing on the cargoes of three shipments of sugar per following vessels: *Gitana*, *Corryureclan* [*Corryvrechan*], *Krimpen von de Lek* [*Krimpen aan de Lek*].

The final result of these shipments, when sold early in 1893, was a profit of
£2326 and 9 pence per *Gitana*.
£2188 5 shillings and 10 pence per *Corryureclan*.
£1879 14 shillings and 1 penny per *Krimpen von de Lek*.
TOTAL £6394 0 shillings and 8 pence.

The *Gitana* profit was paid into our firm in April 1893 but the profits of *Corryureclan* and *Krimpen von de Lek* never came into my hands as they were retained by Messrs Henry Clark & Company to reduce the indebtedness of my partner, Mr George R Leyland, to them in March, April, May 1893. I lost all my interest in these two vessels (one ½ share) having sacrificed it to benefit (vainly) my brother, Mr George R Leyland. In the statement that I made of my assets to Mr N Hill, at the time of making post nuptial settlement, I do not think I mentioned the value of my one ½ share in the business of R W Leyland & Company. This item should have been included in the list deposited with Mr Hill when making settlement in 1892.

The value of the business consists, or consisted, on the possession of a number of 'Agreements as to Management', of a number of sailing ships – with the shareholders in those vessels. We were the managing owners. An idea of the value of this asset may be formed from the fact that my brother Mr George R Leyland sold his one ½ share of the business in May 1893, at the time of our dissolution of partnership, for the sum of £10,000. This was a forced and hurried sale. It should have brought more money, but even taking it at this lower figure – my share therefore would have been £10,000 – or say the two halves together would have been worth £20,000 – a sum of money almost sufficient to have paid off the Bank of Liverpool at the time I made my post nuptial settlement, – quite apart from the shipping shares, and the interest in the estate of the late R Leyland, which at that time the Bank of Liverpool held as a quite sufficient margin of cover for our overdraft account.

Recapitulating the above – if at the time of my post nuptial settlement in November 1892 – my brother's interest and my interest in the firm of R W Leyland & Company had been sold, as a going concern with the benefit of agreements as to management of sundry ships – the commission on the business of the Mutual Insurance Company and Marine insurance brokers business we then had – etc, etc, it would have realised £20,000 at least – enough to have nearly paid off the Bank of Liverpool, which was our only creditor at any moment, and left us all our shares in the ships and other assets, free, quite apart from the subject matter of my settlement.

I must also refer to an item of commissions accrued, but not paid, in November 1892. These were the commissions (management) of various ships homeward bound; possibly these would have amounted to between £2–3000. The ships were on voyages (chartered) and the management commissions, although earned, were not paid into the firm at that date. We did not at that time pay ourselves until the voyages were completed. As a matter of fact though, the commissions were due to us the moment charters were signed.

The only transactions involving a loss at the time I made my post nuptial settlement were the following:

About the time of my sailing for India in November 1892, my firm had opened, with my knowledge and consent, the following:
A parcel of wheat per ship Liverpool (with Cornelius Esq.)
A part of a cargo of flour from Portland, Oregon with William Scott & Company.
6000 bales of cotton (November 9th 1892) bought at 4d 47/64 48/64 49/64 per pound, with Hollins Thomson Melly.
The Liverpool parcels of wheat resulted in a loss of £1074 17 shillings and 8 pence.
The 6000 bales of cotton resulted in a profit of £258 8 shillings and 8 pence on February 10th 1893 and at the time of my settlement in November 1892 the parcel of flour showed no loss although eventually at the end of 1894 it did show a loss, as the arbitration and subsequent settlement, showed.

I have endeavoured to set forth my position fully on the date I made my post nuptial settlement, and I think I have shown that at that date, I was perfectly solvent and so was the firm of R W Leyland & Company.

The day after signing my post nuptial settlement I set off on a 4 months holiday to India, going to London, and sailing P & O Company's steamer *Bengal* for Calcutta.

My brother and partner Mr George R Leyland remained in sole charge of business after my departure. Unhappily he commenced to speculate largely both in the name of the firm and in his own name. The chief contracts entered into were as follows:

Nov 30th 92	*Invergarry*	10,000	Units Walla Walla Wheat
Dec 23rd 92	*Anglesia* [*Anglesea*]	8,000	Units Californian Wheat
Jan 4th 93	*Maschona* [*Mashona*]	17,154	Units Californian Wheat
Dec 31st 92	*Talus*	14,780	Units Californian Wheat
Dec 16th 92	*Allerton*	14,139	Units Californian Wheat
Dec 29th 92	*Grassendale*	12,643	Units Californian Wheat
Dec 16th 92	*Otterspool*	12,669	Units Californian Wheat
Dec 15th 92	*Toxteth*	17,370	Units Californian Wheat
	Centals	106,755	

Beginning 25 November 1892 he bought a further 6700 bales American cotton, on the firm's account, also 5789 bales

of Peruvian cotton on the firm's account in Nov 15th, 18th [sic] 1892.

He also contracted with Russell & Company of Port Glasgow – to build a new ship and entered in December 1892 upon the negotiations regarding Frederick Leyland & Company shares – which ultimately led to a loss of over £7000, and which I have treated on in another letter. The new ship contract I managed to cancel with Messrs Russell on my return home – and the Leyland shares I always repudiated having anything to do with – as I had absolutely nothing to do with the purchase or sale. The losses on the wheat ships accumulated during the spring and summer of 1893, and the amounts are set forth, in our various books, also the losses on the cotton.

All these losses were paid in full, the Bank of Liverpool assisting us to do so, and holding as security what was then considered sufficient to cover them – the shares of (or in) our ships, and a mortgage over our shares in the estate of our father, the late R Leyland. There is no occasion for me to go on with the events of the early part of 1893, which finally led to the disillusion of partnership between my brother Mr George R Leyland, and myself.

I will only remark that the Bank of Liverpool (knowing that Mr George R Leyland had sold his one ½ share in our business for £10,000) made no claim upon the money, and allowed him to keep it, without question, which seems to go to show that they considered even then that the security they held was ample for a debt, which was more than double what it was in November 1892 when I made my post nuptial settlement.

The Old Partnership Dissolved – a New Partnership Begun

At the end of April 1893 the partnership ended and the bank was notified that only R W Leyland was to sign cheques on the firm's accounts or the separate accounts of the various shipping companies, and in May George Leyland sold his share of the partnership. For a short time he went to live in Glasgow and then he returned to Liverpool and formed a new company in his name as a shipbroker and commission merchant and his company was a subscriber to Lloyds Register until 1910. They were agents for a number of overseas firms from San Francisco, Antwerp and elsewhere. However, despite his attempts to do well in business he was never very successful and was continually in debt. For instance in 1897 E D Pochin, who was chairman of the new Leyland Shipping Company, lent G R Leyland £600 but in 1901 the money had not been repaid and the lender was advised to issue a writ for the non repayment of the loan.

A year previously, in 1900, R W Leyland was at the Conservative Club when in error he was handed a writ intended for G R Leyland. He was also managing director of Leyland Thomas & Company and this company were agents for several other companies in Liverpool. In June 1904 certain actions were still pending against G R Leyland and by the December of that year R W Leyland was preparing for his brother's bankruptcy and various measures were being taken to protect his family. They were forced to move from their home, Old House, Grassendale Park, to rent another property in the city. However, in 1905 G R Leyland died and R W Leyland wrote a letter to a gentleman in Antwerp and remarked: 'I regret to say that my brother George has left nothing but debts behind him.' R W Leyland did a great deal to help his late brother's family and made arrangements for contracts that George's firm had entered into to be carried out.

G R Leyland sold his half share in the partnership of R W Leyland & Company to three people. Lorentz Bahr Haddock purchased a ⅜ths share and H Sewallis Winter and Arthur John Preston each purchased a 1/16th share. In this respect it would be interesting to have further details of the partnership agreement and some indication of how decisions were made. The partnership was for 10 years from May 1893 and in the articles of partnership goodwill was valued at £20,000 in the event of R W Leyland's death during the partnership term. His surviving partners had the right to purchase his share and

The *Planet Venus* (I), a steel screw steamer, was built by William Hamilton & Co. She was launched on 5 September 1894 and was owned by R W Leyland & Co for two years prior to being sold to J Holman & Sons and renamed *Birchtor.* Her first journey was to New York where she picked up 130,054 cases of oil which she took to Tokohama, Japan.

BY KIND PERMISSION OF MR WILLIAM LIND

the goodwill at a sum equal to five times the amount of his average annual share of profits for the five preceeding years before his death. Upon the completion of this purchase, Mr Leyland's executors were to have had no further interest in the earnings of the business. However, the partners had agreed at the time of the purchase of their shares in the company that if it was at all possible they would amalgamate the single ship companies into one company and they therefore made provision to vary the articles of partnership.

Lorentz Haddock was a young man with a background in shipping in Liverpool. A J Preston had obviously worked with Leyland for many years by this date and had managed the marine insurance business of the company for 23 years. Sewallis Winter had joined the firm in 1886 and by 1891 had completed his apprenticeship as a clerk in the company. He was a clerk for the firm at this date and in November 1891 the two brothers heard that Sewallis had suddenly got married. His father was somewhat disappointed and Leyland wrote to him saying that the firm had increased his salary immediately to £2 a week as they felt he needed something to supplement his income. Leyland also had him out to his house the Sunday following the news and it was after this event that Leyland wrote saying that the family should be delighted by Sewallis' marriage. Presumably the problem was sorted out and two years later in 1893 at the age of 25 he became a junior partner in the firm.

Early in 1893 when Leyland returned from his trip abroad he managed to cancel the contract for the new ship with Russell & Company, Port Glasgow. However, in November 1893 the new partnership agreed to purchase a new steel sailing ship from Messrs William Hamilton & Company, Port Glasgow, to be named *Riversdale*, for £17,200. This was the last sailing ship for the company, she was launched in March 1894 and Leyland may well have purchased this ship cheaply. At the same time as this vessel was being built, Messrs Workman, Clark & Co, Belfast were building a steamer for the company. This was the *Planet Mercury*, the company's first steamship. She was a steel twin screw vessel of 3250 tons, and was launched on 19 April 1894. Unfortunately she was not destined for a long life, being posted missing in February 1900. All the company's subsequent steamers were to be named after planets.

Although R W Leyland & Company were still expanding their business they were having difficulty in selling shares. At the same time as the *Planet Mercury* was nearing completion, they were trying to persuade William Hamilton & Company to defer until January 1895 the launch of the new steamer that they had on contract for launching in October 1894. They felt the ship would bring less business starting work so late in the year and would be at a disadvantage in Lloyd's Register. Leyland wrote in a letter to the builders:

We are having an experience just now in trying to sell shares

> in our *Planet Mercury*. It is most depressing. People are all either half ruined, with no money to spare, or else so sick of shipping that they will not touch it. Of course this is good for the future – very bad for the present.

Trading in the first year of the new partnership was reasonable and Leyland's share of the profit on 31 December 1894 was £2910. With the launching of a new steamer the company had to look to new lines of communication for work for this steamer. In March 1894 Leyland had had one meeting with a gentleman in Manchester with whom he discussed a new venture and the capital outlay necessary as well as the people who might be interested in a new line of steamers. (Other companies were involved in similar activities, such as McIver who issued a prospectus for a line of steamers to Bombay and Karachi.) Leyland wrote:

> Referring to our recent correspondence and visits to your office, we write to ask you if you think Manchester people more inclined to go into the matter now and whether you would be disposed to take it up as we proposed. We gave you full particulars of what we thought would work best but it would be easy to put forward a company with smaller capital, if that would help matters.

Nothing seems to have come of this venture.

A share certificate of the new company formed in December 1896.

No. 148

THE LEYLAND SHIPPING COMPANY, LIMITED.

R. W. LEYLAND & CO. MANAGERS

LIVERPOOL. 9 June 1898.

To R. W. Leyland Esq
Liverpool

I am directed to send you the annexed Warrant for Dividend as noted below.

Alf. J. Turner,
Secretary.

4 % free of Income Tax
on 9143 Shares of £1 each } £365.14.5

NOTE – THIS PART SHOULD BE RETAINED FOR INCOME TAX PURPOSES.

The steamer *Planet Neptune* under construction.

The Leyland Shipping Company Formed

Towards the end of 1895 the partners with their solicitors were trying to formulate plans for the amalgamation of the different ship companies into one company, to be called the Leyland Shipping Company. Leyland started by arranging an insurance policy on his life on behalf of the partnership for £10,000. The partners had agreed that this was necessary since the value of the goodwill of R W Leyland within the partnership would have been increased by the proposed amalgamation of the single ship companies. Therefore in the event of his death the surviving partners were to pay for his share in the goodwill a sum equal to seven times the amount of his average annual share of profits and also to undertake to pay Mr Leyland's executors one fourth of the annual profits for the remainder of the partnership term. The partners were happy with this new arrangement and in consequence on 1 May 1896 a meeting was held at the headquarters of the company in Exchange Buildings with the purpose of amalgamating the different shipping companies. The new company, The Leyland Shipping Company was registered on 16 May 1896 and on 27 October of the same year all the ships of the different sailing ship companies were transferred to the new company. C W Kellock & Company were responsible for the valuations of the different ships and certain amounts were put aside to represent profits or loss on different voyages. These debts and liabilities were to be deducted from the valuations for the individual ships before shares were apportioned to the shareholders. Shareholders were allotted:

> the number of £1 fully paid up shares which at their par value shall equal the interest of such member, in the amount payable aforesaid (based on the value of each ship after deductions) and if the interest of any such member shall amount to a sum not a multiple of 1, then the amount of such interest in excess of the last multiple of 1 shall be paid by the company to such member in cash.

The company was registered with a capital of £300,000 divided into 300,000 shares of £1 each and by the amalgamation of the different ship companies, 173,804 shares were allocated. The object of the company was listed as:

> To adopt and carry into effect an agreement expressed to be made between R W Leyland, L B Haddock, A J Preston and H S Winter of the one party and this company of the other part, and generally to carry on in all or any of their respective branches of the business of shipowners, shipbrokers, insurance brokers, managers of shipping property, carriers by land and sea etc.

Five directors were appointed and these included Leyland and Haddock and H B Winter with W Clarkson and E D Pochin. A J Turner was appointed secretary to the company.

Each of the individual ship companies had to be liquidated and a meeting held to explain the transfer of the property to the new company. There were a number of these meetings in early 1897 which coincided with the completion of voyages of different ships. The great majority of the 353 named shareholders at the start of the new company were gentlemen and ladies who were not involved in business, but some 54 merchants were listed as owning shares.

However, the new company largely removed the close relationship that had existed between the shareholders and the partners of the firm. The partners were not so closely involved with the subscribing and sale of shares as they had been hitherto. There was now a company secretary and the sale of shares was conducted on the Liverpool Stock Exchange. There are thus very few letters from Leyland to shareholders as this part of the management of the company had changed. In 1897 Mr

A L (later Sir Alfred) Jones was going to put some shares that he held in the company on the market and offered them to R W Leyland first. He replied: 'I am much obliged for your courteous remark about considering our feeling in the matter before placing your shares on the market. I am afraid many shipowners have lost the sense of feeling altogether . . .'.

At the same time as the formation of the new company, Leyland was trying to sort out his debt to the old No 2 account of the previous partnership. At one stage he offered to retire from the partnership and to sell his share in the estate of his late father as well as to sell the shares of his two brothers, in the hope of raising sufficient money to pay off some of his debts. When G R Leyland had sold his share of the partnership in 1893 he did not pay off his debts to the old firm and throughout the 1890s R W Leyland found himself in an awkward situation with his own bank. He made various references to his financial situation in his letters. In one letter Leyland wrote: 'I regret my brother never makes the slightest attempt to reduce his indebtedness to me. My present unfortunate position is the result of his indebtedness to the old No 2 account . . .'.

Although he was caught in this unfortunate situation he wanted, if it was at all possible, to make some form of settlement of his overdraft and the bank had suggested a figure of £30,000 since, inclusive of interest, he owed £43,120. He wrote to the bank saying that he was unable to manage this amount since 'I have absolutely nothing left but what you hold' and asked 'if you would reconsider the matter and mention a sum that would be more within my reach. I am unwilling to let the matter drop if by any chance a settlement of this long outstanding trouble can be arrived at.' As security they had shares in the Leyland Shipping Company with a nominal value of £17,620 as well as a mortgage of his interest in his firm and the mortgages of the interest of himself and his brother in their father's estate.

A final sum was agreed shortly after and in consequence Leyland found himself having paid his debts but without any shares in his old company. Early in 1900 his partner, Lorentz Haddock, agreed to sell him 2000 or 3000 shares at a reasonable price and later in the year he took another 1000 shares in his wife's name.

A Disappointing First Year

The company's first year was a poor one and in January 1897 the price of shares on the Liverpool Stock Exchange was only 12s 6d. The report and accounts for the first year of the company ending 30 April 1897, made disappointing reading and the meeting held in June 1897 discussed the position of the company. The directors reported:

> continued depression in homeward freights from all parts of the world, but they trust to see an improvement in the autumn months, when jute and wheat crops come forward for shipment. Outward freights are firm and at a level which if combined with fair homeward business, would give profitable results.

One reason for this low profit of only £988 was that the auditors had decided that only closed voyages of different ships should be taken into account and only six vessels out of the fleet of 15 vessels had completed their round voyages.

Leyland had tried to reduce the costs of maintaining the fleet and one way to do this was to reduce the premium of insurance. From late in 1896 the company had only insured vessels for their real value instead of the high values which their original worth had demanded. Leyland felt this saving on insurance could be considerable in one year's working of the company.

In their meeting to discuss the annual report Leyland said:

> With reference to the general working of the fleet during the past 12 months, we regret that the course of homeward freights during the latter part of last year, from both East and West, was most disappointing to sailing shipowners generally. We fortunately had no vessels in the East, but we had the *Aigburth* on the West Coast of South America and two due in San Francisco at about the end of the year 1896, which have not come up to our expectations. We had chartered 6 vessels from San Francisco and the neighbouring ports, at about the best average rates of the season but the two San Francisco ships above referred to viz the *Grassendale* and *Halewood* have been a source of disappointment. When we made our estimate of the position of the fleet on September 26th 1896 and assessed earnings, the San Francisco home freights were then about 30 shillings to 31 shillings and threepence; in fact we had just fixed the *Wavertree* at the latter rate. This proves to have been the high watermark of San Francisco freights of 1896, although at that time there was said to be plenty of wheat in California for shipment, and higher freights were looked for. But, for later loading, for which the *Halewood* and *Grassendale* were to have been available, on 26 shillings and threepence to 27 shillings and sixpence was talked of, and while we were negotiating charters at a shade higher rate the market suddenly collapsed and most unexpectedly dropped to one of the lowest ranges on record, namely about 15 shillings per ton, in January 1897; and as these vessels were only ready to load when this rate was about reached, we laid them up, one in Martinez and the other in Oakland Creek, the bay of California, where, as you may have noticed from your monthly list of position of ships, they have since remained, but at very little cost. A gradual recovery is taking place, and the vessels are now fixable at about 22 shillings and sixpence to 23 shillings and 9 pence new crop loading, but with the promise of a large Californian crop, we hope to see a higher range of freights shortly.
>
> Some shareholders may remark, well, what are the prospects for the coming 12 months? We do not wish to be too sanguine, but we think there are reasonable hopes of presenting you with a much better report next year. We are

satisfied that there will be plenty of wheat for shipment in California and Washington territory and we do look for higher freights shortly from that part of the world. The East India freight market has been firmer lately, and with no super abundance of tonnage in that direction, and with the jute crop coming forward, we hope to see a better state of freights ruling. But of the outward freights we are sure, and the following figures will give you an idea of the improvement in which we are participating:

Names of Ships		Present Outward Charters	
Ditton	1897	To San Francisco	£3,337
Leyland Brothers	1897	To Chittagong	£2,860
Liverpool	1897	To Calcutta	£3,790
Riversdale	1897	To Diego Suarez	£3,824
Fulwood	1897	To Monte Video	£2,774
Aigburth	1897	To Java	£2,636
			£19,221

Names of Ships		Last Similar Outward Cargo	
Ditton	1896	To San Francisco	£2,927
Leyland Brothers	1896	If loaded then for Chittagong	£1,800
Liverpool	1895	To Calcutta	£1,885
Riversdale	1896	To Singapore	£1,969
Fulwood	1896	To Portland	£1,811
Aigburth	1895	To Vancouver	£1,950
			£12,342

The wives of the partners.

This photograph was probably taken in 1901 at the launching of the *Planet Neptune*, though it is possible that it was taken a few years later when Leyland took all the office staff across to Hamburg. He went to a meeting of the International Sailing Ship Owners Union of which he was a prominent member.

An office party.

Turning his attention to the value of shares in their company he said:

> Shareholders will have noticed sales of the Leyland Shipping Company's £1 shares on the Liverpool Stock Exchange, at 10 shillings per share, and we think it right to draw their attention to the true position of affairs, and so prevent an unreasonable sacrifice of property which sales at such a price involve. The fleet as you know consists of 15 modern iron and steel sailing ships, of the highest class in Lloyds, with a carrying capacity of about 52,600 tons dead weight. They originally cost £313,280. For the purposes of amalgamation, they were valued by Messrs C W Kellock & Company of this City, in the month of May 1896, at £186,400. From this valuation, certain deductions, amounting to £12,596 were made, and certificates or scrips issued for balance viz: 173,804 shares of £1 each.
>
> Shares sold therefore at 10 shillings per share, are in the proportion of selling the fleet for £86,902 (or say £1 13 shillings per ton dead weight) which about 12 months ago, was valued by Messrs C W Kellock & Company at £173,804. We would therefore suggest that shareholders considered this ratio of prices before selling their property at the very unreasonable price of 10 shillings per share.

At these meetings various management issues were discussed. Both the managers and directors were considering the possibilities of further steamships, having acquired the *Planet Mercury* in 1894. Leyland said at the 1897 General Meeting:

> A great deal is being said regarding the future of sailing vessels, and this is a particularly interesting topic to us, as being essentially sailing ship owners. We are told that our industry is played out, and just as wooden sailing vessels had to give way to the iron and steel ships, so our modern sailing ships must give way to steam. To a certain extent this may be correct, but I have on previous occasions heard the condemnation and extinction of sailing ships pronounced during bad times, and soon afterwards I found the self same vessels enhanced in value, and paying good dividends.
>
> At present very few sailing ships are being built, – so much in our favour. Many are being lost by perils of the sea, and are not being replaced. Many more have been sold to foreigners, but this does not assist us, as they are thereby brought into unfair competition with us by reason of their new owners being allowed to load deeper, and sail with fewer hands, and at less wages than we sail at.
>
> Some of our shareholders have at various times lately spoken to us on the subject of acquiring steamers in place of, or in addition to the sailing vessels.
>
> The consideration of this subject has already engaged the careful attention of your directors, and they have practically decided that any new tonnage added to the fleet should take the form of steam tonnage. They believe too, that in the immediate future, prices of steamers will be at a lower level than has prevailed during the last year or two, and therefore favourable opportunity may present itself for acquiring the most modern type of boats on advantageous terms.

In addition to the question of steamers the managers were considering the sale of smaller vessels owned by the company. At this meeting Leyland said:

We have had it in view to sell the smaller vessels. The *Aigburth* as you know is valued at £8000. She is a vessel that cost £23,400. When she arrived in Hamburg, the directors thought if we could sell her for the valuation, being a small vessel it would be advisable to do so. We put her up for auction. It only cost us £7 or £8 to do so, we would have sold her probably, if we could have obtained £7500. At the auction there were very few people present, and as there were several other vessels for sale in Hamburg at the same time, you may imagine we had not what might be called a fair field and no favour. The first bid for the *Aigburth* was £5000. That was subsequently increased in the afternoon to £6000 and the next morning when we were closely negotiating a charter which the vessel has since secured, we received an offer of £6500 cash for her. It is possible that had the vessel remained in Hamburg a little longer we might have obtained £7500, but as it was uncertain and as there were many other vessels for sale in the port, we deemed it advisable not to keep the ship laid up, but to turn her round and secure this big outward freight of 19 shillings, and send her to Java. If it was good enough for a Scandinavian to buy her for £6500 and with such a big freight in prospect, we thought under these circumstances it was good enough for this company to retain their property at the present. We believe that any vessel under 3000 tons deadweight is not what might be called a desirable merchant vessel. The tendency of the age is in the direction of large tonnage steamers, and the sailing ships that are being built, are all of very large capacity, and to carry the maximum of dead weight on the shallowest draft of water. We quite see the advisability of selling these small merchant vessels, and we shall do so at anything like the valuation or thereabouts that Messrs Kellock and Company have given us.

Court Cases

The managers were involved in several court cases. One of these reached the Court of Appeal in 1896 and concerned an action to recover demurrage for the detention of their sailing vessel *Riversdale* in Cardiff. The vessel was chartered to proceed to Cardiff to load a cargo of Albion Merthyr steam coal for Singapore and the terms of agreement provided that the shipowners would receive 4d per ton on the registered tonnage of the vessel for every day the vessel was detained in port beyond 17 working days. The terms of the guarantee of the coal company provided for only 3d a day. The loading should have been completed on 21 January 1896 but it was completed on 28 January and in consequence the colliery paid to the plaintiff demurrage at 3d a day for six days since the company refused to pay for a Sunday. Therefore the plaintiffs sued the charter party for seven days at 4d a ton. The previous judge had given a decision in favour of the plaintiffs and in the appeal the Master of the Rolls agreed that as the real contract was between the shipowners and the charter party, the latter would have to pay 1d per ton to R W Leyland & Company.

New Lines of Trading

With new personnel and the formation of the Leyland Shipping Company which provided far greater resources for expansion, the managers of R W Leyland & Company, turned their attention to new lines of trading, partly due to the need for different work for their new steamer *Planet Mercury* and for the other steamers that they intended to build. For instance in July 1897 Leyland wrote to the general manager of the Gulf Colorado and Santa Fe Rail Road at Galveston in Texas, USA. He pointed out that all the cattle at that time were shipped to San Louis and Chicago for shipment from there to Europe. He envisaged that shipment could be done much cheaper via Galveston since the cost of transportation of the cattle on the rail road would be smaller as they had to travel less distance. He wondered whether it would be a worthwhile proposition to introduce a monthly service; whether loading could be arranged with the wharf company; whether the rail roads would give a reasonable rate to Galveston to compete with the Eastern port's monopoly and finally whether the merchants and bankers give this line support.

At about the same time in 1897 the company had a contract for the ship *Planet Mercury* for a minor port in India called Negapattinam. The cargo was a large one consisting of five locomotives, boilers, oil, and fittings for a new railway. Leyland's partner, Sewallis Winter, was on board the ship for a short holiday to improve his health and whilst in Glasgow he made a very poor arrangement as regards this cargo and interfered with the captain's business. Leyland wrote him a strongly worded letter: 'The point is to an amount of cargo shut out, by which we are threatened with a very serious loss, possibly some hundreds of pounds – besides a vast amount of trouble and annoyance to Messrs Temperley – to the India office and ourselves.' He enclosed a letter from the charter party which complained that he 'absolutely refused to meet the case or assist in any way by staying a little longer, and taking out say part of bunker coals – or other unimportant cargo – to make way for the important Negapattinam cargo and fittings amounting to 35 tons.' The cargo that they referred to was 2 locomotives, boilers, about 26 cases of machinery, 3 girders, acid, tubes, oil, wire, and instructions. He continued:

> In the first place under the special circumstances of such a special cargo – for an out of the way port like Negapattinam, it was the height of folly and indiscretion to shut out the vital part of the shipment without coming to some arrangement. You had no right to take upon yourself to do so, without consulting us.

Leyland tried to wire the ship but it had already gone. He further wrote:

> I presume you will say that the displacement scale showed that we had 4959 tons on board and that you feared stoppage by Board of Trade on account draft. But a

moments reflection should have shown you that a more important point was involved in stoppage by Board of Trade. By charter party, in the absence of Captain weighing cargo, we have to take shippers weights. You knew (or ought to have known) that shippers weights were not 4959 tons and as we had not weighed cargo, we have to take their weights. 5 locomotives were intended to be shipped by our steamer, but not one can be put together in India, in consequence of your refusng to take the 35 tons – inclusive of the 2 boilers, which you might have done by taking out bunkers coal – or other unimportant cargo!

Changes in the Leyland Fleet

In the company report for the year ending 30 April 1899

The *Fulwood* soon after launching in 1885; she was named after a suburb of Liverpool and was a sistership to the *Wavertree*.
NORSK SJØFARTSMUSEUM

a number of details for the previous year's working were given. The profit and loss account showed the credit balance at £31,420 of which the company decided to write off £20,000 for depreciation and place £3000 in the reserve fund. Therefore the directors recommended a payment of a dividend for the previous year of 4 per cent. The report revealed that the value of sailing ship property had improved distinctly and that freights had been at a higher level. They had ordered a steamer of 10,000 tons deadweight to be built by Messrs Workman, Clark & Company of Belfast but they sold her before launching at a price in excess of the contract price. In October 1898 the company contracted to build a steamer of about 7000 tons deadweight capacity with the Northumberland Shipbuilding Company of Howden on Tyne, with the engines to be built by the Wallsend Slipway and Engineering Company. This was the *Planet Mars*, a steel screw steamer of 4327 tons, launched in 1900. Her dimensions were a little larger than those of the *Planet Mercury* since she had a length of 360ft. The price of shares had risen to about 13s each and early in 1900 Leyland bought shares from his partner L B Haddock at 15s each.

In October 1899 the managers were trying to sell their last remaining small sailing ship, namely the *Doxford*. Leyland wrote to the Bank of Liverpool stating that they were trying to sell her in her present position in Dunkirk for £1275 less 5 per cent, 'but buyers went off.' He believed that the market 'is better again and we have her out at £1400 less 5 per cent with a good hope of succeeding.' However they were unsuccessful at this stage. The smaller vessels such as the *Doxford*, which were never made into limited liability companies, were owned on the 64th principle and they remained so under the new management from 1893. The ship was finally sold in 1903, after a disastrous loss on one voyage, to the Indische Handels Company, Batavia.

Other changes in the company's fleet of ships at this time included the loss of the *Planet Mercury*, which went missing in February 1900 and the *Roby*, burnt at sea. The *Roby* was well covered by insurance; the hull was insured for £14,000 and her outfit and freight for £4250. Leyland mentioned that she had been valued at £12,000 originally 'but of course has much increased in value.' In a letter to one partner he wrote that it was 'very unfortunate following so soon after the *Planet Mercury*.'

Although the company and particularly the managers were sorry to lose these two ships, trading for the year ending in July 1900 had been good. Leyland wrote to Haddock who was involved in the Boer War: 'I am glad to tell you that we have done very well in the business this year. Up to the end of July our profits showed about £1200 better than the end of July 1899 which I hope you will regard as satisfactory.' The effects of the Boer War and the money from the insurance on the lost ships may have encouraged the directors to order two new steamers. The *Planet Venus* (II) was a steel screw steamer of 4329 tons, built in 1900 by Napier & Miller, Glasgow: she had an overall length of 385ft. A year later in 1901, a similar ship of the same size was launched in the same yard and named *Planet Neptune*.

Business with America

For this new trading it was essential that fresh lines of communication were opened and in May 1901 A J Preston was in Philadelphia on behalf of the company in order possibly to form a new company, either with or without an American partner. They were trying to utilise

In dry dock at Antwerp in 1905/06 the *Fulwood* underwent major work to her hull. This was her first visit to European waters for several years, having made two passages from Newcastle, New South Wales to South America. She went missing in 1919, on a passage from Buenos Aires to Korsor.

the existing American interest in shipping to see if the American commercial interest might be disposed to buy cheap tonnage in England. The idea was to build cheap fine class ships in England and R W Leyland & Company had employed lawyers to work on the main legal points of placing British ships under the American flag. Preston visited the agents of the Leyland Shipping Company called Taylors, and they agreed to join the new venture:

> providing we can put something more definite before them in the way of securing employment for the boats when built and they suggested it would be a good thing if you went to Seattle or some other ports in the Pacific and see what could be done with reference to opening new lines.

Leyland felt that once their company was started and the Americans had put some money into it then 'we should have no difficulty in finding the business for the steamers as long as there is any business for other steamers to do.'

Shortly before Preston's visit to the United States, the Leyland Shipping Company had secured an arrangement for their steamers to trade between Philadelphia and Avonmouth. They did not wish to involve any American partner in this service but felt that there must be other lines to develop in connection with the railway companies on the Eastern seaboard of the United States. Leyland had been over in 1900 and in 1901 he was still considering the possibilities of visiting the Pacific coast to make arrangements with railways for terminal facilities. However at this stage Messrs Taylors were suggesting a line from La Palice in Europe to Philadelphia.

This steamer service between Philadelphia and Avonmouth was run jointly with Manchester Liners Limited from 1901. The first sailings were the *Manchester Corporation* and Leyland's *Planet Neptune* to the piers of the Reading Railroad. Each company contributed a ship on alternate weeks and this service ran successfully for three years. In the first four months of 1903 there had been exceptionally severe weather in the North Atlantic which involved the steamers in delay and extra expense. However early in 1904 the company withdrew its steamers from these two lines in the North Atlantic due to the low freights being obtained and they redirected them into the carrying trade.

The Early 1900s

The early years of this century were good years for the company and it was a better period in the trade cycle. Partly as a result of the Boer War there was a greater need for shipping and a number of shipowners took advantage of this and built new vessels. The company ordered two new steamers and, taking advantage of the better prices being obtained for such vessels, sold some of their older and smaller ships. Among these was the 15-year-old *Grassendale* (II), which was sold for £10,000 through Clarkson & Co to G Granland, of Raumo, Finland. Later in 1900 they sold the *Cressington*, which was unloading at Barry, to a Liverpool company. However, in 1902 she was sold again, to Repetto Bros, Genoa, Italy. In 1902 they also lost the *Liverpool*, the flagship of their fleet, when she stranded on the north east end of the island of Alderney during a voyage from Antwerp to San Francisco, and became a total loss.

In the company report for June 1902, the directors announced a profit of £28,924 which was a result of the eight completed voyages of their sailing ships during the financial year and the earnings of three steamers. They recommended a dividend of 5 per cent. However, towards the end of 1902 trading once more became difficult for their shipping fleet and they had to report to shareholders in 1903 that they had suffered 'a year of unique depression in shipping business.' The report continued:

> This unfortunate state of affairs has been brought about in the first place by the abnormal amount of steam tonnage built during the late war in South Africa, and the subsequent liberation of transports, etc. from government employ,

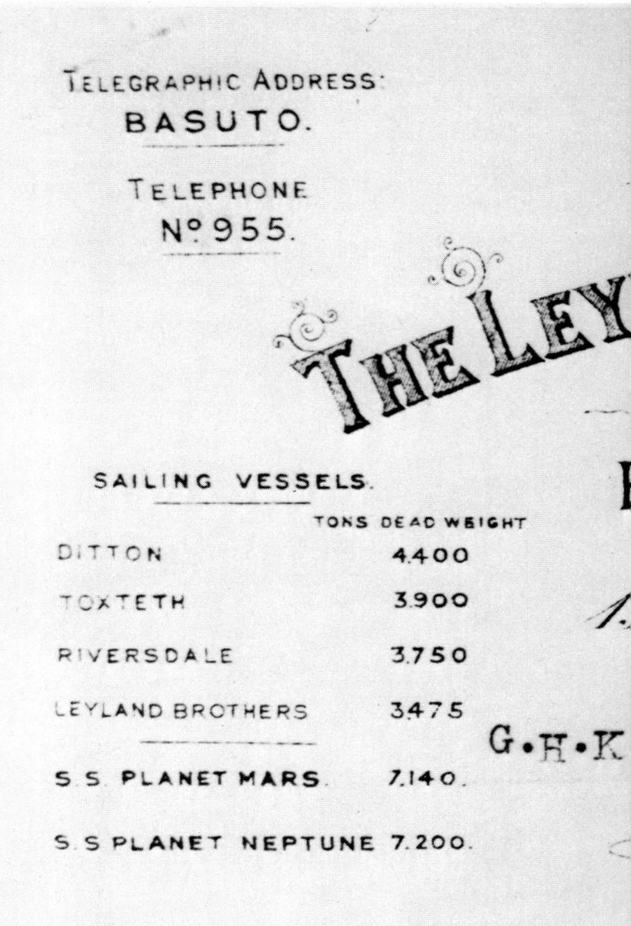

returning to their usual trades and in the second place to the large number of sailing vessels built in France during the last 3 years, to avail themselves of the bounty and mileage (apart from freight considerations) conferred by law on sailing vessels. For these reasons both steam and sail freights have suffered severely but your directors believe that the worst phase of the situation has passed, although there would appear to be no immediate prospect of substantial improvement.

Despite this the company was able to pay a dividend of 4 per cent of which 2 per cent had been paid as an interim dividend in December 1902. Leyland wrote a long letter to *The Times* complaining of the French Bounty System which he believed provided unfair competition for sailing ship owners such as himself in England.

Death of a Partner

On 21 August 1903 Lorentz Haddock died and this was a bitter blow to the management of the company. It was a particularly harsh blow to R W Leyland since they had been close business friends. For instance in 1900 Haddock

There has been some confusion regarding the company's house flag. In all photographs and paintings of the Leyland ships the house flag appears as four globes and the letters RWL & Co. However, the company was known by seamen as the 'hungry goose line' (see A G Spier's *The Wavertree: An Ocean Wanderer*). This referred to the Liver bird, the legendary symbol of Liverpool's connections with the sea. It stands with seaweed in its beak and is derived from the medieval eagle of St John. It was chosen by the burgesses of Liverpool in the thirteenth century as their emblem in tribute to their royal founder King John. The Liver bird was R W Leyland's crest and it appeared on his personal notepaper and was painted on his carriages.

The company's headed notepaper.

CODES.
A.B.C. 5TH ED.
WATKINS' & APPENDIX.
SCOTT'S 1896.
LIEBER'S.
STANDARD.

...ND SHIPPING COMPANY, LIMITED.

RWL & Co

...LEYLAND & CO. MANAGERS.

...0 H & 30 K. Exchange Buildings.
(Lift Entrance 30 K.)

Liverpool. 30th July 1907.

SAILING VESSELS.

	TONS DEAD WEIGHT
WAVERTREE	3300
FULWOOD	3300
HALEWOOD	3300
ALLERTON	3200

S.S. PLANET VENUS, 7120.

had helped Leyland out of his difficult financial situation with the Bank of Liverpool, although exactly how he did this is uncertain. Leyland made only one reference to this assistance in his letters. He wrote to Haddock when he was in South Africa giving him details every week of the partnership and keeping him informed of events. In the 1890s Haddock had been a city councillor and shortly before his death it was intimated that he would be made a Justice of the Peace for the City of Liverpool. He did not live to enjoy this honour.

Leyland now turned his attention to helping his late partner's brother, George Bahr Haddock and almost immediately he tried to use his influence to secure George Haddock's election to be a Justice of the Peace. Firstly he asked a friend to use his influence with Lord Derby and the authorities who would make the appointment. Then at a meeting of the City Council early in September 1903 the Lord Mayor paid tribute to the late Lorentz Haddock. In consequence of this Leyland wrote to the Lord Mayor regarding his late partner:

> The first point that I venture to bring before you is, that having regard to his heroic self devotion in giving up as he did, all that goes to make life happy and comfortable, by going out to South Africa to fight in defence of his country and probably by that sacrifice having materially developed the terrible disease from which he eventually died – by continuous exposure on the Veldt – whether we ought not as Liverpool men to make some public recognition of his services.

He then specifically referred to the possibility of George Bahr Haddock receiving the appointment in his brother's place. He wrote:

> He [Lorentz] has however not lived to enjoy the honour but I venture to say that it would be a graceful act, if his brother Mr George Haddock, who has lived with him all his life, were appointed to the Magistracy, which unfortunately Mr L B Haddock has been unable to enjoy.

This seems to be particularly significant bearing in mind the split in the partnership in later years.

As well as helping George Haddock to secure his appointment to the Liverpool bench he also paved the way for him to enter into the partnership of R W Leyland & Company in his brother's place. It was necessary for the surviving partners of the company to purchase from the executors of L B Haddock his share in the firm and then sell to his brother. At the time George Haddock mentioned that he thought it had been his brother's wish that he should join the firm in his place. Although George Haddock was quite well known in Liverpool not everyone was happy about him entering the firm. For instance George Barker, from whom Leyland had borrowed some money and who was a shareholder of the company, strongly advised Leyland not to have George Haddock in the management of R W Leyland & Company. Why precisely he should advise against this course of action is unclear. It is known that the Haddocks had what could be termed an 'interesting' background.

George Bahr Haddock and Lorentz Bahr Haddock were the nephews of George William Bahr (1822–1880) who was a partner in the firm of Bahr Behrend & Company. George Bahr had retired from the firm in 1879 to stand for Parliament as the Liberal candidate for Preston but had died of cancer in May 1880. He lived with his two unmarried sisters near the Dingle which was a fashionable area of Liverpool. His immense fortune of about £160,000 came mainly from property owned in James' Street, Alexandra Buildings and Old Castle Buildings in Liverpool. By his will made in August 1878, the estate was divided between his three sisters although the ultimate beneficiaries were his nephews George Bahr Haddock and Lorentz Bahr Haddock, who were the sons of his married sister Jane. He desired that George, who was born about 1871, should enter his old partnership of Bahr Behrend & Company on reaching manhood. Before his retirement he nominated his trustee and friend Gordon Ross, an iron merchant and therefore not in shipping, to become a partner in his place, presumably with the consent of his partner, George Behrend.

From this company's viewpoint the appointment of Gordon Ross was a very big mistake which caused a drastic split in their partnership in 1889 and considerably reduced the business of the company. However George Haddock did join the firm for a short time before, surprisingly, Ross moved him on out of the firm. The reason for this is most unclear but he certainly never looked back, for his political ambitions were fulfilled when he was made MP for the North Lonsdale Division of Lancashire from 1906 until 1918; he died in 1930. Perhaps George Barker knew more about the dismissal of George Haddock in the early 1890s from Bahr Behrend & Company and it may be for this reason that he advised Leyland not to accept him into the partnership of R W Leyland & Company.

Depression Difficulties

When George Haddock joined the partnership late in 1903, the company was suffering from severe competition and although trading had been difficult from late in 1902, there was a depression in shipping for the next few years. In a report to the shareholders of June 1904, the directors related that the depression in the shipping business had continued since their previous meeting. The report stated:

> Steam and sail freights remain at an unremunerative level, especially sailing ship freights, which have been unduly lowered in consequence of severe competition by foreign bounty fed vessels. Ships assisted by the bounty are able to work and pay their way at rates of freight that are ruinous to the English vessels, and your directors view with concern the unequal contest.

In consequence the results of the year's trading of the company showed a loss of £3802 on the completed voyages of sailing ships and steamers and with various other losses this amounted to a total loss of £9232. They also felt that the various sailing vessels that were trading abroad would at the current rates of freight show losses on their arrival home, and the directors estimated that this would be about £6000.

Due to the poor state of shipping it was very difficult for the company to find sufficient work for their fleet and all vessels including the steamers were now involved in the carrying (tramping) trade. This meant that the ships were often away from their home ports for several years and it was more difficult to keep a check on the maintenance of the vessel and the financial business of each ship. For instance, the *Wavertree* went from Newcastle to San Francisco with an outward cargo early in 1904 and this was her last visit to European waters for nearly five years before she returned to Ellesmere Port in 1908.

Leyland was ill for some considerable time, probably from October 1903 to June 1904 and he found that his income was seriously reduced. In a letter of June 1905 he wrote:

> We have been going through a very bad time in my business for the last three years. I daresay you will have had similar complaints from other shipowners. The company has paid no dividends for two years and in fact our balance sheet just out shows a loss on trading during the last two years of £37,681. My income is very seriously diminished . . .

Leyland tried to find work for his fleet. He was a prominent member of the International Sailing Shipowners Union which was an international body of owners formed to stand against uneconomic freights, but it did not last long. In 1906 the members of the union agreed not to accept nitrates at less than 21s 3d a ton freight. This was barely achieved. In consequence Leyland made C W Kellock value their fleet early in January 1906, and they based their figures on an offer of G Windram & Company of £6000 for the Leyland ship *Fulwood*. They only valued the nine sailing vessels that remained of the firm; the *Aigburth* had been wrecked in 1904 and the *Speke* was wrecked soon after this valuation in 1906. C W Kellock & Company referred to it as a 'rough idea for Mr Leyland' and the fleet of sailing ships at this date was valued at £66,750. A year later Leyland was thinking of selling the *Toxteth* when she was valued at £8250.

In July 1907 the company reported to shareholders the results of the previous year's trading and they actually made a profit of about £2500. The report stated:

> Steam ship freights were fairly steady during the currency of 1906 but the enormous amount of steamers launched during the year added to the super abundance of tonnage already afloat, militated against the possibility of making satisfactory profits. The directors regret that the estimated probable profits on 4 of the company's sailing ships have not accrued. The *Leyland Brothers* lost a home charter through making an abnormally long passage out from Antwerp to San Francisco, and three other vessels had to leave the West Coast of South America seeking, being unable to obtain the minimum nitrate rate home. The *Ditton* experienced great detention at Antofagasta, and the claim for a substantial sum of demurrage and expenses has been lodged against consignees of inward cargo, and the case is at present before the Courts in Chile. This year's working, therefore, of the sailing ships shows a loss in excess of the provision made last year, and a further amount set aside in respect of estimated losses in connection with present year's accounts of £6000. Outward sailing ship freights from this country and the principal North European ports have materially improved, and if their homeward freights could be secured sailing vessels might yet be worked on a profitable basis.

However trading had not really improved by the middle of 1908. The year's working showed a small profit on the steamers of £2276 but a larger sum was placed against this on interest and charges over the whole fleet. The previous year the company had set aside £6000 for estimated losses on the uncompleted voyages of the sailing ships but this had not proved to be sufficient and they had to put a further sum of £5000 aside in the hope that this would be sufficient to cover the losses on the sailing ship losses. They reported:

> Shipping generally has passed through a year of extremely low freights, dear coal, and detention in all parts of the world; in fact expenses all round have increased, while rates of freight have decreased. At the present moment the steamer *Planet Neptune* is laid up at Hamburg and the *Leyland Brothers* at Portland, Oregon. The directors recognise that while the present low freights continue, this is the best course to pursue. They do not look for any rise in freights before the autumn, when it is hoped business will improve, and with fair freights from the North Pacific and West Coast of South America, the sailing ship fleet is well placed to take advantage of same. The directors have it in view to sell one or more of the sailing ships, but owing to the present state of business it is very difficult to get any reasonable offers.

Loss of the *Toxteth*

On 2 March 1908 the ship *Toxteth* had left Port Talbot with a large cargo of 3906 tons of coal supplied by the North Navigation Collieries. However she went missing and probably foundered off Cape Horn. In the opinion of the court which met in late July 1909 it was concluded that she had probably collided with an iceberg. Captain Jenkins for the Board of Trade surveyed and checked the vessel before her last voyage and found deficiencies in lights and lifeboats and the medicine chest, but these were put right. The company had also had her dry docked for a special survey in January 1908 and £971 was spent on requirements for her. Although she was probably valued at no more that £7000 by this date, the insurances on the vessel were £12,550 and this is a good example of how the company maintained their vessels throughout these difficult years despite the fact they were ships employed throughout the world and rarely visited their home ports.

The directors commented on the maintenance of the fleet by the company in their report in 1908 and they revealed that four of their sailing vessels and one steamer had passed through periodical surveys during the year and that they had meanwhile maintained the whole fleet in first class condition.

R W Leyland Retires

Late in 1908 R W Leyland retired from the partnership due to ill health. He had suffered from periodic bouts of illness throughout his business career. There was very little time left before the renewal of their partnership agreement anyway, and the partners probably came to some arrangement over the purchase of his share in the company. Leyland also had redeemed his insurance policy, which he was entitled to under the partnership agreement. In consequence his income was very seriously diminished, for he no longer was to receive the benefits of his partnership and the company had not paid any dividends for some time. The early years of this century were very difficult for shipping.

The *Halewood* served the company well for 25 years before being sold to a Norwegian company in 1910. She was a sistership to the *Woolton* and was built by Oswald, Mordaunt & Co. She had her share of adventures, being involved in a collision in 1902 in San Francisco Bay while lying berthed ready for sea. Her hull was struck by the steamship *Quito* of Greenock, abaft the main rigging on her port side, causing damage to her plates.

NATIONAL MARITIME MUSEUM

CHAPTER FOUR
Final Years

The surviving partners tried to find some solution to their difficulties in the business and they started by having the whole fleet valued by C W Kellock & Company, obtaining opinions from both the London and Liverpool branches of this firm. It is interesting to compare the valuations for the sailing ships in February 1906 when they were previously valued and then in January 1909 when the partners decided that a forced sale was necessary. Excluding the *Speke* and the *Toxteth*, since the first was wrecked and the second lost at sea, the value of the seven sailing vessels in 1906 was £49,000, whereas three years later the value of the same ships was only £28,000, and most of them were sold subsequently at prices much lower than their estimated value. This was a period of unique depression.

Valuation of the Fleet

The London office of C W Kellock & Company wrote a letter to their Liverpool house in January 1909 which read:

> R W Leyland & Company Limited Fleet.
>
> We have now looked into this matter and the following are our ideas of the value
>
> | | | |
> |---|---|---|
> | *Halewood* | £3500 | |
> | *Leyland Brothers* | £3000 | |
> | *Fulwood* | £3600 | We have not taken into account where any of these vessels are lying |
> | *Wavertree* | £3500 | |
> | *Allerton* | £3250 | |
> | *Ditton* | £6000 | |
> | *Riversdale* | £5750 | |
>
> We would call your particular attention to the figure we have put on the *Leyland Brothers* as the lowness of it may very likely in your opinion require explanation, which is as follows:
>
> We find that although she is the youngest and biggest ship of the fleet, she is due for her No 3 survey in 1911, and has not yet passed her No 2. Added to this, she has been lying for 9 months on the West Coast of South America, which means that it must be 12 months since she was docked, and, as a rule, tropical waters are detrimental to iron vessels. We cannot allow the position of this ship to pass without some notice being taken of it.
>
> Steamers – our ideas are: *Planet Neptune* £18,000
> *Planet Venus* £18,000
>
> Our figures on the above boats may possibly appear to you to be low but we have borne very fully in mind that what is asked for is forced sale value, and have based our calculations on what we were given to understand the *Inchmaree* can be bought for, namely, £13,000. To take this figure, we have made a calculation on the basis of what we think similar steamers could be built for, namely: 5 guineas per ton. The average of these 2 calculations comes out at about what we have put on, namely, £18,000 each.
>
> *Planet Mars*. We cannot even give you an idea regarding this boat as we have no particulars as to her dead weight, speed, etc, but from her dimensions, we should say she is very much of the tub order, and as her engines are considerably smaller than those of the other 2 boats, she looks like a very small boat, and would therefore probably be a difficult craft to dispose of, except at an abnormally low figure. In addition to these draw backs we notice that she is due for her No 2 survey. If you will furnish us with more details, and wish us to go further into the matter, we shall do so with pleasure, but situated as we are we think perhaps it is judicious to refrain from even giving you an idea.

With the figures produced by their Liverpool house, C W Kellock & Company were able to produce an average for the valuation of the Leyland fleet of £92,233. On this basis, and bearing in mind the debts of the company, the board of directors decided to hold a general meeting of shareholders and on 10 February 1909 the secretary of the company, Alf Turner, wrote a letter to shareholders explaining the position. The letter read:

> It will be within your recollection that at the last General Meeting of the shareholders the directors stated that the financial position of the company was receiving their most careful consideration, and that should there be no improvement in the prospects of shipping generally, the shareholders would be called together at an early date.
>
> I am now instructed to inform you that in spite of the utmost endeavours of the Board and of the managers, it has been found impossible, in the presence of the existing

unprecedented and universal depression in shipping, to find profitable employment for the fleet. In these circumstances, the directors deem it their duty to place the whole position before the shareholders.

On the best estimates that can be formed, the present value of the company's assets does not exceed £100,000, whilst its indebtedness is not less than £75,000; but the directors advise that, on a liquidation and forced sale of the assets, in the face of the existing depression, it is probable that, after the liabilities and the attendant expenses had been met there would be little, if any, surplus available for distribution amongst the shareholders. In these circumstances the directors cannot advise liquidation.

If the business is to be continued further capital must be found.

The directors have been in communication with some of the principal shareholders and it is manifest that there are difficulties in the way of obtaining the capital needed from the present shareholders. The directors have therefore been in negotiation, with a view of finding the capital required from some other source and as the result of these negotiations they are now able to place before the shareholders 2 alternative schemes.

The first of these schemes provides for the shareholders themselves finding the further capital required, namely, £25,000, in proportion to their holdings to the shares; contribution on this basis being at the rate of 2 shillings and 10 pence for each £1.00 share. In exchange for the amount so found, the company would issue bonds carrying interest at the rate of 5% and ranking in priority to the share capital, but it would not be possible, without entirely destroying the company's credit, to secure such bonds by a charge on the company's assets. The details of this scheme and the conditions under which the bonds could be issued are set forth in the provisional agreement, a print of which accompanies the enclosed notice and is marked with the letter A. As will be seen from this agreement, in order to carry through this scheme it will be necessary for practically all the shareholders to subscribe for the bonds in proportion to their holdings in the shares of the company.

If this proposal does not commend itself to the shareholders, then, under the alternative scheme, the well known firm of shipowners, Messrs J H Welsford & Company, Liverpool, acting in conjunction with Mr G B Haddock, are prepared to find the £25,000 upon bonds of the company issued subject to the conditions embodied in the provisional agreement, a print of which accompanies the enclosed notice and is marked with the letter B, and subject, also, to 85% of the existing shareholders accepting such bonds, when fully paid, in exchange for their shares in the company.

If this alternative arrangement is carried into effect, then Messrs J H Welsford & Company, in conjunction with Mr G B Haddock, will take over the existing management agreements and resume the control of the company's business, whilst the existing shareholders will, on the completion of the exchange, become the holders of the bonds of the company, and Messrs J H Welsford & Company and Mr G B Haddock will become the holders of the share capital of the company.

Under either scheme it will be necessary to cancel the share capital which has been lost or is unrepresented by available assets. To do this the directors submit to the shareholders a resolution by which the capital of the £173,804 would be written down to £24,622 4 shillings and 8 pence. It is proposed to convert the share capital into stock after the reduction has been carried out to avoid the awkwardness of shares of 2 shillings and 10 pence each.

It is with very great regret that the directors have to record such a serious loss of capital, but they are satisfied that in view of the extraordinary depreciation there has been in the value of shipping property, during recent years, it is a loss which must be faced and dealt with. They trust that if the capital of the company is rearranged on the lines above indicated it will be possible to maintain the business, and that, ultimately, the shareholders will receive in full the present value of the surplus assets.

Management of the Company Taken Over

Somewhat naturally the shareholders were unable to agree to the first arrangement and therefore there was a reduction in the capital assets of the company and they agreed to the second arrangement whereby, through George Haddock, the management of the company was taken over by J H Welsford & Company. This scheme

The *Leyland Brothers* recorded one of the slowest and one of the fastest passages. She was built by Oswald, Mordaunt & Co in 1886; the owners named the ship after themselves rather than after a Liverpool suburb.

allowed for the previous partners to continue under new management.

Over the next three years the rest of the Leyland sailing ships were sold and they were dispersed throughout the world. Seven vessels realised a total of £27,300. The three steamers were retained under the new management.

When J H Welsford & Company took over the Leyland Shipping Company fleet in 1909 they had already acquired a fleet of nine cargo vessels. Under the name of the Gulf Transport Line their ships were largely engaged in the cotton trade between Liverpool and Galveston. At one time J H Welsford & Company had an office in Texas. James Hugh Welsford JP who was the principal owner of the company, in 1911, also bought control of the Union Steam Ship Company of Vancouver by purchasing the majority of shares, amounting to nearly $400,000. However, J H Welsford died suddenly at his London residence on 1 May 1917, aged 53. George Haddock, now an MP succeeded J H Welsford and was chairman of Welsfords until 1930 when he died. During this period the Union Steam Ship Company was really the brightest prospect of J H Welsford & Company's operations. Richard Welsford, J H Welsford's son became president of the Union Steam Ship Company in 1922 and remained in this position until 1931 when he died tragically at the age of 35. Thus by 1931 the firm of J H Welsford & Company was largely in the hands of family trustees, and in 1937 the majority of the Welsford interest in the Union Steam Ship Company was bought by a group of prominent Vancouver businessmen. The last Leyland steamer to survive under the Welsford management, the *Planet Neptune* which had been renamed the *Ikala*, was sold to the Industry Steam Ship Company, before being sold to Italians. The Leyland Shipping Company was dissolved in 1922.

The amalgamation of the Leyland Line with the Gulf Transport Line was not quite the end of the story as far as R W Leyland was concerned for 'on the last day but one of 1914' he issued a writ alleging fraud against G B Haddock and negligence against all three partners. Leyland tried to prove that his position had been prejudiced by the breach of contracts of his late partners. Leyland claimed that Haddock had

> by his acts depreciated the financial position of the firm; that he kept vessels laid up instead of chartering or selling them, thereby incurring large expense; that he gave notice to the manager of Parr's Bank that cheques drawn should not be recognised unless signed by himself or the defendant, Mr Preston, and as a result of this the confidence of the bank was shaken and on or about 6 January 1909, reduction of the Company's overdraft was called.

Leyland also complained that Haddock 'wrecked the company, that he kept back negotiations which he had with other people which would have saved the company, and that he did these things deliberately to get the Plaintiff out of the company.' This case reached the Court of Appeal in February and May 1920, when Leyland appealed against an earlier judgment because he had been required to give details, dates and items which could only be found in documents held by G B Haddock and the Welsford company.

Since the records of the company are no longer available for examination, it is difficult to draw definite conclusions. There is evidence of vessels being laid up, such as the *Halewood* at Esquimault late in 1908, the *Leyland Brothers* which was at Portland, Oregon from April 1908, and the *Wavertree* at Ellesmere Port in 1908, but the question is whether work could be found for the sailing ship fleet. Certainly J H Welsford & Company had no problems in selling the vessels in the three years after the change in management. Most of the vessels were sold at prices that were well below the valuations that had been given in 1909. Leyland believed that these vessels should either have been sold in 1906 or possibly in 1907. When trading improved a few years later the *Ditton* was sold for about £55,000. The events of late 1908 and early 1909 strongly suggest that Leyland could find facts to support his case, but history does not relate the outcome since his friends persuaded him to drop his accusations, due to ill health. He died within a year of the last court hearing in March 1921 at the age of 79.

R W Leyland – an Influential Shipowner

R W Leyland had a long and very remarkable life. He stands out as a successful entrepreneur in the sailing ship world of the late nineteenth century and as an unlucky steamship owner. If he had not suffered from the financial difficulties of 1893 that caused continual problems for the succeeding years, and if he had not been prone to ill health for most of his business life, the Leyland Shipping Company might have survived the difficult years at the turn of the century. He created his own distinctive style of sailing ship and was the managing owner of the largest iron sailing ship firm in the United Kingdom. He helped to pave the way for other shipowners in their competition against steamers both in Liverpool shipping circles and through the International Sailing Shipowners Union, of which he was an influential member. Although R W Leyland stands out as one of the most prominent late nineteenth century sailing ship owners, as with other companies of the same period, the Leyland Shipping Company did not survive without the inspiration of its founder. Many British sailing ship companies had already disappeared from business by 1908 when Leyland retired. Although he had tried to adapt his shipping business by selling the sailing vessels and purchasing steamers, times had changed as had the manner of business, so that their days as a well known company were already numbered.

The *Allerton* served the company for 26 years before she was sold. Like the Leyland Shipping Company, J H Welsford & Co could not make sailing ships pay their way and she was eventually converted into a hulk in Valparaiso, Chile.

Part Two

The Shipowner

Ralph Watts Leyland in the early 1890s. He is dressed in a morning suit, as he would have been seen on the Exchange. He always wore a buttonhole camelia which was given to him by his head gardener each morning.

This photograph, taken about 1857, shows R W Leyland (standing left) with his younger brother and later partner in the firm, George Richardson Leyland (standing right) and their grandmother, Ellen Richardson (1777–1838). Their sister died quite young.

CHAPTER FIVE

R W Leyland – a Portrait

Our knowledge of the early life of many shipowners of the nineteenth century often comes from indirect evidence. Rarely did shipowners, later in life, write autobiographies – though Sir Alfred Jones did, and described his childhood as happy and uneventful. Thus, much evidence comes from newspaper articles or from references and letters written by the shipowner. This is certainly true of Ralph Watts Leyland, the figurehead and senior partner of R W Leyland & Company. The most important information about his early life comes from newspaper articles of the 1890s, by which time he was well known in Liverpool. However, often the writers of these columns may have felt it was unimportant to dwell too much on his birth but to concentrate more on his rise and claim to fame.

The background of many Liverpool shipowners was similar. James Baines, who was one of the principal partners of the Black Ball Line, was the son of a sugar refiner who operated a small business in Jackson Lane, Liverpool. His mother ran a confectionery shop in Duke Street, otherwise his childhood is a complete mystery. Sir Alfred Jones' father was a courier who through marriage and his own father, had a number of useful connections. Few can have experienced poverty but their relatively modest backgrounds may have had a great effect on their desire to succeed.

The first interesting comment on Leyland's birth comes from one Liverpool newspaper in 1892, when he was almost 50. It recalls 'Mr Leyland is a son of the late Ralph Leyland Esq., builder of Everton.' He was the first son and was the third Ralph in a direct line. His grandfather, Ralph Leyland (1776–1839), moved to Liverpool in the 1790s and worked in Dale Street as a grocer. In the register for 1810 he is listed as a wholesale grocer at 31 Richmond Row, but it has not yet been established where he came from. The most likely place is the village of Knowsley, near Liverpool.

Early Life

R W Leyland was born in 1842 in his parents house in Field Street, Everton, and he was baptised just over a month after his birth in the main and oldest Liverpool church of St Nicholas. His mother was Adèle (née) Watts. His father was listed in the register as being a plumber which was no doubt considered a lower class job. Nevertheless, between this date and his death in 1881 Ralph Leyland rose quickly up the social scale. This is shown by the value of his estate when he died; also the title of gentleman in Gore's *Directory of the City*, as well as the rapid change of residence in R W Leyland's early years, finally finishing at the prestigous Grassendale Park, Aigburth.

From such writers as Picton and Sir William B Forwood (later a relation by marriage of R W Leyland) one is able to learn some details of the now much changed district of Everton, where Leyland spent the first five years of his life. Picton speaks of Everton as a suburb of which in 1821 Liverpool was justly proud. He said that Everton 'reached the height of its beauty and attraction about the year 1821. From the umbrageous foliage of the gardens, noble mansions in tier about tier, looked out on a lovely landscape.' Forwood speaks of Everton in 1840 as containing fashionable late Georgian houses but states that the town of Liverpool was pushing its way to Everton and that in time the more fashionable areas were Aigburth, Princes Park and Edge Lane.

When R W Leyland was three months old the family moved house to Mary Ann Street, the name of which changed later to Mitford Street. This was one of several moves in his early boyhood before moving to Grassendale Park in 1847. Although the family was increasing in size with the birth of George Richardson Leyland (later partner in the firm of R W Leyland & Company), it appears that the five years between 1842 and 1847 were the most important years for his father in his business. How Ralph Leyland elevated himself from plumber to builder is difficult to determine but it would appear that he gradually invested in property. By 1881 his properties were worth a total of £40,000 and consisted of both shops and houses. It is probably no coincidence that in 1847, when 300,000 desperately poor Irish people landed in the port of Liverpool, that the family moved to Grassendale

Park. Ralph Leyland may well have taken advantage of purchasing cheap property in Everton. Everton thus became, as Engels would have commented, one of those 'separate territories assigned to poverty. Removed from the site of the happier classes poverty may struggle as long as it can.' A report of 1842 said: 'More filth, worse physical suffering and moral disorder than Howard describes as affecting the prisons, are to be found among the cellar population of the working people of Liverpool.' In this environment cholera and typhoid were still common and the annual death rate was about 65 per 1000 of the population. Life expectancy of a new born child, in the middle years of nineteenth century Liverpool was said to be 17. All this may have encouraged Ralph Leyland to move his family home.

With Ralph Leyland's rise in the social scale, he was able to afford a good private education for his son. Perhaps it was an education he sorely missed. First he went to a small school in Aigburth whose headmaster was the Reverend Barber. Later he went to Basingstoke College, whose headmaster was the Reverend W Lightfoot, brother of the Bishop of Durham. There is no indication to suggest that he did very well at school but he did complete his education up to the age of 18, for in one letter some 30 or more years later he recalled being confirmed at Basingstoke in 1860.

By this stage his physical features were fully formed and it is interesting to note the impression he had on those people he met. One newspaper article described Leyland as 'tall, stalwart, broad shouldered and of Saxon fairness, his Herculean form distinguishes him from the general crowd of commercial notabilities. He may be said to be a giant among pigmies . . .' The average height of a Victorian gentleman has been estimated at 5ft 4in. Another newspaper said 'If the people abroad among whom he mixed, imagine that Mr Leyland is an ordinary sample of an Englishman, they must come to the conclusion that Britain is inhabited by a race of giants. Mr Leyland stands over 6ft high in his stockings and possesses enormous breadth of shoulder.'

There are fewer details of the other members of the family. His father died in 1881, a wealthy man. However, he died too early to see his son successful in business. Their mother Adèle, died very shortly after her husband. In a letter dated 28 March 1883, R W Leyland speaks of his mother having returned from Italy 'poisoned we fear by drains or something of the sort' and that a Dr Gall has been called up from London. She died soon after and on 4 May, Leyland wrote to a monument cutter in Walton to arrange an additional inscription to be added to his father's stone for the family grave in the Anfield Cemetery.

Of the six children, four boys and two girls, the details of Ralph Watts Leyland are the most well known. He had a sister two years older than himself called Mary Parker Leyland who married John Bethune Thompson and at the end of the nineteenth century they were living in Grantham. This gentleman was a shareholder in one of Leyland's early ships, the *San Luis*, and the couple invested money in other ships of the company or made loans to R W Leyland at difficult times. George Richardson Leyland, who was the third child and five years younger than Ralph, joined him in business. He married Ella Gladstone, a cousin to the premier, W E Gladstone, and they lived in the family home in Grassendale Park, Aigburth, called 'Fairholme'.

The Leyland family had known the Gladstones for many years and had commercial connections with J M Gladstone. He was a shipowner and his company made the sails for Leyland ships. He gave four beautiful etchings (his own works) to R W Leyland when he married in 1885. George and Ella Leyland had three children, all girls, named Ella, Norah and Ethel. Henry Leyland, the third son, married Agnes Leyland and they had two children, Doris and Clarice. He was not really involved in business even though he managed his father's estate on behalf of the family. Occasionally he seems to have helped out in the shipping firm when R W Leyland was abroad. He worked at the Shipowners Stores Supply Association. The other daughter, Ellen, married Colonel Harrison and they lived in Dover towards the end of the nineteenth century. They had two sons, Arthur and Percy. The eldest, Arthur Harrison, was killed in 1918. Lieutenant Commander Harrison served on HMS *Vindictive*, one of the ships taking part in the operation aimed at blocking Zeebrugge and the entrance to Ostend Harbour in 1918. They were involved in the attack on the Zeebrugge Mole, the bombardment of Zeebrugge and the Ostend defences, all of which were designed to cover the main purpose of blocking the harbours. The 12 miles of German defences between the two ports included over 225 guns. Apparently the destruction of the Mole defences was not as thorough as they had hoped but at least 23 torpedo craft and 12 submarines were sealed up at Brugge.

Lieutenant-Commander Harrison was severely wounded in the head on board the *Vindictive* but directly he recovered consciousness he joined his section on the Mole. There he led a rush and was killed by machine-gun fire but this last act of gallantry earned him the VC, since by his efforts he was able to keep the battery at the Mole head from coming into action. Finally, the youngest child of Ralph and Adèle Leyland died in 1880, probably in his early twenties.

There are few details about the relationship between the children and their parents, but one point which perhaps illustrates the traditions or practices of the age and the way in which R W Leyland was brought up occurred in the 1850s. Indeed, it goes a long way to explain why he was a traditionalist and disciplinarian, and why he had considerable difficulty with his own sons in a different period, for he had very fixed views about young people. Ralph and his brother George shared a room in the family home at Grassendale Park. On one occasion the story goes that Ralph had done something particularly naughty and had been warned by his father that he would be whipped when he was in bed that night. Ralph obviously fearing the consequences and knowing his father to be a hard man, decided to make an arrangement with his brother who knew nothing of the forthcoming whipping. He successfully persuaded the unsuspecting George to swap places with him. At the appointed hour their father came up the stairs with his whip and walking over to the side of the bed where he thought Ralph lay, proceeded to give him a sound whipping. One can imagine the horrified son with this unexpected beating and the screams of protest. Evidently this beating was a regular fixture and for many years after Ralph talked about his father's 'great big whip' and of his frequent beatings.

Leyland may have been ill during his school days, and throughout his long life he suffered from various ailments. Soon after leaving school, probably in 1861, his father sent him away from disease stricken Liverpool for the benefit of his health. He was away until at least 1867. In the six years he was abroad he visited the Mediterranean ports, in particular Constantinople. After some time there, he travelled to South America. He lived on the Pampas and in Buenos Aires where for three years he saw and learnt a great deal about sheep farming, horse breaking and riding. It was here that his great interest in horses was born, and this experience seems to have had a great deal to do with his treatment of horses later in life when back in Liverpool.

To send his son away for six years must have cost a little money even if Leyland did support himself abroad, at any rate in South America. By the time he returned to England in 1867, possibly completing a circuit of the world in the process, he certainly had not saved sufficiently to start up in business but the experience must have been very valuable to his later work. He may even have been involved with sailing ships for a while. By 1869 he was beginning to make tentative approaches into the shipping and merchant business world and it is possible that he started his insurance business in 1869 rather than the following year. He certainly opened an account with the Bank of Liverpool in this year, in the name of R W Leyland & Company.

Until his marriage in 1885 R W Leyland's lifestyle reflected his bachelor existence and the pursuit of his own interests, which he was able to carry out because of the leisurely manner of his business. He was quite well known but was yet to achieve fame as a shipowner. His standard of living reflected that of a comfortably well-off middle class bachelor. He travelled abroad every two years, had his own servants and drove a carriage and four.

This photograph was taken early in 1885 when Leyland announced his engagement to 17-year-old Letitia Heyn, who was the daughter of a local shipbroker, Gustavus Heyn.

Leyland's Travels

R W Leyland was a globetrotter in the fullest sense and up to 1893 we have a full account of his travels and a chronology of his foreign trips. In 1891 at the age of 49 he wrote 'I have been in the habit all my life of going every second year on a voyage or travel abroad for the sake of a perfect rest and change from business and for the sake of my health. I have been 3 times round the world and to most countries in it.' He published two books about his travels and there is also a diary of his trip to Calcutta and to Upper Burma in late 1892 and early 1893. In 1872 he travelled to Italy and explored the Italian lakes. In 1874 he visited New Orleans, the Southern States, Chicago, Niagara and the Eastern seaboard of the United States. In 1876 he made another trip, possibly around the world and in 1878 he circuited the world in 124 days, which resulted in a book published in 1880 with the title *Round the World in 124 days*. A critic wrote:

This is a book which, when once taken up it is difficult to put down again. Beginning with the overland route from London to Bombay, it describes a stay of 16 days in India, the journey from Bombay to Shanghai, via Galle, Penang, Singapore, Hong Kong and Canton. The reader is then taken from Shanghai to Nagasaki, Kobe, Kioto, Yokohama and Yeddo; thence 4600 miles across the Pacific Ocean from Yokohama to San Francisco, through California and across the North American continent to England.

It is a delightful book, as instructive as it is entertaining. It aspires to no great heights of descriptive style, to no profundity of observation, nor philosophical reflection. It is written in a modest, privy and attractive manner and conveys a very clear and interesting bird's eye view of the journey, with such added comments as one might expect from a clear visioned, well travelled Englishman, with the gift of putting his experiences in graceful and unaffected language.

The front cover of Leyland's second book, entitled *A Holiday in South Africa*. It was beautifully bound in red and gold.

His second book entitled *A Holiday in South Africa* was the result of a most interesting tour of this region in 1880. It was received favourably by the newspaper critics, but he did write a couple of apologies to people who complained of some opinions expressed in the book. It deserves close study because of the date of the trip and the inumerable hardships and adventures he experienced. It is also interesting for its accounts of the people he met and with whom he talked. These included Sir Theophilus Shepstone, Bishop Colenso at Pietermaritzburg, and Ketchwayo in prison in Cape Town. He wrote:

> The war against Ketchwayo was waged for the purpose of breaking a great native power which was considered to be dangerous to the safety of the white inhabitants, which stood in the way of Confederation. As to the outrages alleged to have been committed by Ketchwayo and his Zulus, they are not worthy of the name. A perusal of the facts would soon settle this point in the mind of any impartial hearer and as the ultimatum and its requirements, backed by the approach of a vast armed force at 4 points of the Zulu kingdom, it could scarcely be expected that an independent monarch would quietly collapse without striking a blow to resist the invaders of his country, although I believe that at the time Ketchwayo was prepared to concede all that he could reasonably do and as far as his chiefs and army would allow him.

On the whole he avoided political questions or matters of controversy but it would appear that he was decidedly adverse to the policy of Sir Bartle Frere. He believed that Great Britain gained little from the annexation of the Transvaal although he believed that the latter did benefit. His findings and his visit to a place such as Rorke's Drift where regiments of Zulus crossed the Buffalo river, helped to change his political persuasion toward the end of the 1880s from Liberal to Conservative.

One critic wrote:

> There are probably a few people still residing in England who have never crossed its borders, who do not desire to do so, and to whom solitary confinement for a few weeks in Kirkdale jail would seem vastly preferable to a voyage of 22 days in a first class steamer. To people of this sedentary disposition, the manners and customs of R W Leyland will appear to savour slightly of lunacy; at all events they will regard him as a wild eccentric being, perhaps lineally descended from the wandering Jew. In the days of demoniac possession one might have supposed him subject to a travelling evil spirit, who insisted on his rushing about for three months, every alternate year, over the greatest space possible in that period. After the manner of most enthusiastic travellers, he exhaults all readers to his book to make a tour without delay in Southern Africa, as being about the most charming thing out. Unfortunately the number of those who can spare the time and money for such an expedition is extremely limited; but we must candidly say that though Mr Leyland makes his adventures as interesting as the nature of things permits, we do not feel fetched at all, and shall defer

our trip to Natal indefinitely, though, if we had to do it, we should like to secure him as a companion, provided we wished to combine the maximum of sight seeing with the minimum of food and sleep.

In spite of his enthusiasm it strikes us that Natal, the Transvaal and South Africa generally must be intensely uncomfortable to the flesh and only moderately pleasing to the spirit. Certainly many of Mr Leyland's adventures were very exciting, and though he never boasts of them, he seems to have gone through as many dangers as hardships.

Upton Manor

R W Leyland's home life only really becomes of interest when he moves into Upton Manor after his marriage and from his letters one can learn some fascinating details of Victorian life at his level of society. His private letters show clearly two different periods of prosperity. The first is from 1884 to about 1894. The second is from 1902 to 1911. There are fewer details for this second period but the letters which have survived show a sharp contrast between Leyland's lifestyles, as a direct result of the poor state of his shipping business in the early years of this century.

In the seventeenth and eighteenth centuries, Upton village near Birkenhead became the most important village of the Wirral and a seat of the gentry in the 1800s. With the introduction of a regular ferry service, wealthy Liverpool businessmen moved over the water. One of these was William Inman, the builder of Upton Manor and the owner of the Inman Steam Ship Company. The village was right out in the country but not inaccessible, for not only was the village close to the ferry for Liverpool but it was also at the junction of five neighbouring villages. In the nineteenth century the village contained five large mansions – too many possibly for a small village – one of which was Upton Hall (subsequently the Convent School), which Inman purchased prior to building and moving to the Manor, the fifth large mansion.

The railway which ran under the Mersey attracted many middle class people to the area, and a number of new houses were built to cater for this influx. Nevertheless it was to this village that Leyland moved in 1885. The house was elegant and suitable for a man of his position and he played an influential part in the Wirral district. In one late nineteenth century newspaper he is actually referred to as 'The Lord of Upton Manor'.

The Manor house and grounds first came onto the market sometime after the death of Mr William Inman in 1881 but it was not until 1883 that Leyland showed any interest in its purchase. It is thought that until this year

Upton Manor was probably first inhabited in about 1863. It was built for the well known steamship owner William Inman of the Inman Steam Ship Company.

▲ The dining room. When the Leylands moved into the Manor they purchased the dining room table and chairs from the Inmans. There were 24 chairs and two carvers.

One of the two carver chairs at the Manor. ▶

Although this photograph of the staircase and galleried landing was taken in the 1950s, it had not been altered much since the house was ▼ built.

The Italian garden in about 1950 looking very different to when the Leylands lived there. The unusually shaped lake with its exotic fountain had long since gone and had been replaced by an ornamental pond. The tower of the Manor can also be seen in the top right corner. This was built so that Inman could see his ships approaching the Mersey, before their arrival was announced by telegraph flags on Bidston Hill. ▶

Leyland lived at the family home in Grassendale Park with his mother (if he did not live with his mother at this stage he at any rate lived nearby in a family property). Upon her death George Richardson Leyland and his family, moved in and Leyland moved across the water to Birkenhead. He had stables in Claughton village and at one time gave his address as the Queens Hotel, Claughton. He certainly lived for a time in Hamilton Square in Birkenhead.

In the early 1950s several comments on the date of the construction of Upton Manor appeared in the *Liverpool Daily Post*, when the house was due to change ownership again. At first it was thought that the house was built in

The Italian garden as it was originally created. This photograph was taken in about 1903 when the family had moved back into the house, after several years living in Grassendale. ▶

1830 but in the course of this investigation it was found that Mr Inman, who was responsible for building the Manor, was born in 1825. Therefore the date of building must have been considerably later and the house was probably first occupied in 1863. Mr Inman was a well known steamship owner and one of the unusual architectural features of the house was the tower. Mr Inman had this constructed so that he could look out over the Mersey and see when his ships were coming in. He was thus able to obtain information before the flags which were flown on Bidston Hill indicated the arrival of his vessel.

Mr Inman owned a considerable amount of land with the house as well as several cottages and a farm of approximately 400 acres. When Leyland bought the house he was not interested in the extra land even though he did purchase a few more acres, to the north of the house, a little later. The house was an imposing residence: 'fit for a gentleman'. There were four pillars at the front of the house and large glasshouses with a sloping area on their immediate left. The grounds, which were designed and developed by Inman, included fruit, flower and vegetable gardens, pleasure grounds and an Italian garden with fountain. The beauty of all these was that

Leyland on the box of his carriage and four outside the Manor in 1884.

A view from the tower looking towards the sea. In the foreground are the extensive conservatories and the large stables.

The reception hall looking towards the front entrance.

they were blended into one, rather than being separate units within the walled perimeter. Inside the house there were five reception rooms and 18 bedrooms.

Although the contract for the purchase of the house no longer exists, one is able to learn some of its clauses from Leyland's letters. The house and grounds cost Leyland £11,650 but to build it is thought to have cost Mr Inman £25,000. Leyland paid a 10 per cent deposit and then a further sum leaving a mortgage of £5000, the interest for which was to be paid half yearly at 4 per cent to the Inman Land Company.

Marriage

About the same time as Leyland was looking to purchase Upton Manor in August and September 1884 he was making plans to visit Buenos Aires to see some old acquaintances and in one letter to them he wrote 'I am still a bachelor alas.' Yet by early January of 1885 he knew he was to be married. He was married to Letitia Heyn on 12 June 1885 at Bidston Church by his uncle the Reverend Richard Watts, the Rector of Nailstone, Leicestershire and the Reverend Bachelor. Apparently this wedding was the talk of the town as she was aged only

17 and he was 43. Therefore, not surprisingly, there was an unofficial turn-out to see the couple on their wedding day, so the Leylands took a small tour around the villages near Upton – places such as Bidston, Moreton, Kirby, Thurston and Heswell. The villagers responded to this gesture by decorating the route taken by the carriage. The couple travelled to Norway for their honeymoon and were away nearly two months, returning on 13 August.

Letitia Heyn was born in 1868, the daughter of Gustavus Heyn who worked as an agent in Liverpool for Harland & Wolff. G H O Heyn gave his occupation as a shipbroker and lived at 3 Old Church Yard, Liverpool. Although her father and Leyland knew each other quite well beforehand there is no indication from Leyland's letter or from subsequent events to suggest that any new business arrangements were connected with the new marriage. Her formal education must have been minimal for in her early teens she caught scarlet fever and was ill for some considerable time. From an early age she had been nicknamed 'Madam Contarini' because she was so strong minded.

Leyland had to carry out some repairs to his property, Upton Manor, as the house had been empty for nearly four years and several matters had been neglected. His letters show him being over-particular about some of the work done and insisting on a high standard, stating the work would have to be re-done if he was not satisfied. It took a year to repair the house. One of the main causes for this late entry into the house was the lack of a proper water supply. The couple wished to move into the house two weeks after they returned from their honeymoon on 25 August. However, by 7 September they were still waiting for the pump and well to be repaired. They probably moved on 16 September for there are two letters, one referring to them as having moved in, the other as just about to.

In the grounds he carried out considerable repair work and re-planting, and completely re-fenced the shrubbery, which had a perimeter of 220 yards. He purchased a few dozen fir trees and a number of plants including roses, which he acquired by the hundred. At the same time as buying roses he was anxious to acquire some privet and thorn for hedging about 200 yards. Nothing was done on a small scale. Next he purchased 300 plant pots to supplement the existing ones in his greenhouses.

They left much of the furnishing work until after they had moved in and it is interesting to compare the prices of some furnishings and the priorities that they accorded to them. For instance, it cost only £4 10s to furnish one servant's room. This was probably the equivalent to one month's wages of a servant. In the price was included 'bed, mattresses, chest of drawers, toilet table and a chair', with one or two other pieces. Whereas for his wife and himself he wanted a black and brass bed of 'large solid pattern' which cost over £6 and this price did not include the mattresses. He was prepared to pay £70 for a good billiards table and £150 for a piano. Both of these must have been beautiful pieces. A Chesterfield sofa cost just under £12. It took some time to furnish this mansion and after paying a large bill for furniture eight months after they had moved in, he realised that he still needed more.

The first year of their marriage must have been difficult for them both, for Leyland was very involved with the financing and chartering of six new ships at Southampton, and of course they moved into the Manor house. It seems a remarkable achievement for Letitia, at the age of 17, to have taken over the welfare of the servants and the everyday organisation of this vast house.

From Leyland's letters one is able to establish the number of servants they had at the Manor in 1885, as well as their attitudes to them. From the start of their occupancy until they moved to Aigburth for a few years in October 1893, when they took some of their servants with them, there appear to have been nine servants in the house and gardens. Leyland was firm about the number of servants needed when he wrote 'As far as servants are concerned, five women servants in the house mean comfort – and every additional servant – less comfort'. They were certainly given accommodation but there is no indication as to how much he paid them. Leyland seems to have had at least four male servants, two of whom were labourers; the other two were classified as gardeners but had extra duties, and acted as footmen for his carriage. His foreman was a Mr Hodgson, and a Mr Talbot, who was also cashier for the firm, was secretary at the house. In 1897 the head gardener was paid 28s per week; the second gardener 25s per week and the other two 21s per week. Presumably the servants employed inside the house were paid similar amounts.

A year later, in 1886, Leyland parted with one gardener. Why, is unclear but this quote from a letter requesting another gardener may give some indication: 'Can you recommend one to me – thoroughly competent to take charge of glass – sober, quiet and will do what he is told to do.' Similarly in another letter: 'I don't care what the man's religion may be nor whether he be married or single. I have no cottage for him to live in – and as to wages, I want the best man I can get at the lowest wages he can be attained for.'

Business Life

From his letters one can learn some of the details of the daily business life of a shipowner. He appears to have worked four days a week in Liverpool and travelled by carriage to Birkenhead to cross the Mersey on those days. He seems to have been at home until about 11 o'clock each day. In Liverpool he was on 'Change at midday and at 4 o'clock when shipowners and other commercial dignitaries met to discuss business. In between these hours he worked in his office in Exchange Buildings. Leyland was a traditionalist in his clothing and certainly wore a tailcoat and silk hat when at the Liverpool Exchange. Prior to leaving the Manor, each day, the head gardener would bring him a camelia for his buttonhole. Another interesting practice of Leyland's was reported in the *Birkenhead News*:

> That it is a good notion of Mr R W Leyland to have the flag flying from the top of the house at Upton when he is at home. This royal custom has a three fold benefit, it adds variety to the landscape, saves his visitors purposeless journeys and enables Mr Leyland to at times enjoy his own grounds when he is not 'at home'. He can be like Sir Boyle Roche's bird, in 2 places at once – at home and not 'at home'.

From his private letters one can learn something of the manner in which he treated people. He was courteous and business-like in his approach and expected the same from people in return. In one letter he writes 'It would be more business like to write acknowledging communication to say nothing of courtesy'. In another: 'I have been put to trouble and expense by your extraordinary behaviour for which you will receive debit note in due course'. In another incident he decides his own bill when he believes the one sent to him is too much. He deplored drunkenness and only decided not to sack one of his most famous captains (Captain Stap ex *Great Britain*) because he was honest enough to reveal all details of the incident. He expected to be treated with respect and was quite prepared to take legal action if he was not satisfied. In a letter to a landowner in Cressington he wrote:

> I trust you will take the necessary steps in this matter to ensure its not being repeated, and unless I have a written apology from the park keeper, I shall place the matter in my solicitor's hands to proceed against him for exceeding his duty, using insulting language, and being guilty of conduct conducive to a breach of the peace.

Social Activities

He regularly entertained Liverpool dignitaries, such as the Lairds, for supper and offered his hospitality, house and grounds to charities, political and social groups. Shortly after moving into the Manor, Leyland purchased large quantities of cutlery at discount prices for his parties and details of these arrangements are found in his letters.

In this earlier period he entertained many children of the Poor Childrens Mission that was organised by Charles Thompson in Birkenhead. As long ago as 1862 he had been a founder member of this mission and served on the committee for many years. There is a very moving account of the party at Upton Manor in 1887. The Leylands arranged a number of games in a nearby field and provided a large tea before the children went back to Birkenhead at 7.30pm. A reporter wrote 'It was indeed a beautiful sight to see those 19 carts full of children, all so happy, a great many without shoes or stockings, and scarcely a rag on their backs, while others, you could see their clothes patched and mended, yet very clean.' In connection with the work of Charles Thompson, the Poor Childrens Mission purchased, a building in Hemingford Street, Birkenhead for the furtherance of the work of the mission and work of a benevolent and philanthropic nature. By this time in 1892 A J Preston, of Leyland's firm, was the Honorary Secretary and Treasurer of the movement and R W Leyland was supposed to open the building. However, he was ill and unable to attend so the building was opened by John Hope Simpson, the manager of the Bank of Liverpool.

In 1887 and again in 1890, Leyland invited all the men employed in the Woodside Ferry to the Manor for dinner. This was followed by outside games of tug-of-war and bowls, and later Leyland played the piano while his brothers sang to amuse the audience. Their appreciation of Leyland's hospitality was recorded in the *Birkenhead Advertiser*.

In 1891, Leyland invited all the members of the Central Council of the Working Mens Conservatives Association of Liverpool to spend a day at the Manor. In the afternoon they enjoyed the relaxed surroundings of the Manor parkland and conservatories as well as bowls and croquet. In the evening they had dinner and Leyland, in his speech, recognised the voluntary work of the association to further the political interest of the city. This event was repeated a year later when Sir George Baden-Powell delivered a speech.

It was after the association's first visit to the Manor that a well written piece of poetry appeared in the *Liverpool Citizen* mocking Leyland's speech to the Association, in which he ridiculed talk about equality and said 'No gentlemen, we don't want this. We want to be men, fighting, striving, carving out each man his own life; grieving, loving, doing foolish deeds, doing great deeds, failing, struggling, helping one another – living.'

> Good friends, I'm proud to see you here
> On this my wide demesne,
> And now that you've imbibed some beer
> And feasted well, I ween,
> Take heed unto the words I say,
> And the same ponder o'er;
> You live in parlous times to-day
> And counsel need full sore.
>
> Beware of anarchists who prate
> About equality
> And picture a new social state
> Where you may masters be.
> By stupid fools be not dismayed,
> Nor listen to their rot.
> How will you get your wages paid
> When men like me are not?
>
> How could my riches make you glad
> As they are doing now
> If e'en the wealthiest only had
> Three acres and a cow?
> Where could you go, at any rate,
> For aid, and counsel, too,
> If all the people in the State
> Were ignorant as you?

Then bless the Providence that made
The rich to rule the poor,
And be not of dull Rads. afraid –
They'll ne'er prevail, I'm sure.
England expects – well, you know what;
Let each of you obey,
And be contented with his lot
And grin as best he may!

And bless the Tories, who uphold
Imperial unity,
Whose foreign policy is bold
And keeps old England free.
You may be serfs at home, 'tis true,
But so you'll always be;
And placidly endure it, too,
If you will credit *me*!

See how the native Yankee scoffs
At our old monarchy;
And yet how he admires the toffs
And peers of high degree!
So heed not the Gladstonian crew
And Socialistic fuss;
Believe me 'twill be best for you,
And also best for *us*!

Leyland enjoyed entertaining people and having different groups of people to the Manor. After dinner he often played the piano for his guests and if his brothers were present they accompanied him by singing. At his son's 21st birthday party in 1907 he played the piano for the whole evening without music. He was quite an accomplished musician and wrote and composed a number of pieces that were printed by J B Cramer and Company of Liverpool, such as 'The Grassendale Quadrilles', 'The White Flag', 'The Silvery Star', and an Anthem of the 111th Psalm for four voices called 'Praise Ye The Lord'.

When Leyland allowed social functions to take place at his house there were always a number of references in newspapers to the gardens which visitors had seen and enjoyed. Certainly Leyland spent a considerable sum of money improving the garden and grounds when he first bought the Manor. There are also frequent references to his gardeners and labourers and we know that Mr Joseph Godwin, the head gardener for a number of years, was the main architect behind their beauty. One writer described these gardens as follows:

> At the back of the garden there is an extensive plateau, which has been designed and cultivated so to have now become one of the best specimens of picturesque gardening to be seen for miles around. A pretty lake and artistic fountain complete the view to be seen from the back windows. A great deal of space has also been covered in with glass and gardeners are always at work raising grapes, peaches and other hot house growths.

Leyland was particularly proud of his conservatory and the glasshouses which included a large centre house. An aerial view of these from the Manor house tower dated 1884 has survived together with a number of photographs of the inside. The vines were removed in the winter of 1901 after the house had been empty for four years, even though the gardeners still worked there. Otherwise until 1910 the gardens, grounds and hot houses remained unaltered and very well cultivated until the Leylands left the Manor. Leyland was so often away from home that it caused the aforesaid writer to comment:

> Mr Leyland has cultivated his garden and orchards to such a pitch that the brigands of the vicinity pay them a great deal of attention in the early hours of the morning, and taking the whole year round, they perhaps receive more benefit from the efforts of the gardeners than does the owner himself.

Interest in Horses

One of Leyland's main loves was his horses, an interest which he seems to have developed when he was abroad in the 1860s. While he was in South America he learnt about horse breaking and riding on the Pampas, and the methods and skills learnt here formed his views on his own team of horses when back in England. For instance he never went to the Grand National as he believed it was harmful for the horses.

In June 1881 he hired stables at £25 per annum in Claughton Square which included accommodation for his groom. From this date until he moved from Upton in 1893 to live in Grassendale for a few years, intermingled with his business contracts, are letters about his horses and their peculiarities; of rents for stables, of new carriages, and in June 1884 of trying to find a new groom. In a letter to a gentleman in Birmingham who thinks he had a suitable man to be his groom, he lists all the duties and then wrote 'I give a livery once a year – stable suit – and top boots and wages about 23 shillings per week, though for a really good man – a shilling or two extra might be given.' There exists a photograph of Leyland at Upton Manor in 1884 with his team, coach and two footmen. (See p67.) From his letters one can even establish the names of three of these horses – Black Prince, Castor and Zulu. In 1886 he had three carriages; two with four wheels and one with two wheels. One of them was probably a landau he had purchased the previous year for £40. Also he mentioned paying 70s for a top coat for a coachman.

In 1887 he seems to have purchased a new brougham and it may be this coach that was referred to in an article in the *Birkenhead News*:

> it was pleasant last Saturday to see once again Mr R W Leyland's grand four-in-hand, which has become one of the institutions of the district. His lovely black horses were, as usual, in splendid condition when he drove round the Birkenhead Park, stopping for a time to witness the Birkenhead Park and Sefton cricketers at play. There are not

many more perfect four-in-hands in the country and there are not many better whips than Mr Leyland.

In May 1889 Leyland took the four-in-hand and his two footmen to London for 10 days. He probably went to the Coaching Club meeting on 29 May. The next year he spent two weeks in Southport with the coach. Although he was not riding in 1891 an article on Leyland in this year included a long passage on the coach and horses and as this is a largely forgotten form of transport, it makes interesting reading. It read:

> Attached to Upton Manor are some remarkably fine stables, where a stud is kept of six horses, and it need scarcely be said that, horses and driving being Mr Leyland's hobby, the stables and appurtenances are not neglected. The masterpiece of this department is a magnificent coach used for four-in-hand, which is made with superb skill and elegance.
>
> Into this are yoked four highly bred horses, and away they swing through the country roads with their owner on the box and a couple of very trim looking footmen at the back. Being seated so high up in air, and being drawn by such a powerful team, have the effect of causing a feeling of the greatest exhilaration.
>
> At the Chester and Wirral races, and on other occasions, 'Leyland's Coach' is always one of the lions of the day.
>
> Driving four-in-hand is quite a fine art, very much more so than anyone would imagine who has had no intimate experience of the work. The exact moment for using the brake, the uniformity of the horses' movements, the turning of corners and a perfect knowledge of the temper, capabilities and peculiarities of each horse are absolutely necessary to become a master hand at the work. To this knowledge must be added very considerable muscular power, the strain on the wrist and arm caused by 4 horses is very heavy. In this, however, Mr Ralph Leyland, is admittedly *facile princeps* for he has reduced the matter almost to a science. Under his skilful guidance one scarcely feels the motion of the vehicle and the sensation is more like that of sailing than of driving and in the turning of even abruptly difficult corners there is no inconvenience or irregularity. The horses glide round the corners with a beautifully calculated bend. Mr Leyland is opposed to the use of the whip believing, that those who properly understand their cattle can control them by the gentler method of word of mouth.

Political Activities

Leyland played a leading role in local politics and was certainly one of the most prominent Liverpool Conservatives of the late nineteenth century. However, political life was always second to his business interests and he might well have been Lord Mayor of Liverpool or have entered Parliament if he had so desired. On many occasions it was illness and the necessity for travelling abroad frequently for the benefit of his health that deterred him from entering higher office.

In 1890 he was approached by the City Magistrates Office of Dale Street and he was elected a Justice of the Peace soon afterwards. In 1891 he was one of several magistrates who met in a special session to consider 'the transfer of Public House and Beer House and other licences' and from 1892 he was on the Licensing Committee. In 1899 several people were trying to discredit him and the newspaper *The Porcupine* tried to correct a few facts. They believed him to be 'one of the most independent and fearless of the city's JPs' and pinpointed some instances of his impartiality.

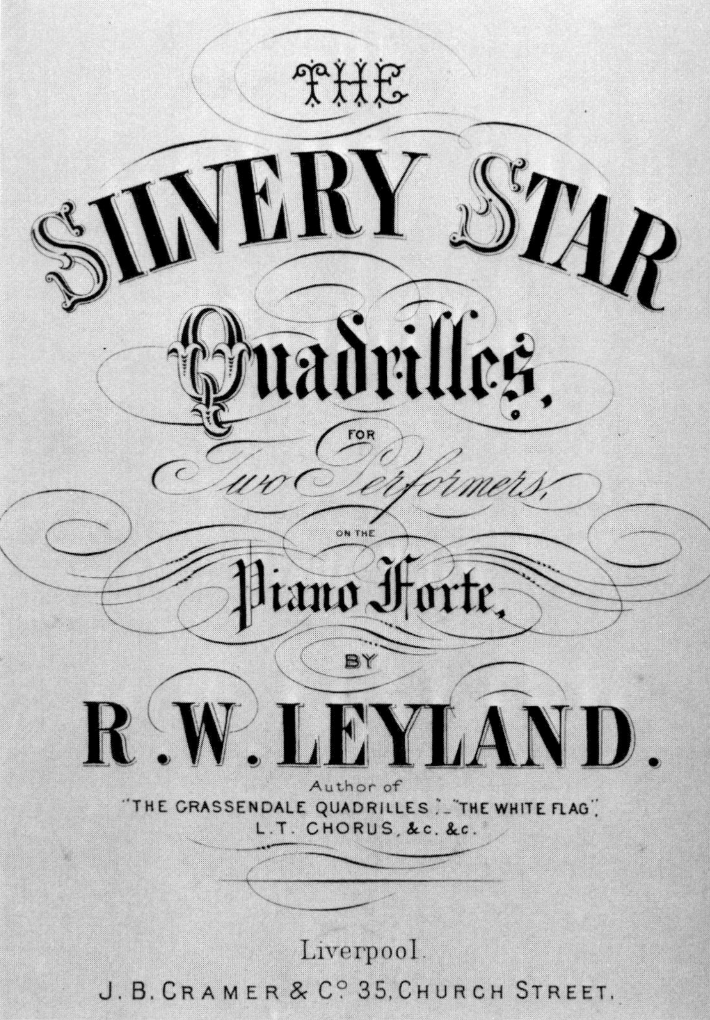

The cover of 'The Silvery Star', a piece of music composed by R W Leyland.

Leyland first entered local political life in 1888 when the city councillor R W Preston decided that if the Exchange ward was to be contested then he would retire. Just five hours before the closure time for nominations, Leyland was persuaded by a group of electors to stand on behalf of the Conservative cause for Exchange ward. This ward was the most important commercial division in the city and ratepayers believed it was essential that someone

LEYLAND for EVER!

Electors of Everton and Kirkdale.

You are called upon to elect a Representative to take the place of your late honoured Member, Mr. EDWARD WHITLEY.

Election, Tuesday, 16th February, from 8 a.m. to 8 p.m.

Consider well the responsibility of selecting a REPRESENTATIVE WHO CAN WORTHILY FOLLOW in MR. WHITLEY'S FOOTSTEPS.

THE ELECTED REPRESENTATIVES of the Ward, through its various organisations, have unanimously adopted

MR. RALPH WATTS LEYLAND, J.P.

SAILING SHIP OWNER.

The Liverpool Working Men's Conservative Association has passed a resolution **endorsing** the action of the Ward Branches in their choice of Mr. R. W. Leyland, the Conservative Candidate, and **pledged itself to secure his triumphant return.**

Your **hearty** support and votes on **behalf of Mr. Leyland** are respectfully invited on the following grounds :—

1. He is engaged in the **Trade of the Port of Liverpool.**
2. As one of the largest **Sailing-ship Owners in the World,** he employs **and well pays nearly 1000 men.**
3. **His Ships** are brought **to Liverpool,** their **Cargoes are** discharged here and loaded; five of these Ships came to Liverpool last year.
4. **All his repairs** are done in Liverpool by Liverpool Workmen.
5. **The propelling power** of his Sailing Ships is obtained in Liverpool, and he never uses any other but Sails **made by Liverpool Sailmakers.**
6. **The Tradesmen of Liverpool supply his goods.**
7. He has **never had any** dispute with his Men.
8. He is in cordial sympathy with all **Working Men** and at his home at Upton Hall he frequently welcomes bodies of Working Men from Birkenhead and Liverpool.
9. He is **the only Conservative Candidate** before the Constituency, and the Ward's adoption.
10. He is **a gentleman** with immense influence.
11. **He has had** experience in the Council on important Committees, and has the respect of men of all shades of politics.
12. **He is just the man for Everton and Kirkdale,** with its teeming population of those who daily toil for their bread.
13. He **was respected** and esteemed by your late Member **Mr. Whitley.**
14. He is a **consistent** man, and **supports largely all** objects for **good, irrespective of Creed or section.**
15. He is a **supporter of the Established Church.**
16. His firm owns **21 Sailing Ships** (mostly bearing Liverpool names), with a total registered tonnage of 39,858, and burden 60,400 tons.
17. **His influence** will help to secure you an **equitable representation in the Council.**
18. He is supported by your present **excellent Representatives Mr. J. Barkeley Smith and Mr. John Houlding.**
19. **He will loyally co-operate** with them for the welfare and **prosperity** of you all.
20. **He is courteous, generous, a true type of an Englishman,** and the **most thorough-going Representative you can have.**

VOTE FOR LEYLAND
AND
A GLORIOUS VICTORY.

JOHN HOULDING, Chairman Everton Division.
D. DUNLOP COSTINE, Chairman Kirkdale Division.

Printed and Published by C. Tinling & Co., 53, Victoria Street, Liverpool.

with their commercial interests should be elected. Here it was that Liverpool commerce was conducted and Leyland was one of the most significant men on the Exchange. In his first speech he recognised the importance of the ward when he said 'The influence of the Liverpool exchange is not confined to local or even national limits, it is far reaching and wide spreading and is recognised throughout the World.' The Liberal candidate was Edwin Morris, a solicitor. The *Liverpool Courier* believed that the parties were 'pretty equally balanced in this ward, and although the greater proportion of the electors are businessmen, there is a considerable labouring class element mostly Irish in race and in sentiment.' Therefore the fight for supremacy was close and keen, with Leyland just securing the seat by 17 votes.

Some newspaper columnists viewed Leyland in very favourable terms. 'A better representative for such a ward it would be impossible to secure. Compared with such a man Mr Edwin Morris sinks into insignificance, and the ratepayers will be dull indeed if they do not secure to public life so highly desirable a recruit.' However, in 1891 when elections were held again, one writer listed all Leyland's attributes and then wrote 'But he has not done a good day's work as a councillor during the whole of his three years' term of office.' On the other hand the Conservatives were very pleased with his work. They believed he had not only been an asset in the Council for the party but had also helped the moderates of all parties. In this election of 1891 in the Exchange ward, much attention centred around why Leyland became a Tory some years earlier. In a letter in May 1884 Leyland wrote to the local Liberal Association whom he supported and said: 'I must confess to having lost all sympathy in the Liberal programme as foreshadowed by Mr Chamberlain and other advanced politicians. In my opinion it is not true Liberalism and the interests of the country are not best served.'

In consequence in June 1884 he resigned from the Reform Club in Liverpool. In a speech in 1891, he mentioned that he served on several sub-committees, spent one year on the Health Committee and had attended most of the meetings of the Contracts Committee. His change in political colour had apparently taken place because he objected to Gladstone's policy in the Transvaal and protested against the Liberal party when the 10,000 men sent out to Cape Town were brought back. He had also complained against the agitation of Mr Chamberlain towards shipowners and he found himself in the position of 'supporting a party with whose foreign policy he was entirely at variance, who would touch his pocket . . . as well as the pocket of everyone else.' He remarked that like Mr Chamberlain he would have left the party in 1886 anyway and come out of it as a strong Unionist.

A political poster. Leyland won this election to the City Council in 1892 with a comfortable majority but ill health forced him to retire shortly after.

In the election of 1891 Leyland lost by 17 votes, the same number by which he had won in 1888. He was probably displaced by the Irish Nationalist votes of the Exchange ward who voted for a man 'pledged to the separatist projects of Mr Gladstone.'

In a political comment on the different candidates and on Leyland's defeat in the election the *Liverpool FairPlay* wrote:

> Truth is stranger than fiction, it is recorded, and here is an example of the truth of the old saying. Mr R W Leyland who was defeated in Exchange ward last Monday by 17 votes, won the ward by exactly 17 votes three years ago. He was born on the 17th of a month, married his wife in her 17th

Ralph Leyland jnr (Rallie), aged four in 1890, is seen here in a typical boy's sailors uniform. He was sent to sea for three years at the tender age of 11, as an apprentice on his father's ships.

George Leyland, finely dressed for a portrait in a Liverpool studio, was two years younger than his brother.

This delightful photograph of Leyland and his daughter was taken in 1894.

year on the 17th of a month and his elder son was born on the 17th of a month. This is remarkable, but Mr John Hand, of the Liverpool School Board, beats the record. He was born on the 25th of a month, landed in England from Ireland on the 25th of a month, was married on the 25th of a month, had two sons and one daughter each born on the 25th of a month, his mother died on the 25th of a month and his father died on the 25th of a month. Mr Tom M'Cracken will now have to take a back seat in the matter of coincidences in his family . . .

During the election of 1891 it was rumoured in Liverpool that Leyland had been asked to be Mayor. This was one of several occasions he was asked to accept the city's highest civic honour and several commentators believed he sacrificed the mayoralty to a sense of fair play in the forthcoming election. One reporter wrote:

> Mr R W Leyland is probably the most popular man in local public life today and his refusal to be approached on the subject of the mayoralty is probably due to his desire to avoid all appearance of soliciting the votes of Exchange Ward by any side issue or by any extraneous influence.

Early in 1892 there was a municipal election for the Everton and Kirkdale ward owing to the death of the representative, Mr Whitley, and Leyland was nominated. The great bulk of the electorate shared his anti Home Rule sentiments. However, there were four candidates. The strongest rival, Mr Tom M'Cracken was a great friend of the late councillor and he stood as an Independent Conservative. This interesting contest caught the public's attention in the largest ward of the city for some weeks. About one third of the city's voters came from this one ward so it was a very important seat. M'Cracken was standing in protest against the despotic rule of the Conservative Association. Leyland won with a comfortable majority of 1424 votes but he had all the advantages of being the official Conservative candidate.

In the city the Conservatives were divided and newspaper reporters saw this as a bad omen and as a distinct advantage for the Liberals. One wrote 'The fact that the Conservatives are a disunited body and in no mood to extinguish their differences, should be a stimulus to the party of progress to contest every division in Liverpool at the General Election.'

Early in October Leyland was suffering from rheumatic gout and was forced to retire due to ill health. Shortly after this he went to India to recover and Mr Austin Taylor was elected to replace him.

On 20 April 1892 Leyland had been the main speaker at the Primrose Day celebrations near the Beaconsfield Statue. At this anniversary people in many parts of the Empire recognised 'the patriotic aims of the statesman who was radically described as "More English than the English" '. In the second city of the Empire and the busiest port of the world, the Liverpool Working Mens Conservative Association organised a rally in the evening near the statue. Apparently several thousand people attended the meeting. Leyland was Chairman at this meeting and the Chairman of the Conservative Association, the well known Mr A T Salvidge, proposed the first resolution to the memory of Lord Beaconsfield.

1892 was the peak year of Leyland's fame and popularity in Liverpool. He was asked to be Mayor as well as to stand for Parliament. In an interview he was pressed for a reason why he would not enter Parliament and he said 'I cannot afford the time. My business requires all my attention. Besides, entre nous, I am not much of a politician.' If he had so desired he might well have become a politician of international reputation but it was both his illness and his business problems that started in 1893 which caused him to take a less prominent role in politics and allow others to take his place.

Travel to India and Burma

In November 1892 the Leylands went to India and Upper Burma so that R W Leyland could have a rest from business and recover his health. His diary of this voyage has some very interesting passages, including one about Everest. The couple travelled along the Northern Bengal State Railway to Siliguri and then started the ascent on the Darjeeling-Himalayan Railway. He described in fascinating detail the course of the railway

Letitia with her two sons, Rallie (centre) and George (right). After serving as an apprentice on his father's ships, Rallie entered his father's office. When the firm was taken over, he was too young to become a partner and so there was no chance of there being a second generation of Leylands within the company. George had an unhappy time at school and yearned to go abroad. His father found him work on a farm in Canada for a year in 1905. However, on his return to England he quarrelled with his father and within a month returned to Canada, never again to see England or any of his family.

Adèle and Hal playing croquet on the front lawn.

A picture of Adèle, reputed to be one of the most eligible and attractive young ladies in Liverpool before the First World War.

and the views of the plains beneath as well as the differences between the hill people and the natives of the plain. Just before reaching Darjeeling, the clouds opened and they saw the summit of Kinchinjunga (28,156ft high). It was

> lifted up by the setting sun and looked like a mass of burnished gold in the heavens. For a moment or two I was puzzled as to what it might be, as the cloud surrounded us, but the conviction of what it must be soon forced itself upon me, as surely there can be nothing anywhere else to compare.

They reached Darjeeling and their hotel veranda overlooked the mountain range. Despite getting up from bed at 5.30am to see the sun rising over the mountain range, they were unable to see Everest itself because of the cloud. Of Everest he wrote:

> This Everest is said to be the highest of the Himalayan range. It is said to be 107 miles distant from Darjeeling and its height is 29,002ft. It is well to be particular, and as the measurement is so accurate in respect of the 2ft who can doubt about the odd 29,000.[!]

Changing Fortunes

It was on their return from this journey early in 1893 that Leyland discovered that all was not well in his shipping business. It may well be financial reasons and the fact that George Leyland had moved from Grassendale, that encouraged Leyland to move back to his family home – Fairholme, in Grassendale Park. He described his unfortunate position with the Bank of Liverpool as 'altogether helpless'.

Leyland put his carriages up for sale and tried to reduce his standard of living. He decided to rent the Manor to Colonel Herbert Robinson of Hoylake who lived there for three years. The Leyland family lived in Grassendale for nearly 10 years. Thus apart from a few details concerning the tenancy of the Manor, little is known of their home life before they moved back to the Manor in 1902, as their letters have not survived. Colonel Robinson rented the Manor House at £400 per annum whereas Leyland rented the family house from his father's estate for £70 per annum.

Once again he got himself involved in local politics and from 1894 he was Chairman of the Exchange Ward Conservative Association which illustrates his pre-eminence in the commercial world. Throughout the 1890s he seems to have had a very great influence in Conservative Party affairs in Liverpool. He also became involved in the affairs of the Aigburth, Grassendale and Garston districts. In 1903 Sir Alfred Jones of the Elder Dempster Line presented Leyland with a portrait of himself on behalf of the residents of Aigburth and Grassendale. In his presentation, Sir Alfred Jones said: 'The tendency of Liverpool was to expand and while land was cheap it should be secured, so that the beautiful parts could be preserved for future generations. Mr Leyland had always been in the forefront in work which has this object.' It was pointed out that Leyland started the Ratepayers Association for the district and was the moving spirit behind its work. It seems that Sir Alfred Jones was referring to the fact that through Leyland's work Aigburth and Garston had been added to the City of Liverpool. Details of the incorporation of Garston and

Hal Leyland was one of the first to sign up with the 'Liverpool Pals' to fight for their country in the First World War. Sadly he was killed shortly before the end of the war.

Ralph and Letitia playing croquet.

of the official inquiry can be found in the newspapers for 1900.

The ratepayers also recognised Leyland's work in preventing certain disadvantages being inflicted on the neighbourhood: 'notably the proposal to erect a refuse destructor at a point which would have interfered with the amenities of the locality.' This was certainly a major issue in the Garston Urban District Council Election of 1898. He had also objected most strongly to the building of an infectious disease hospital in the district. He wrote in one letter: 'It would be most unreasonable to build a hospital in a neighbourhood which produces no fever patients' and 'it would depreciate the value of property and so reduce the rates to say nothing of possibly damaging the prospects of the district as a good residential centre.'

In 1897 Leyland, through his solicitors, tried to obtain compensation from Colonel Robinson for damage at the Manor. An addendum to this letter shows that Leyland was thinking of selling the house for an hotel or alternatively for scholastic use. In *The Times* of 15 May 1897 it was advertised to let. He was anxious to find a purchaser and wanted to sell the house for about £20,000. However, he was unsuccessful and by May 1901 the house had been empty for four years. Leyland decided that if he could not sell it he would let it for three years. The best offer received was £250 per annum with a vast expenditure. Similarly he was prepared to sell the house for £14,000 at this date but the highest offer was only £10,200. Therefore in the early summer of 1902 he moved back into Upton Manor.

Family Life

In 1902 when they moved back to the Manor their four children were all at school. Ralph, the eldest was born in the year after they were married in 1886. In a letter of 1897 there is mention of him at school in Grassendale Park and Leyland speaks of his handwriting as being 'remarkably bad' and he asked the headmaster that he may be taught 'to acquire the habit of letter writing'. He was withdrawn from the school in September 1897 and was sent to the Liverpool Institute but within a month the headmaster was complaining of untruthfulness and of Ralph not completing his work. In June 1898 the doctor thought he had just escaped typhoid and Leyland decided to send him on one of the firm's ships to recover his health. He must have travelled around the world, for in a letter of October 1899, Leyland speaks of his son's return from this voyage; so at the tender age of 12 he started his career in shipping on his father's ships. In an article (*Sea Breezes*, vol 14, July–Dec 1952, Oct issue, p266 onwards) written some fifty years later Ralph Leyland junior speaks of this voyage: 'The first voyage was in the *Grassendale* from Hamburg to Melbourne, the passage taking 112 days around the Cape of Good Hope and then home to Falmouth around the Horn in 108 days,' He was at the Rossall School near Fleetwood briefly until the end of 1902 and then in 1903 he entered his father's firm, and with his practical knowledge of life on board ship, he was within a couple of years promoted to Stores Supply Officer for the Leyland Shipping Company.

In February 1908 R W Leyland wrote to Sir Thomas Sutherland, the Chairman of the P&O Steam Navigation Company in London, asking him to take his son Ralph into their employment on one of the steamers in their Australian Line as Ralph wished to gain some more experience. So when the firm of R W Leyland & Company was taken over by new management in 1909, Ralph Leyland was too young to take over under the terms of the partnership agreement.

George Leyland was born in 1888 and was educated at a local school with his younger sister, Adèle, who was born in 1892. In 1899 he was sent to Cranleigh School in Surrey, at which time Adèle left her Grassendale school. His first school report stated that 'he is inclined to be idle and inattentive' and his handwriting 'very bad'. In September 1901 Leyland wrote to the headmaster to report that George would be late back due to the delayed arrival of one of his ships. Apparently he had been sent off to Philadelphia on one of the company's steamers. Early in 1902 George was removed from Cranleigh School. Why, is difficult to determine because the letters on the matter have been removed but three years earlier he had been caught stealing. He completed his education at Birkenhead School but in 1905 Leyland was trying to obtain a farming position for him in Canada. In one letter R W Leyland wrote 'I have not been able, up to the present, to find suitable location for him, and he is rather young to go out alone unless I could depend upon the person to whom he may be sent. I think it just as well that he should stay a little longer in the old country.'

Shortly after this he went to Canada where he stayed a year and then came home. He quarrelled with his father and returned to Canada within a month, never again to see England.

Adèle went to the Convent in Upton (the old Upton Hall) throughout the second period of the occupation of the Manor. She died in August 1979, and so it is that much of the oral evidence for this period has come from her. Hal, who was born in 1895, like George did poorly at school. Later he worked in a cotton office in Liverpool before joining the Army and he was killed shortly before the end of the First World War.

Although they all had happy childhoods, none of them did very well at school. The boys clashed with their father for he was a very strict disciplinarian and he had very fixed views on how they should be brought up, but Adèle spoke of him as a very good father. In one letter sent to the headmaster at the Liverpool Institute about Ralph he wrote: 'You have my full permission to punish him in any way you think fit if he deserves it. I believe in a good sound caning when circumstances such as you have described arise.' In another letter a few years later, this time when there was a problem with George at school, Leyland wrote: 'I shall be the last to encourage disobedience to properly constituted authority as I am too much of a disciplinarian myself.'

From Adèle I was able to learn a number of details about life at the Manor and of the servants. She spoke of her mother with respect but not much affection. She recognised her as very capable and believed that she managed the Manor very well. She remembered that in 1910 there were four servants in the house which included Mrs Lloyd the cook, Katherine the housemaid and Ellen, the waitress. All of them had worked with the family for some time so there were difficulties when they moved house to Mount Road in Upton, as they needed only one servant. Katherine wanted to go with the family but Ellen had served them longer (a total of 18 years) so she joined them. Joseph, the gardener, his wife Sarah and three children lived in the flat upstairs. One of them, Maggie, combed Adèle's long hair every morning for her. Even at this stage there seem to have been five gardeners.

Many of the servants seem to have served the Leyland family for a number of years. Joseph Godwin, the head gardener in 1910, was certainly working for them in 1897. In this year he was made caretaker at a wage of a guinea a week. When Leyland moved back to the Manor in 1902 he referred to his foreman as a Mr Hodgson who had certainly been foreman for Leyland since 1886. Mr Talbot, who was his secretary at the house and cashier for the firm in 1885, was certainly there in 1892 and he may well have continued like his colleague, Mr Turner, till the firm was amalgamated in 1909.

One reason for this long service must be that they were well treated and their rights respected. For instance in later years, on no account were any of the children allowed into the domestic quarters unless they had previously knocked on the door and their call been answered. However, the household was run in an authoritarian manner by Mrs Leyland, as is illustrated by this letter of 1904:

> Mrs Leyland has to inform Mrs Lewis that her daughter Maggie returned to Upton last week after a holiday and immediately asked for an increase of wages. This was refused. Yesterday she stated she would give up looking after the children so she was immediately given a month's notice, as Mrs Leyland prefers to regulate her own household. She will return home at the expiry of that period.

Later Years

With the family to look after, the Leylands travelled less in later years. Occasionally Leyland combined business with pleasure and certainly in some cases he was anxious to have first hand evidence of ports, facilities and commercial potential. So he made several trips to America in the early years of the century, generally to arrange contracts for his steamers. He very rarely travelled on his own ships, not because he did not trust them but he never wished to interfere with the running of one of his own vessels. However, in 1906 after a trip with the whole family to Amsterdam, Rotterdam, the Hague and Hamburg, he did return on one of the *Planet* steamers. On another occasion, this time in 1904, Sir Alfred Jones offered them a cabin on his steamship *Kingston* which was due to sail to Jamaica in November. In return he asked Leyland to advocate his line and to write some articles.

He still played an important part in Liverpool public

life. He had been a fellow of the Royal Geographical Society of London certainly from 1878 until he resigned his membership in 1889. He was one of the founder members of the Geographical Society in Liverpool and notification of the formation of the society was recorded in the *Liverpool Courier*. Leyland was appointed to the Council with the Earl of Derby, Sir W B Forwood, William Rathbone MP, Thomas Royden MP, J Hope Simpson and other shipowners including A L Jones (later Sir Alfred Jones) who seconded R W Leyland's motion to procure funds for the society.

In the early 1900s Leyland carried on work in the Exchange division as chairman of the ward, in local associations and probably in the Wirral. Certainly in 1914 he called a meeting in Upton School to ask for volunteers to join the Army and his son, Hal Leyland, stood up and announced to the assembled company that he had signed up with the 'Liverpool Pals' that day.

Although a picture of happy family life at the Manor can be painted, for Leyland business in the shipping world after 1902 was very unsettled and this may have brushed off on his children. Ralph after all worked in his father's office from 1903 to 1908. Leyland's private letters give frequent references to the poor state of shipping. For instance in 1902 he wrote: 'We have fallen upon very bad times in shipping with poor prospects in the near future', and there are a number of references to Leyland trying to sell the house to raise money. On 30 January 1906 he recorded that £12,000 had been offered for the house. On 24 June 1908 the house was due to be auctioned, but Leyland failed to sell it.

Late in 1908 he had retired from the firm due to ill health and on 24 February 1909 it was announced that the Leyland Shipping Company had been taken over. Within a very short time his income was seriously reduced. In 1910–1911 Leyland, who had been unhealthy throughout his life, suffered his worst illness

.. PARTICULARS. ..

The Handsome Stone-Built Residence known as Upton Manor, Upton, Cheshire.

Approached by a well-planted Carriage Drive, standing on high ground, and commanding Beautiful Views over Wirral, together with Stabling, Good Fruit, Flower and Vegetable Gardens, Conservatory, Glass Houses, Plantations and Paddock, comprising in all about

11 Acres, 2 Roods, 18 Perches Statute of Freehold Land,

and situated about six minutes' drive or sixteen minutes' walk from Moreton (Hoylake and West Kirby line) or Upton (Wrexham and Connah's Quay Railway) Stations, connecting with Liverpool and Manchester and within easy range of the Golf Links of Hoylake and Wallasey.

THE HOUSE

is of imposing appearance and contains on the **Ground Floor**, Vestibule, leading into Square Entrance Hall lighted by dome at top of house. Dining Room, 30 feet 6 inches by 22 feet with Service Room, Drawing Room, 42 feet by 30 feet, Billiard Room, Library and Morning Room, Servants' Hall, Lavatory, Two Kitchens and Scullery and usual Domestic Offices.

FIRST FLOOR:—Nine Bedrooms, Boudoir, Three Bathrooms, Two Dressing Rooms, Linen Closet, &c.

ABOVE:—Nine Bedrooms and Store Rooms and room in Tower.

BASEMENT:—Ample Cellarage.

. THE GARDENS .

comprise good Fruit, Flower and Vegetable Gardens, Pleasure Grounds, Italian Garden with Fountain, Conservatory, Glass Houses, including large centre House, well stocked with Vines and Fruit Trees, Plantations, &c.

. THE STABLING .

includes Stalls for Five Horses, Harness Room, Coachhouse with Coachman's Rooms over.

The Property is Freehold and has a valuable frontage to the main road.

In 1908, Upton Manor was put up for auction, as Leyland's shipping business was still in a depression. However, it failed to reach the reserve price.

Widowed at the age of 52, Letitia was never quite able to accept her situation in life after moving from the Manor. She rarely wore any other colour than black and lived for long periods of time in a hotel in Parkgate, Cheshire, as well as with her daughter and son-in-law in their vicarage.

and he was confined to Upton Manor for six months. In the circumstances Leyland had to sell the house quickly and tragically did so for little over £3000 to the Stern family in 1911.

The family moved to a much smaller, semi-detached house in Mount Road in Upton. Leyland once more became involved in politics and in the shipping world; he was asked to write his memoirs in the Exchange Buildings but it is not known if he ever did. It is a tragedy that he outlived his own generation for most of the old shipowners had died by 1911. Adèle summed up his life in the following way:

> A very intelligent, thoughtful man. He was a kind father to me. He travelled worldwide. He was a marvellous character who could speak on any subject. He was a very great Chairman and did some great work in Liverpool. Although not a bitter man, after the terrible loss of the Manor, brilliant early childhood and losing his business, he seemed to lose his individuality and lost his interest in life. I feel that after his very bad operation [1910] he just lived out the last years of his life.

He died in 1921 at the age of 79. It is probable that Adèle received £600 from him in his will but it was rumoured that his estate was found to have only £1 left after all debts had been paid. Liverpool had largely forgotten him and his obituary in the *Liverpool Daily Post* was only a few lines long. This was a sad epitaph indeed, to one of the most important late nineteenth century sailing ship owners.

When the Leylands found themselves in financial difficulties and were forced to sell the Manor, they moved to a much smaller semi-detached house in Mount Road, Upton. Letitia had refused to move from the area, despite the fact they were rejected by many of their former friends.

The *Aigburth* loading cargo, probably at Seattle or another NW American port.
COURTESY J H REID

Part Three

The Shipping

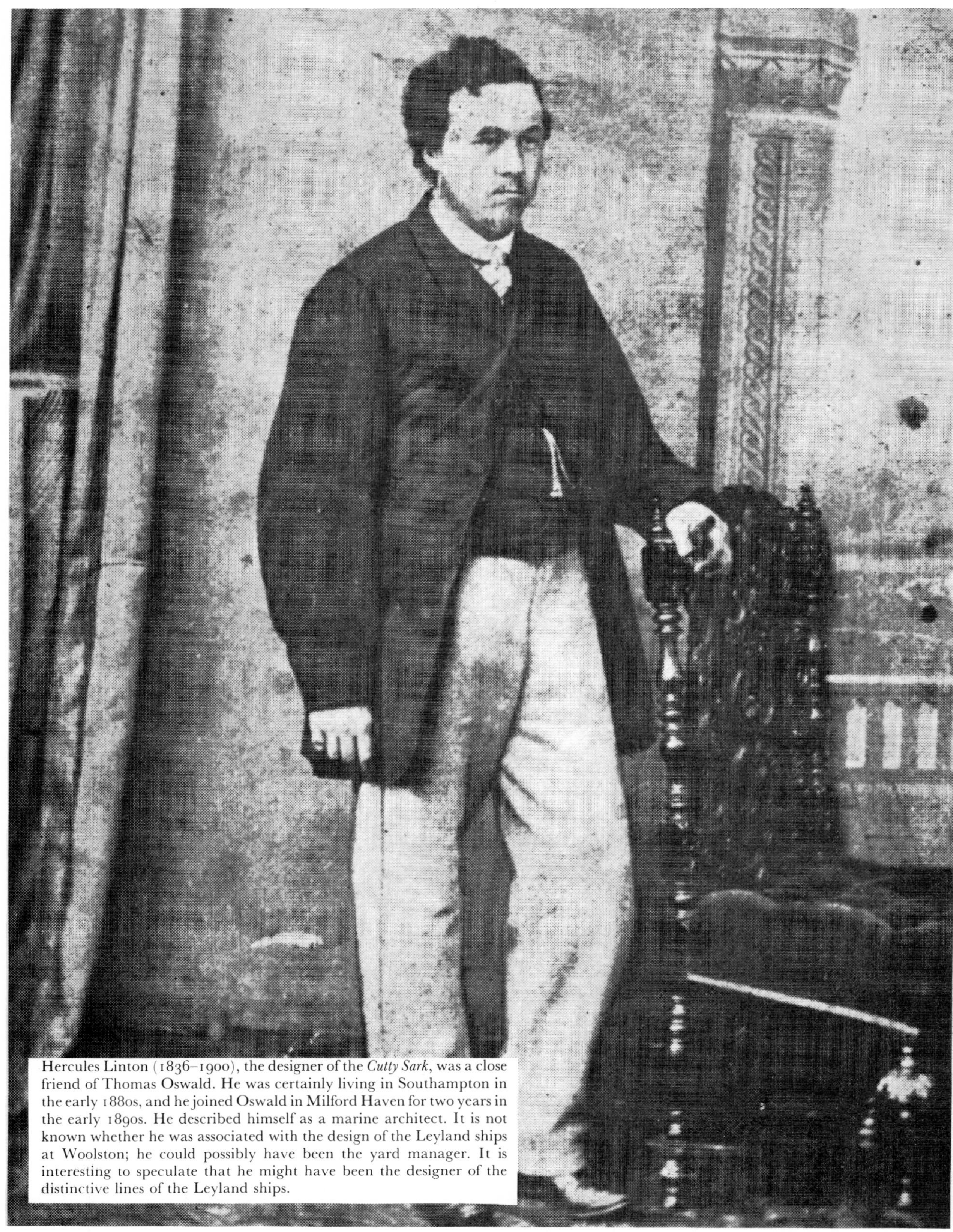

Hercules Linton (1836–1900), the designer of the *Cutty Sark*, was a close friend of Thomas Oswald. He was certainly living in Southampton in the early 1880s, and he joined Oswald in Milford Haven for two years in the early 1890s. He described himself as a marine architect. It is not known whether he was associated with the design of the Leyland ships at Woolston; he could possibly have been the yard manager. It is interesting to speculate that he might have been the designer of the distinctive lines of the Leyland ships.

CHAPTER SIX
Ships and Builders

During the 1880s and early 1890s R W Leyland & Company created a reputation for three-masted full-rigged sailing ships most of which were built by Oswald, Mordaunt & Company of Southampton. At this time many shipowners on the Clyde and elsewhere were declaring that these big carriers were uneconomical, besides being unhandy and high-masted. The Leyland ships were carriers with no pretensions to speed and in their rig they started a fashion by doing away with the spanker boom. Most of them carried very large single topgallant sails, royals, and several had a main skysail.

On at least four of the sailing ships (the *Toxteth*, *Liverpool*, *Ditton* and *Speke*), the officers' accommodation and the bridge were built amidships. This was an uncommon arrangement for accommodation and was called the Liverpool house; it was known also as a three-island type ship. (For details on the Liverpool house see pages 143–144). In practice this meant that the ships were helmed from amidships because the officer of the watch was then close to the man at the wheel and able to keep an eye on steering. However an emergency steering position was usually provided under the poop. When the officer's accommodation was aft and under the poop the wheel was as a rule right aft on the poop deck, where the helmsman could get a much better view of all three masts and would therefore be able to watch the wind movements and also the mizzen royal, so keeping all sails drawing properly.

Although these ships were large carriers with no pretensions to speed, some of them made very fine passages. Ralph Leyland jnr wrote in an article that the *Grassendale* (II) was one of the slowest ships afloat. He sailed in her from Hamburg to Melbourne by way of the Cape of Good Hope on a passage which took 112 days, and came home to Falmouth around the Horn in 108 days. He recalled that if she made 10 knots with a Force 5–6 soldier's wind she was doing well. In his second voyage, the *Wavertree* went from Hamburg to Calcutta carrying salt, from Calcutta to Mauritius with coal, then to South Africa, and from there to Australia and on to the west coast of South America before coming home. He remembered that she was quite a fast ship under favourable conditions, and recalled that they used to log as much as 15 knots with a strong wind of perhaps Force 6–7 on the quarter. Several fast passages of Leyland ships included the voyage of the *Fulwood* from Calcutta to San Francisco in 1895 which took 105 days. In 1899 the *Toxteth* made the best passage of the year from Calcutta to New York in 99 days. In 1907 the *Leyland Brothers* sailed from San Francisco to Sydney in 46 days, and back in 1895 the same ship ran from the Thames to the Lizard in 56 hours on a passage to Melbourne which she made in 90 days. On another occasion she anchored in the Mersey 101 days after leaving San Francisco. However there were slow passages as well. In 1897 the *Loch Torridor* made a passage of 46 days from Newcastle, New South Wales to San Francisco but the *Cressington* took 106 days. Although the Leyland ships were large carriers and were different to the clipper ships of the *Cutty Sark* era, they could make some good passages themselves.

The *Woolton*

Some idea of the size of these ships can be obtained from reports on the vessels shortly after they were completed. For instance the iron ship *Woolton* came in for special mention in one London newspaper on 21 July 1886 (paragraphing has been added). The correspondent wrote:

> This splendid vessel which is now lying in the Alexandra dock, is attracting considerable attention. She is one of the largest ships that has ever visited the port and is of the newest design. The *Woolton* was launched last year at Southampton and loaded a cargo of coal for San Francisco. From the latter port she sailed direct for Hull, being the largest sailing ship that has ever done so. The *Woolton* is 274 feet long between the perpendiculars, 42 feet broad and 29 feet deep. Her nett registered tonnage is 2101 tons and she is designed to carry 3350 tons of cargo with a freeboard of about 5 feet 8 inches. She brought from San Francisco a cargo of 50,708 sacks of wheat which weighed 62,173 hundredweight imported by Messrs C Roberts & Company of Hull. The ship is consigned to W R Johnson. She is owned by Messrs R W Leyland &

The *Woolton* was launched in 1885 at the yard of Oswald, Mordaunt & Co. She caused some excitement in the newspapers when she visited London for the first time.
NATIONAL MARITIME MUSEUM

Company, the well-known ship owners of Liverpool, who have a large fleet of vessels, amongst which may be mentioned the *Allerton*, which has just left Hull for California, taking the largest cargo of coal ever shipped at Hull.

In order that our readers might have some idea of the size of the *Woolton*, we may mention that her fore and main yards are nearly as long as the monument is high, being 90 feet in length. The length of her other main yards are as follows: lower topsail 81 feet, upper topsail 72 feet, topgallant 58 feet, royal 41 feet, and skysail 34 feet. The *Woolton* has three masts, the height of which and the depth are as follows: the length of the *Woolton* spanker boom is 47 feet. She has a horn bowsprit which disposes with the need for jib boom. This forms a great contrast with the ancient vessels, which had tremendous jib booms and even flying jib booms, with wonderous gear; the simplicity of this arrangement provides that, even with the crew half seas over, the ship can proceed to sea with little trouble. There are four hatches of great capacity for the discharging of cargo. The anchor is hove up with a capstan windlass and there is a double capstan on the main deck. There is admirable accommodation under a large forecastle for stores, with the crew and petty officers both berthed in a long deck house amidships. The other officers' quarters are arranged under the poop and are of a very superior description. The saloon is a good apartment, fitted with state rooms, and captain's room and bathroom, whilst under the poop are also large store rooms and sail rooms.

The vessel is built more as a carrier than a swift sailer; nevertheless, she makes her 12 knots and has sailed 270 miles in a day. She has not, however, been in perfect trim and a fair chance has not yet been given to test her sailing qualities, but it is expected that better results will be obtained. She made the passage from San Francisco to the Lizard in a very good time of 120 days. The *Woolton* has a crew of 32 hands, who are commanded by Captain Wilcox, a gentleman who has been in Messrs Leyland's employ for six years, but has had 40 years experience of the sea – 20 years of which have been as Master. He has an excellent reputation both for courage, skill, and courtesy, which has gained him much popularity. He previously visited Hull in command of the ship. On his last voyage he had amongst his crew the ruffian who turned Queen's evidence in the celebrated case of the Pirates of the Flowery Land. The *Woolton* will take on board at Hull a quantity of iron for Melbourne, for which port she is ultimately bound; but she will also load at Hull a cargo of about 1000 tons of coal which she will take to Frederickstadt, at which port she will load a cargo of wood for Melbourne.

Shipowners and Shipbuilders

From the shipowner's letters we can learn some details about the relationship between the company and their shipbuilders. The first letters concerning shipbuilders referred to the launching of a new ship, the *Grassendale*, in January 1882 at £12 15s per ton (a total of £22,400). Shortly after, they agreed the construction of another ship, the *Aigburth*, with the same company, R Williamson of Workington. The payments were to be in three instalments, the first being on 1 June 1882, the second on launching which was expected in July, and the third on completion of the vessel which was expected in August

1882. At the same time as these bills for the *Aigburth*, the company had two bills outstanding on the *Grassendale* for £5150 which were due on 4 August. The company asked for a change in the payment of bills and delayed paying one of the bills on the *Grassendale* by shifting the amount of the bill onto the *Aigburth* contract.

When the shipping company contracted with R Williamson & Company in January 1883 for the *Garston* to be built, they agreed to payments of £4000 when half plated, and another £4000 when launched, and the balance in cash on completion. However,

> it is further understood that any money we get from the co-owners above the amounts we agree to pay it to you – it is also understood that if we require six months bill for any amount up to £4500 for the final payment we are to have it on paying you the discount at the rate of 4% giving necessary security.

Thus Leylands were able to defer the payment for the completion of their ships and they had more time to obtain shareholders or co-owners in their vessels.

For the next vessel the Leyland brothers looked to Palmers Shipbuilding & Iron Company Limited, Jarrow, to build their ship *Otterspool*, but in July 1884 they came back to their original builders R Williamson & Company. In a letter of 11 July Leyland wrote:

> We have now to say that if you could see your way to accepting £9 per ton to be commenced October 1884 and launched September 1885, about 1800 tons, we should be disposed to do business and take the whole ship ourselves – subject to an arrangement with you as to payments . . .

and they were prepared to waive the 1 per cent builder's commission. Over the course of two years of negotiations with R Williamson & Company, Leyland were able to build cheaper ships, to the same high specification, partly due to the downward trend in the shipbuilding industry. However, at this juncture Williamson were not prepared to accept the proposition of Leyland, and Leyland for his part was not prepared to take on any new contract whilst he had 45 shares to be sold on the *Otterspool*. He wrote again to Williamson saying:

> Before making any new contracts elsewhere we will communicate with you again and perhaps then you will be better able to come to terms, as we feel certain that wages will be reduced at the ship building yards very considerably before long. It will be, however, quite impossible to discuss your quotation of July 5th, viz £9 12s 5d. That figure we can get very much reduced with other first class builders – for future work and delivery. What we offered to you was equal to about £9 2s less 1 per cent but we still hold to £9, no commission off, as being the outside we shall pay. Meanwhile we consider the matter off between us, but if you see your way to accept our terms shortly – let us hear from you.

Obviously R W Leyland proved to be correct because by November 1884 Williamson came back to Leyland and the cost of shipbuilding was reduced even further. On 5 November 1884, there was an agreement in R W Leyland's hand in his private letter book:

A close up view of the poop of the *Allerton*, seen here lying at South Street, New York, around the turn of the century. Within this structure, under a skylight which provided both air and light, were the officers' quarters and saloon. The rounded plating of the poop was designed to restrict boarding seas.

Memo of agreement between Messrs R W Leyland & Company of Liverpool and Messrs R Williamson & Son of Workington. Whereas the former agree to buy and the latter agree to build and sell, an iron sailing ship of about 1825 tons nett registered for the nett sum of £16,000. Any tonnage registered beyond the 1825 tons will not be paid for by purchasers – but should the nett register be less than 1815 tons then the sum of £16,000 to be reduced pro rata £8 16s 3d per ton for each ton under 1815 tons. The vessel number 81 in Messrs Williamson's yard is now fully framed and has about 20 plates already laid in the bottom of the ship, but not yet riveted. The vessel not to be launched before June 1st 1885 but not later than September 15th 1885, specifications to be the same as *Garston* except where otherwise stated. Payment as follows:– £200 in 10 days after signing. £2800 on March 1st 1885 by bill at months – estimated date of launch. £3500 on launching. £9500 balance on completion with option to buyers of giving a bill for £5000 for six months and further option of £2500 for further six months, made equal to cash. In all cases the rate of discount to be 4 per cent. Specifications to be submitted and mutually agreed. R W Leyland & Company. R Williamson & Son.

This ship when built was named *Grassendale*, following the loss of the previous ship of this name.

In May 1886 there was some disagreement as to the payment of bills and Williamson expected some security for the money outstanding on the *Grassendale*. Leyland was not keen on issuing Williamson with 15 shares of the *Grassendale* since a transaction of this sort needed to be registered and cost half a per cent. However he agreed to hold 15 shares in the ship in case bills were not met. Leyland wrote: 'Your asking for this is certainly not in the spirit we should have expected from the nature of previous transactions – and the large amount of business we have placed your way'. Finally, a couple of months later Leyland decided to keep £500 of a bill outstanding for a further six months and his annoyance is perhaps best shown when he wrote: 'We know you always have more money than you know what to do with.'

Oswald, Mordaunt & Company

In 1883 R W Leyland & Company turned to Oswald, Mordaunt & Company, to build their ship the *Cressington* but it was not until May 1885 that there was the first

A photograph of the second *Grassendale*, probably taken at the turn of the century and sailing under the Finnish flag.

A view across the Woolston yard looking west to Southampton docks taken during the 1870s.
SOUTHAMPTON CITY MUSEUMS

reference in Leyland's letters to this shipbuilding firm in Woolston near Southampton. The classic Leyland ships of the mid-1880s were from this yard.

The building of ships commenced at Woolston in 1876 when the shipbuilding yard of T R Oswald opened and was known as the Southampton Ship Building Engineering and Repair Works. Thomas Ridley Oswald had already had an impressive career. He was born in 1836 on Teeside. He was the nephew of the well known Sunderland shipbuilder James Laing and he entered his uncle's yard at the age of 16, as an apprentice, to acquire the knowledge of the building of ships. Later he moved to the Thames where he worked on the *Great Eastern*, then building at Scott Russell's Millwall yard. Possibly by the age of 19, but certainly by the year 1857, Oswald had opened his own yard at Pallion, Sunderland on the south bank of the Wear, known as High Yard. He confined his building to iron sailing ships and barques in the 500–600 ton range as this was a business in which he was well qualified. The site was actually owned by Christopher Maling Webster, whose daughter Oswald had married and it is highly probable that the young shipbuilder obtained financial help from his father-in-law.

Shortly he opened a second yard, this time at the North Dock, and because he was a builder of iron ships, his premises had to be equipped with plant and machinery far in advance of that required for wood shipbuilding. In his first year of operation at Pallion eight barques and four full-rigged ships were built, each of which were about 500 tons. By 1861 Oswald had encountered the

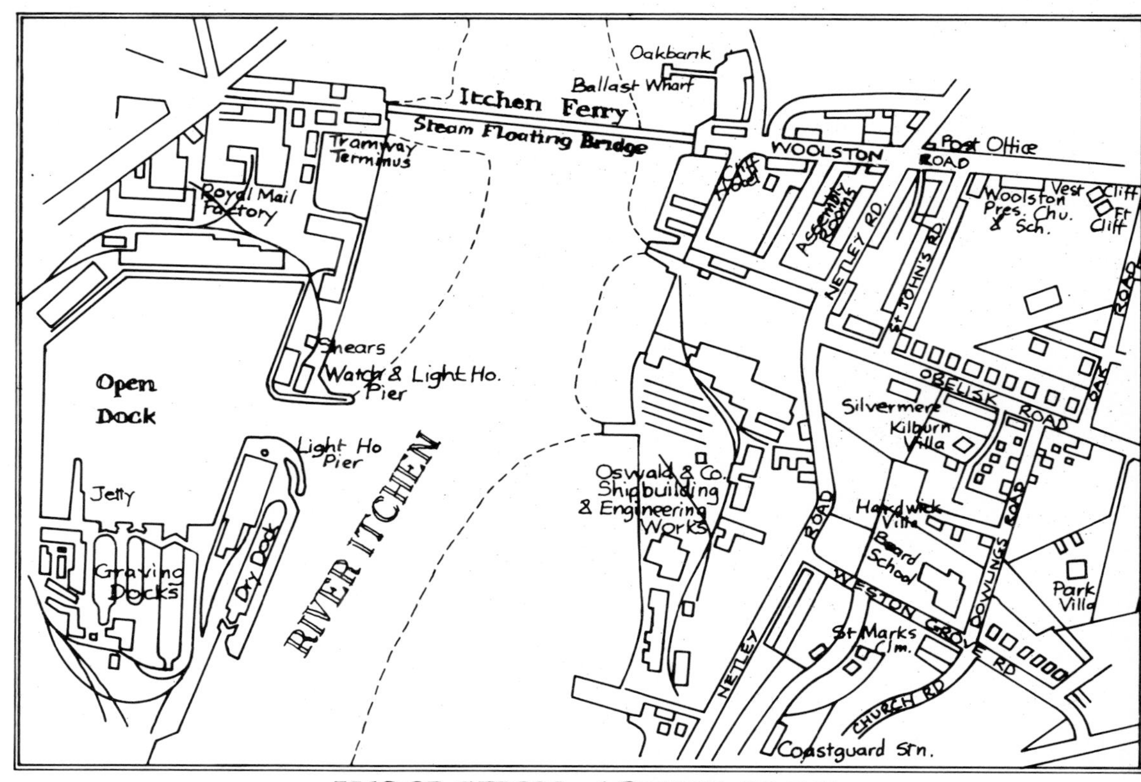

WOOLSTON ABOUT 1885

first of his financial difficulties. Within a few months of his first failure, however, he was again building iron sailing ships for noted owners in London and Liverpool, even though he had given up his North Dock yard. Oswald took advantage of the trend in the late 1860s to build iron clippers designed for the transport of emigrants and goods to Australia and New Zealand.

The great move in the early 1870s was to acquire facilities for building engines and boilers, as well as hulls. Oswald went further than just shipbuilding, therefore, when he built his own ironworks and rolling mills at Castletown on the north side of the river. Here, he imported iron ore from Spain for the plates from which his ships were fashioned, and the engines and boilers to power those ships. His engine works were completed in 1871 and his hundredth ship was also built that year. However, in 1872 Oswald was in debt for £300,000. In consequence the Castletown works and Pallion High Yard were closed and Oswald's father-in-law, who had lost faith in his son-in-law's financial if not shipbuilding abilities, advertised the lease of the Pallion Yard. Oswald, as determined as ever, within a year was operating two yards on the Pallion side and once more was launching iron clippers for London and Liverpool owners. Among the ships that Oswald completely built were the *Zulu* and *Namaqua* for the Union Line in 1872 and the RMSP *Severn* in the following year. In 1875 he launched the clipper ship *Sierra Morena* for the famous Sierra Shipping

Company owned by Thompson & Anderson, and this was the last ship he built in Sunderland. Within two years of this new operation his creditors were again pressing him, and his career on Wearside was ended, even though he had built seven first class sailing ships, of which the smallest was 1425 tons, in his final year at Sunderland. During the previous sixteen years he had built 149 ships. The Sunderland yard was sold to Boolds & Sharer.

However, the Pallion yard was dismantled and shipped to Woolston, near Southampton and a new yard was opened in 1876. The first vessel to be built there was the barque *Aberfoyle* of 853 tons gross, which was given the yard number 150. Her frames were brought from Sunderland, already bent to shape. The next year the firm became known as Oswald, Mordaunt & Company when Thomas Oswald took on a partner. Oswald lived locally at New Place House, Bedford Place, Southampton, whereas his partner Mordaunt lived on the other side of the river at Midanbury.

It was here at Woolston that Oswald was able to continue his reputation for building large iron sailing ships. According to Frank Bowen (*Shipbuilding and Shipping Record*, 24 Jan 1946, 'Shipbuilders of Other Days'), despite the partnership of Oswald, Mordaunt & Company:

> Oswald remained the moving spirit and was acknowledged to be one of the leading and most enterprising shipbuilders in the country. His ideas were not always readily accepted by the industry, but they were always listened to with attention as for instance, when he put before the Institution of Naval Architects an entirely new system of construction, which

A map showing the yard of Oswald, Mordaunt & Co and the surrounding area of the Itchen river. The yard occupied about 20 acres and at one time employed nearly 1000 men.

The *Albyn* in the outer dock at Southampton probably in April/May 1883. She is moored at the jetty near Dry Dock No 1.
SOUTHAMPTON CITY MUSEUMS

included the abolition of floors and their replacement by extra keelsons attached directly to the frames. One of the principal opponents of that scheme was Oswald's old employer, Scott Russell, and it did not receive any strong support. Sailing ships of more normal design and steamers for firms such as Lamport and Holts and the Union Line were launched in rapid succession; with reliability, good construction and good carrying power being their great qualities.

The firm did not hesitate to lay down ships on speculation when orders were scarce, running them under their own flag until purchasers appeared. [One of these was the sailing ship *Jubilee* which Leyland purchased from Oswald and renamed *Roby*.] They also took over a number of old ships in part payment for new ones, re-engined and modernised them and sold them again at a good price. The firm accepted a number of unusual contracts, including one for one of the many of the small vessels which were specially built for the Nile expedition for the relief of General Gordon.

In 1887 the yard launched its first steel steamer, *Benita* of 1160 tons, for Spanish owners and after that their output was practically confined to steel ships. In 1888 the firm started to build steam trawlers, with the *Romulus* and *Remus*, and also tankers with the 3225 steamer *Rock Light* and the 1254 ton sailing ship *Ville de Dieppe* for French owners.

Contracts

The business letters of Leyland to Oswald, Mordaunt & Company cover a period of 18 months from May 1885 and they clearly show that Leyland enabled Oswald to carry on building ships with flexible contracts and the chance for Oswald to sell ships prior to completion or shortly after. This option to sell ships was against the judgement of Leyland but in order to help the shipbuilders. In consequence Leyland probably got vessels at cheaper prices and also some profit on the sale of

The *Milverton*, 2141 tons, was originally built as No 231B at the Oswald, Mordaunt & Co yard, and known as *Leyland Brothers*. However, prior to completion she was sold to F & A Nodin. She made some good passages and Basil Lubbock mentions a passage of 89 days from Melbourne to London. She was bought by the Finns in 1914 and finally broken up July 1925 in Sunderland.

the vessels as well as a small commission for allowing Oswald to build these ships. The commission that Leyland received generally amounted to one per cent of the selling price but was sometimes rather more if it was sold just prior to completion. This could provide complications in that Leyland might be uncertain whether he had to find finance for the payment of bills by certain dates. For instance on 10 April 1886 he wrote:

> We were quite under the impression on commencement of this week that we should take up this vessel 231B and at great trouble to ourselves had to make all financial arrangements for that purpose. Everything had been arranged, and it is no relief to us now to have to undo the work for your benefit.

Leyland expected the full one per cent commission for their troubles when he wrote:

> We think too that on reconsideration, you will see that we are morally entitled to what we ask – as in addition to the four ships we have paid you for in the last twelve months – we have given you accommodation to build and sell three others.

As well as the sailing ships Leyland were involved in the construction of one steamer at Southampton during this period.

LEYLAND SHIPS BUILT BY OSWALD, MORDAUNT & CO

Yard no	Ship name
212	*Cressington*
224	*Allerton*
226 }	*Woolton*
227 }	*Halewood*
229A	*Bactria* Sold prior to completion as *Fulwood* to T & J Brocklebank
229B	*Fulwood*
230	*Toxteth*, later renumbered. Became 238
231	*Toxteth*, renamed *Southgate* (later *Wavertree*) sold prior to completion to Chadwick & Pritchard. Renumbered 237
231B	*Leyland Brothers* (1) sold prior to completion to F Nodin, renamed *Milverton*
231C	*Leyland Brothers* – later renumbered. Became 241
238	*Toxteth*. See 230
241	*Leyland Brothers* See 231C
243	*Jubilee* later *Roby*
259 }	*Speke* Built by T R Oswald & Co,
260 }	*Ditton* Milford Haven

The problem of contracting for vessels in this way was that it could involve disputes as to what was meant by commission on contracts. At the end of December 1885 Leyland wrote a strongly worded letter to Oswald:

> Dear Sirs, we have your favour of 28th instant and are surprised beyond measure that you should make such a statement so that you fail to see how commission is due to us unless you sell 231 to us. We feel so indignant at such a statement that perhaps we had better not record on paper our first thoughts – suffice it to say however that if you reiterate the statement the whole matter shall go into our lawyer's hands and we will test the legality of the agreement, although we thought an honourable agreement of such a nature when it was quite understood what was meant – was quite sufficient. However we are having a rude awakening.

> You know just as well as we do that to oblige you, we accepted your bills to enable you to build a ship which you hoped to sell to someone before the end of this year – and that you agreed to pay us one per cent for so doing. You know perfectly well that we dislike this whole business intensely – but to oblige you we waived our scruples. Now you have not sold the ship you wish to saddle us with a vessel dating this year but not due before April of next year and furthermore you would rob us of the miserable commission that we have earned to oblige you!

However towards the end of January 1886 their differences were patched up and a new arrangement was agreed.

These rearrangements and delays in launching vessels were not really surprising considering the difficulty in obtaining shareholders in an already saturated market. Leyland wrote in a letter July 1886 when he heard that Chadwick and Pritchard were not meeting one of the bills on the *Southgate*: 'In the present extraordinarily congested state of shipping affairs it would have been better for all concerned to have had even one less – large ship – building. However in this respect we are entirely in your hands.' However, Leyland carried on building quite merrily throughout the middle years of the 1880s and his success was largely due to his building 10 vessels of the highest class during a depression. However he fully recognised the depression and there are references to it in a number of letters. On 29 May 1885 he wrote a letter wanting to defer the launching of one ship and offered Oswald, Mordaunt & Company £500 additional money for so doing to prevent having two ships coming in November and December 1885. He wrote: 'Surely this is not asking very much under the circumstances of such extreme depression and difficulty in getting people to go into ships.' And a little later he wrote: 'We don't quite think you are treating us altogether nicely considering the difficulty there is just now in getting shareholders.' They were still arguing about ship 230 in June 1885 when he said again: 'When you consider the difficulty of getting people to take shares just now you will understand why we wish to cover ourselves in this manner.'

There were complications on the ship 229 as well. She had been sold prior to completion as the *Fulwood* to T & J Brocklebank who had renamed her *Bactria*. In August 1885 the new 229B, also called the *Fulwood*, was already being plated when Oswald, Mordaunt & Company suggested postponing delivery, and a couple of months later in October 1885 Oswald, Mordaunt & Company had the prospect of selling both the new *Fulwood* and the *Southgate*, the latter which he subsequently sold. The continued depression caused R W Leyland to write:

> We would very much like to dispose of 229 and obtain delivery of a new one in February but we cannot. It would, we greatly fear, compromise us in the eyes of our shareholders as already we have had difficulty in explaining to some shareholders Brocklebank's purchase of the first 229. We must push along and sell the shares and take delivery of the present 229.

They often took an option to pay their final bill on the completion, six months after it was due and in the case of the *Fulwood* the contract provided that the final quarter cost of the vessel could be paid for by R W Leyland & Company if they so wished either in cash or by six months bill. The amount of this payment was £4562 10s and they decided to take advantage of the bill option. The company's reply from Southampton was that they agreed to this option but that the interest should be at six per cent, which Leyland felt was prohibitive when the bank rate was only four per cent. Therefore he wrote: 'We must decline to pay it.' It was on the strength of this that Leyland wondered whether there were problems with Oswald, Mordaunt & Company at the end of December 1885:

> We don't quite like the tone of your letters regarding bills during the last few days and we would like to know if there is anything in the wind to cause a difficulty with them; we ask you for nothing but what we are entitled to; and hitherto the accommodation has been given entirely by us. We trust things are going alright in Southampton.

Oswald, Mordaunt & Company had actually launched the ship *Toxteth*, later the *Southgate*, on 15 December, four days before this letter and Leyland was not prepared in the following letters to accept bills on her when she was due for launching on the 15 April 1886. This resulted in the problems of commission and selling of the vessel to Chadwick and Pritchard which was mentioned earlier.

The *Leyland Brothers*, number 231B, was sold prior to completion to F Nodin and renamed *Milverton* on 8 April 1886 and at the same time Leyland took the opportunity of requesting that there should be a delay in the launching date of the ship 231C, the *Leyland Brothers*, set for 25 August, and the ship *Toxteth*, which was due for launching on 20 March 1887. He wrote: 'We would like to have put them off as late as possible – say as many months as you like to name from present arrangements.'

Problems at Southampton

In July 1886 Leyland may have heard rumours as to difficulties at Southampton for apparently he had asked for contract number 238 to be cancelled; Oswald, Mordaunt & Company had refused. Secondly in September 1886 Leyland had received a communication from his captain of the *British India*. Apparently the captain had heard by letter from a friend of his, Mr Alder, who was in the employ of R W Leyland & Company at one stage, that there were problems at Southampton. The captain communicated to R W Leyland what he had heard and Leyland approached Oswald, Mordaunt on the subject. Oswald was annoyed that Leyland was 'encouraging our people to get information up there to you'. Leyland maintained that

The *Manydown*, 2381 tons, was built for another Liverpool shipowner, E Bates & Sons in 1884. Leyland bought one of this company's early ships, the *Twilight*.

NATIONAL MARITIME MUSEUM

The *Claverdon* was originally built for J Coupland as the *Alexandra*. She was subsequently owned by F & A Nodin. In 1902 she made an abnormally long passage of 218 days from Cuxhaven to San Francisco Bay.

NATIONAL MARITIME MUSEUM ▼

The staff of Oswald, Mordaunt & Co during their outing to the New Forest in 1884. Oswald is standing in the back row; Mordaunt is seated in the middle row.

SOUTHAMPTON CITY MUSEUMS

he had not harmed the interests of Oswald, Mordaunt & Company in any way since he had only reported frankly what he had heard from his captain. Certainly there is a letter of 11 July 1887 in which Leyland stated that he was not prepared to go any further in taking up ships by bills and therefore he was not contracting for ships to enable Oswald, Mordaunt & Company to carry on building. The last ship that Leyland had built at Southampton was the *Toxteth*.

Oswald, Mordaunt & Company also built a large number of vessels for other Liverpool sailing ship owners as they had developed a reputation for iron sailing tramp ships which were efficient deadweight carriers. These included E Bates & Son, T R Williams & Company, H Fernie & Sons, and J Coupland. Leyland stuck roughly to the same size and rig for all his ships built at Southampton since he preferred the '2100 size, being easier to manipulate for insurance and chartering.'

Of the letters to Thomas Oswald from R W Leyland, the majority are business letters concerning the price of the vessels and the payment of bills. The three letters of a private nature are each replies to personal letters from Oswald when he was in financial difficulties. Oswald, Mordaunt & Company were in liquidation in 1881, and in 1886 there was an attempt to form the business into a limited liability company but this failed. Leyland's letter of 4 September 1886 shows some surprise at the present position of the works at Southampton and states that he had only heard that the estate was being wound up. Leyland hoped that Oswald might 'be able to arrange matters so as to be enabled to carry on your business as before at Southampton'. This he was able to do until 1888 when the company stopped trading with debts of over £100,000.

In 1888 a receiver, Mr William Beckett Hill, who was a member of the firm of Allen Bros & Company and a creditor of Oswald, Mordaunt & Company was appointed by the Liverpool and West Coast Trade to receive the old company. In February 1889 Leyland, in a letter to Oswald, revealed that Mr Kellock of C W Kellock & Company had approached him asking whether he would be a director and take some shares in a new scheme which was brought forward to buy the Southampton works and form a company. Apparently Leyland had replied that he would, only if Oswald was the manager and there was to be a meeting on the subject in the middle of February. Leyland wrote: 'I should be glad to see you established at the works again in Pallion if it can be arranged – the creditors will want some cash from you first I think.' So obviously Oswald had contemplated going back up north.

In December 1889 a new company was formed under the chairmanship of stockbroker Edward Coates, and largely promoted by the receiver William Beckett Hill, to acquire the business of Oswald, Mordaunt & Company at Southampton. The value of the business was supposed to be £175,500. Mr James Wallace-Cox was an iron merchant and shareholder of Oswald, Mordaunt & Company and he was appointed managing director of the new company, the Southampton Naval Works Limited, which took over the yard. Mr John Harvard Biles was appointed manager of the yard. However, this company also failed largely because they were cutting profit margins; they were trying to obtain work at too low a price for shipbuilding. This led to a court hearing at the London Bankruptcy Court in March 1893.

Oswald Moves to Milford Haven

However, by the end of the year 1889 Oswald had moved to Milford Haven, where he took over an existing yard which had been unoccupied for some time, and opened as T R Oswald & Company, for shipbuilding, marine engineering, and repairs. Once again he was building very large sailing ships. It was here that Leyland contracted through Oswald to build the two largest three-masted sailing ships of the Leyland line and the largest merchantmen afloat for some years, namely the *Ditton* and *Speke*. There are only three letters in Leyland's

The *Andrina* proved how well-built these Southampton square-riggers were. She was a four-masted barque built for E F & W Roberts of Liverpool. In 1899 she ran ashore in Policarpo Cove on a passage from Antwerp to San Francisco. Over the next twenty years she remained in this position and was gradually stripped of her gear and wood work. In 1918, with a shortage of shipping, the Menendez family of Punta Arenas bought her, for the transport of wool, and after a period of four months' work she was safely refloated with very little damage. She was re-rigged and sailed for several more years.

NATIONAL MARITIME MUSEUM

The figurehead of the ship, *Allerton*. This was probably the work of the wood carver, Dick Cowell.

The *Scottish Lochs* was built at Southampton for W H Ross & Co. R W Leyland had close friends in this firm and it is through Leyland's patronage of Oswald, Mordaunt & Co that the shipbuilders received the contracts for this ship and the *Scottish Glens*. The *Scottish Glens* probably carried the figurehead that Dick Cowell carved of Mrs Leyland.
NATIONAL MARITIME MUSEUM

private letters to Oswald during this period at Milford Haven. The third, written 24 November 1891 concerns a business proposition, probably to help finance Oswald to keep going in Milford Haven. Leyland wrote:

> As you know my brother and myself are not financiers, and we are not large capitalists. Neither have we the time to devote to a concern which is beyond our own business. We therefore cannot entertain the proposal contained in your letter but we shall be glad to hear that you have been able to place the debentures and we wish you all success.

In consequence of Oswald's financial difficulties the company went into liquidation in 1892. Once again the firm returned to its original title of T R Oswald. This was not quite his final year in shipbuilding for he completed some smaller vessels, and in 1895 he built his last ship, the steam trawler *Seamew*, before the yard was closed. Oswald lived until 1916 when he died at the age of 80 in Blackheath.

Hercules Linton, who was the designer of the *Cutty Sark*, had a strong connection with Thomas Oswald and it is interesting to note that the designs of the ships of R W Leyland & Company may owe a great deal to his work. Hercules Linton went to Woolston in 1880 and apparently stayed there until the end of 1884, and he certainly joined Oswald in Milford Haven for two years in the early 1890s. In the time between leaving Southampton and working in Milford Haven, in which his address can be traced in Montrose, his occupation is given as marine architect. It is not known, however, what his capacity was with Oswald, Mordaunt & Company, but he may have acted as yard manager or been involved in the design of ships.

An Apprentice's Recollections

In the 1950s, Jimmy Angel recorded his time as an apprentice at the yard of Oswald, Mordaunt & Company from 30 September 1883 until the yard closed. He recalled the broad-spoken, hard-muscled men from Clydeside and Tyneside who enjoyed their few spare hours racing their whippets on Peartree Green or playing

A photograph looking aft along the deck of the *Planet Neptune*. She had a deadweight carrying capacity of 7000 tons.

football at the Antelope Ground in St Mary's Road. He said:

They formed a big brass band to play at the frequent launching ceremonies, and brought down from the North new and radical ideas in trading and started their own co-operative shops. My mother was frightened when I joined Oswald, Mordaunt because they were known as the Slaughter House. They had a lot of fatalities. Hardly a week went by without someone being killed or maimed. The trouble was there were few precautions like guard rails over machinery. Odd times when ships were on the stocks stuff was dropped on the heads of workmen.

I thought my time had come when we were building the *Bitterne*. I was carrying some panelling when the wind blew me off the jetty. The tide wasn't full so I dropped in the mud and after they had fished me out I was sent home for a week's holiday.

Once while one of the three (*Scottish Lochs*, *Scottish Dales*, and *Scottish Hills*) was being built, I was working in the Mould Loft when Mr Leyland and his fifteen-year-old daughter were brought in by Mr Thomas Oswald. The visitors were introduced to the wood carver, Dick Cowell, who was left with a photograph of Miss Leyland and told to make a figurehead in her likeness for a clipper then under construction. A beautiful job he made of it. It was over life size and made a grand figurehead. When Mr Leyland came down again and saw the finished article, he was so pleased he gave Dick Cowell a five-pound note. As soon as Mr Leyland had left, Dick sent me off to the boozer to buy some beer so that we could wet Miss Leyland's nose. I was just a slip of a lad – they called me Wee Jimmy – so I was able to get through a loose paling and return with the beer without anyone noticing.

He also recalled the hard regime of Oswald, Mordaunt where the drinking of beer, tea, or coffee and smoking in the yard was strictly prohibited. Men who started at 6am and knocked off at 5pm with a short break for dinner were not even allowed to brew themselves a cup of tea.

The story of R W Leyland going down to Southampton probably concerns a visit that he made early in 1885 but the lady he took down with him was not his daughter but his seventeen-year old fiancée, Miss Letitia Heyn. The ship most likely to have borne this figurehead was the *Scottish Glens*, owned by W H Ross & Company. When T R Oswald & Company went into liquidation in 1892 in Milford Haven, Leyland turned to the firm of William Hamilton & Company, Port Glasgow for his last sailing ship, the *Riversdale*.

Steamer Building

At the same time as Leyland built his last sailing ship, he started to turn his attention to the construction of steamers. From the same yard, William Hamilton & Company, Port Glasgow he ordered a steamer, named *Planet Venus* (I), which he sold prior to completion to J Holman & Sons for a profit of £2000 in 1896/97. In the same year he ordered the *Planet Mercury* from Workman Clark & Company, Belfast. This was a typical tramp steamer which sadly only had a short life, as she went missing in February 1900. She was a steel twin screw vessel of 3250 tons with a length of 335 feet. As well as these two ships Leyland built three other steamers that had long lives and served the company until it was taken over by J H Welsford & Company in 1909. These were the *Planet Mars*, *Planet Neptune*, and *Planet Venus* (II); all the steamers that Leyland built for the company were named after planets. The *Planet Mars* was a steel screw vessel, as were the other two, of 4320 gross tons built in 1900 by the Northumberland Shipbuilding Company Ltd at Newcastle. Her overall dimensions were 360ft x 48ft with a depth of 20.2ft whereas the *Planet Neptune* and the *Planet Venus* were built by Napier & Miller, Glasgow with similar lengths of 385ft. The *Planet Venus* was completed in 1900 and the *Planet Neptune* in 1901. Here again a gradual increase can be seen in the size of the tramp steamers built for the company. The company owned only four steamers, apart from the one they sold prior to completion, but for a short time in the 1880s they had owned a small steam vessel named *Londos*. In the *Lloyd's Shipping Gazette Weekly Summary* for 1901 there is a short report on the launch of the *Planet Nepture*. It reads:

On June 7th Messrs Napier & Miller Ltd, launched at Yoker, on the Clyde, the steel screw steamer *Planet Neptune* for Messrs R W Leyland & Company of Liverpool. Her dimensions are: length between perpendiculars, 385ft, breadth moulded 48ft 6 inches; depth moulded 29ft 9 inches, having a deadweight carrying capacity of about 7000 tons and a gross tonnage of 4400 tons. The vessel is built to the highest class of the British Corporation. Machinery is being supplied by Messrs Dunsmuir and Jackson. The engines are triple expansion, with cylinders 27, 43 and 72 inches with a 48 inch stroke and the two boilers of large size with a working pressure of 180lbs. During construction the hull and machinery have been under the personal supervision of Messrs Maxton and Sinclair, Consulting Engineers, Liverpool, and Captain J A Bromley, Commodore Captain of Messrs Leyland, who will take command of the vessel when finished.

Thus R W Leyland's letters and the contracts that have survived provide some fascinating reading. (See the contract for *Riversdale*, page 182).

The launching of the *Planet Neptune* took place in Glasgow in 1901 at Napier and Miller's yard. She was a tramp steamer and initially she was put into service in the bi-monthly North American service run jointly by the Leyland Shipping Company and Manchester Liners.

CHAPTER SEVEN

Captains and Crews

From various sources we can learn of the relationship between the company and its captains. In the last days of sail R W Leyland & Company tried to uphold certain standards. For instance, Captain Holmes in his book *Voyaging* wrote: 'Leylands of Liverpool were the last sailing ship firm to insist that all their Captains wear full gold braid uniforms and if any master appeared in their office in ordinary dress he was fired instantly.' These standards drew comment in a San Francisco journal, and a Liverpool newspaper commented on this shipping article as follows:

> The journal pays a high compliment to the owners and Captain Farmer [master of the *Allerton*, in port April to June 1894] for the remarkably smart appearance of the ship and for the discipline observed by all on board; and then goes on to say that the discipline observed on these vessels (Leyland's Line) is something unheard of before on a sailing vessel and approaches that of the Man of War.

The newspaper continued:

> Such a praise-worthy notice must be very gratifying to a firm of shipowners who have always done their utmost to send their vessels to sea fully equipped and in a perfectly seaworthy condition, and also have them properly governed while at sea. We understand that each of Messrs Leylands' sailing ships is provided with a set of the company's printed rules which have to be strictly observed and one of these rules provides that the crew shall be exercised in fire and boat drill at least once a week at sea or in port. With such admirable arrangements for the safety of their vessels we should think that Messrs Leylands' fleet are highly thought of by underwriters.

Discipline

The company also took a hard line on captains being found under the influence of alcohol. One of the company's most well known masters was Captain Henry Stap who had been master of the *Great Britain* on her last voyage in 1886 when she had to put back to the Falklands and never sailed again. In 1895 Captain Stap was master of the Leyland ship *Ditton* and it had been reported to the company that he had been intoxicated when the ship was taken by pilot to Penarth Roads at Swansea. Captain Stap admitted to Leyland that he had been under the influence of drink on this occasion and Leyland in a strongly worded letter wrote:

> It is a source of great regret to know that you have been in such a condition and that a comment should have been made on the fact. We have always held you in such high esteem that the confirmation of the report is of great sorrow to us. If it had been the case of a junior captain or a man new to us we should have instantly dismissed him. This being your first offence (as far as we know) we intend to overlook it, on the clear and distinct promise that it shall never happen again. Of course the repetition of such a condition would involve your leaving us but we sincerely hope that there will be no occasion to refer to the matter again after this date.

Another practice the company felt strongly about concerned gratuities and bribes to the captains by which the masters were able to supplement their meagre incomes. In 1902 Leyland wrote to Captain Toye of the *Allerton*:

> There is no doubt that you did wrong and not in accordance with your agreement with us, in not distinctly stating that you had received a gratuity from Messrs Balfour, Guthrie & Company in connection with the outturn of cargo on last voyage. I am glad to see that on consideration your cônscience has prompted you to make a disclosure which is somewhat late and is to a great extent a breach of faith. I am pleased to see that you have had courage to confess the fault and under the circumstances – and with the distinct understanding that nothing of the sort will occur again – I accept your letter in the spirit it is written. You know we consider the system of bribes and gratuities most pernicious and you can seen how ship owners' interests may be prejudiced by such action. Of course we cannot prevent men tendering commissions and gratuities to our captains but as you know we stipulate that the captains when making engagements with us shall return all discounts, commissions, brokerages, gratuities, etc. and we expect all honourable men to do so.

Leyland captains wore full gold braid uniforms similar to this.

Court Actions

On another occasion, in 1898 in the Liverpool County Court Thomas Calder, who had been a master on Leyland ships for some years, brought a case against the company on account of £99 in wages and disbursements that he had not been paid. The company had resisted paying the plaintiff while he was master of their ship *Planet Mercury* because he had traded on his own account, accepting gratuities secretly in breach of his agreement. It was therefore urged that he had forfeited his wages and he had at any rate lost his job. A counter claim was also put in by the defendant for the gratuities which the plaintiff had received and failed to disclose. In the judgment on the case it was conceded that Captain Calder had obviously been corrupt in his dealings with his employers in deliberately omitting to disclose gratuities. However, it was felt that it could not be said that his conduct was so corrupt as to warrant a forfeiture of his wages. So it was decided that judgment should be given for the claim of Thomas Calder but the defendants were to receive the amount in gratuities that Thomas Calder had not disclosed. Although this was an old practice of masters the Leyland Shipping Company were not prepared to tolerate it, and legally made sure in their agreements signed between the masters and the company that their financial interests were protected.

In October 1898 Norman Campbell brought a case against the company at the Liverpool Court of Passage for an amount owed to him in wages and disbursements and the result was found in his favour for a certain amount. Leyland subsequently sent a letter to the weekly newspaper *Fairplay* stating that owing to the way in which the case ended in the Court of Passage, their defence did not fully appear and they thought in fairness

Captain Stap (fourth from right, in front of the wheel) on board the ss *Great Britain*. Leyland complained that Stap was drunk when in charge of the *Ditton* in 1895. He served as master of the ss *Great Britain*, for several voyages under the ownership of Antony Gibbs, Sons & Co, and on her last voyage in 1886. During his first passage to Montevideo in 1882 he wrote in a letter to his brother 'I almost wish now that I had not taken the command . . . The men are all afraid of her, and a more useless lot I never was with, half a dozen of them no sailors at all, substitutes shipped on board at the last moment with only what they stood upright in and are no earthly use on board.' The day after their arrival, 19 men deserted.

ss *GREAT BRITAIN*, BRISTOL

it should be put forward. Campbell therefore decided in December 1898 to sue for libel against the shipowners. Apparently the *Doxford* had been laden at Rosario in 1893 contrary to the instructions of the owners and had therefore been detained in that port for four months. As their captain had been unable to find any substitute for the charter that he had been offered, he considered he was obliged to load and did so. The delay in getting to sea was due to a revolution and to abnormally low water in the river which caused the vessel to ground three times. Whatever the facts of the case may have been the letter to the newspaper made no sort of charge against the captain. The fact was that after the action had been tried in the Court of Passage the defendants were attacked for having set up a 'mean and petty-fogging and improper defence.' The defendants stated that they had sufficient evidence to support their claim since the captain had been instructed not to charter the ship at any time without the authority of the defendants, and undoubtedly he did commit an error in disregarding that instruction of the owners, whether he acted in his judgement in the best interest of the owners or not. Therefore the jury found in favour of the defendants.

From their earliest days as shipowners the Leyland line tried to encourage captains to take an interest in

The crew of the *Wavertree*, pictured here in Portland, Oregon before her journey to Liverpool in December 1907. Each person in this photo has been identified. George Spiers (standing with arms folded in front of ladder) wrote a remarkable account of this journey, next to him is Mr Connors, the first mate, and his nephew, Captain William Masson stands in the middle.

SOUTH STREET SEAPORT MUSEUM

their ships. Indeed originally the purchase of some shares in one of their ships was part of the agreement for the command of the vessel. For instance, the first master of the *Nelson* after Leyland purchased her in April 1880 was Captain Watkins, and with his agreement to command the ship he was obliged to purchase $^{6}/_{64}$ths of the vessel.

This amounted to the considerable sum of £703.

There were disagreements occasionally with captains over the non-delivery of cargo. In March 1886 Leyland sent a telegram to Captain Bonfield of the *Garston* berthed at London. It read:

> Merchants at Plymouth receivers of *Garston* wheat cargo decline to pay for certain short number of bags delivered. It appears that you sent some more bags on shore after you left quayside. Merchants allege these bags or part of them were bought in the town by you or others in the ship and were tended improperly. Let us have the truth of this story. Did you tender to them any other bags than were brought home in the ship?

Despite the tough treatment of Leyland & Company towards its masters several of them stayed with the company for many years. Masters such as Calder, Reid, Bromley and Tilston served on a number of Leyland ships. We can follow the career of William Masson who joined the steamship *Planet Neptune* as third officer in July 1901. Within a short while he was appointed master of the sailing ship *Ditton* and he remained in that vessel until August 1903 when he was discharged in hospital on account of injury. In March 1904 he was appointed second officer of the *Planet Mars* in which position he served for eight months and was then made chief officer. In 1906 he resigned from the *Planet Mars* and later signed an agreement to go to Sydney in New South Wales to the sailing ship *Wavertree* to take command, and he remained in command of the *Wavertree* until November 1908. For his dedicated service to the company he received a good recommendation when the management of the vessels was taken over in 1909 and hence he lost his position. In the testimonial Leyland wrote:

> During the whole time of Mr Masson's employment with us we have been perfectly satisfied with him and whilst as master of the sailing ships we have been pleased with the manner in which he has looked after the expenses at foreign ports and in regard to crew etc. So far as our experience of Mr Masson goes we have always found him to be a sober and capable ship master. His intention originally was to endeavour to obtain command in steam but so far we have not had a vacancy to which we could appoint him. In lieu of this we offered him command of a sailing ship which he took, but he now wishes to go back in steam.

Although the evidence suggests that Captain Masson performed in a most extraordinary way on board the ship *Wavertree* on her voyage 1907/1908 he had served the company well. When he left its service in 1909 he was only 35 and this was another example of a young captain moving out of sail into steam.

The company treated their officers extremely well and rewarded them for their services. Captain John Bromley, for instance, who was born in Liverpool, took his master's certificate in 1879. Shortly after he joined the firm, certainly in 1883, he was master of the *Cressington* on her first voyage from Cardiff to San Francisco and remained with this vessel until 1890. He then served in various other sailing ships including the *Wavertree* before rising to become the commodore captain of the Leyland fleet. In July 1901 he took command of the newly completed vessel *Planet Neptune* on her first voyage. Bromley

Captain John Reid. An excellent seaman but an unlucky master.
COURTESY J H REID

obviously had a good relationship with the company and he brought back from his journeys presents for R W Leyland's daughter, Adèle. He was also entrusted with the care of Ralph Leyland when he went as a youngster on the ship *Wavertree*.

Troublesome Incidents

Leyland & Company had its share of unsuccessful masters. Captain John Reid was unfortunate in that in 1900 his ship the *Otterspool* was destroyed by fire under his command. Less than two years later when he had command of the *Aigburth* he stranded the ship on the South Arklow Bank in the Irish Sea, and found himself suspended for three months. In 1904 he was again in command of the *Aigburth* when she was wrecked off Rooke Island. A little later he was given command of the *Toxteth* and the log survives for the journey from Newcastle, New South Wales, starting in July 1906 to Antwerp, April 1907. The official log makes fascinating reading and although it is written in the hand of the master one gets a very vivid impression of life on board this unhappy vessel. Take the case of Patrick Shean.

During their time in Valparaiso there is an entry in the log which reads:

> It was reported to me ashore at 3pm that six of my men had refused duty. I was coming off at the time and enquired of the mate what was wrong. He said one hand was doing all the talking and as far as he could see he was the ring leader of the lot. I sent for the ring leader Patrick Shean to come in the cabin to see what was the matter. He refused to come in any – cabin and seen any – skipper. He wanted to get ashore and see if he could see the British Consul. I got him aft after a lot of trouble and put the irons on him. As soon as he was in irons he commenced to plead he wanted to get out of them again; after all the trouble he had given me I did not want to let him out but he pleaded so hard to me I let him go as long as he would behave himself. He faithfully promised to do so. I asked the other five hands after Shean went away to see what they had refused duty for and the only reply I got was that Shean told them they had got to stop with him and do what he says, he refused duty and they had to do the same. I kept two of them in irons all night as they still refused.

A few days later Patrick Shean stole the ship's boat and deserted. He went ashore and left the boat on the rocks.

At Caldera, Timothy Regan 'said he would not work at nothing on the grub he was getting,' and two months later a note was made in the log saying that three men had deserted including Regan and that this was his sixth attempt. In Caldera ten of the men refused to work but the master was able to take four of them to the police who kept them in prison on judge's orders until the ship was due to leave and the rest were locked up. One of those put in jail at this time was a man named Marsh who later escaped and nothing more was heard of him until three weeks later. In the log was written:

> Marsh was found somewhere on the railway line almost starved to death. The police wanted to put him aboard the ship. I refused to take him. He is a deserter not only from me, but out of jail also and I thought too ill to be taken aboard.

Three days later Marsh died in hospital 'death being due to privation suffered in desert'.

José Rosiques in Caldera

> refused duty this afternoon and wanted to be paid off. I reported him to the Consul and he told me to keep him aboard for the time. I called him aft last night to give some advice and did not intend to keep him fast, but when he came aft, he was that insolent and used such bad words and threatened me with the knife, and told me I dared not put the irons on him. I put them on him however and got him in the aft end of tween deck and locked him up there. He must have had some drink to carry on like a mad man as he did. He has sworn he will cut me up when he gets out of irons . . .

The final entry before they left the west coast of South America for Antwerp was that the Consul had protested against the master for delaying the ship after she was loaded. However the Consul would not have known that the ship was short of ten sailors and by the time she left seven days later she had only got seven replacements.

Of course one only seems to hear the details of some of the worst relationships between captains and crews. For instance in 1892 the *Chile* was on her way to the United

The *Toxteth* being towed through the Schelde near Antwerp. Captain John Reid was master of her, during the voyage from Newcastle, NSW to Antwerp, and the log that survives of this journey is in his hand.
NATIONAL MARITIME MUSEUM

Kingdom with a cargo of 800 tons of nitrate when she was destroyed by fire at sea. In the inquiry held later in the year the court were unable to ascertain the origin of the fire except that there was little ventilation to the cargo. However it was found out that the crew had refused duty and that at the time of the fire, they were still in a state of open mutiny.

In the *Fulwood*'s official log for July 1907 the master recorded repeated instances of abusive and foul language being addressed to him and the first mate, Mr Braine, who were the only Britons in a crew of foreigners. Conduct such as flat refusal to obey orders and jeers and insolence whenever an order was given appeared to be daily occurrences. Certainly conditions on board ship were pretty bad in the early years of this century. There were problems with foreign crews but often the masters seemed to have brought the problems on themselves. In the log of the *Leyland Brothers* in 1909 at Valparaiso there is a report from the Consul which reads:

> I hereby certify that the Master has, in my opinion, disregarded the wellbeing of three of the seamen who were certified sick by a competent English doctor though it was his duty to procure them hospital treatment. I found him very indifferent in this respect and was obliged to bring pressure to bear on him before he would move at all in the matter and I have not received the assistance from him I have a right to expect. This entry is made in case anything should happen to any of these seamen, or others later on, during the voyage.

However there is no entry in the log of sick seamen at this time.

The journey of the *Speke* between Barry (June 1901) and Antwerp (September 1903) under the command of Captain Stott does not seem to have been much better. Before she left Barry 14 men had been fined one day's pay for turning up late and five had failed to join. A week later the carpenter was said to be incompetent and his wages were reduced to £3 10s per month and a month later the captain wrote in the log:

> I find that he is thoroughly incompetent and incapable of performing his duties, he having no tools suitable for his work and he does not even know names of the same, and having no knowledge of carpenter's work whatsoever and I now reduce him to the rating of boy. Wages 10s 0d per month from the date of joining.

The crew of the ship *Fulwood* during her visit to San Francisco in 1888. Captain Owen Jones (standing in the centre of the back row) came from a line of seafarers from Portmadoc. His father, Richard, was master of the Portmadoc schooner *Edward* when she was lost with all hands on a passage from Liverpool to her home port in 1868. Owen was born at Criccieth in 1846 and was master of the *Fulwood* from 7 May 1887. He was taken ill on one voyage and landed at Cape Town. He was brought home to Criccieth where he died on 27 March 1890. To the left of Owen Jones, is Ellis, aged 11, his eldest son who also grew up to command his own vessel.

COURTESY O A MORRIS

For the poor seamen whose wages were reduced to this level, there was no appeal. The captain was master of his own vessel while at sea. When she arrived at anchor at the entrance of Rio de Janeiro on 14 August 1901, 20 seamen refused to keep anchor watch both as a group and individually, and the captain reported the 'ship is now in a dangerous position'. A month later still in the same port 13 men refused duty and after they had been to see the Consul, refused to join the ship again.

In the section of the journey from Port Adelaide to Cape Town lasting about 11 months there are 63 sailors listed in the ship's log. Even before she had left Port Adelaide ten men were stated to be refusing duty and the rest of the crew were unhappy to proceed to sea with so

Fulwood's crew during her Norwegian ownership. In her heyday as a sailing vessel her crew rarely reached this size.
NATIONAL MARITIME MUSEUM

few men. These ten men were eventually brought before the local magistrate William Johnson of the City of Port Adelaide on a charge of continued wilful disobedience of lawful commands and were sentenced to 6 weeks in prison.

A little while later on the voyage there is a long entry about the sail-maker called Terry with whom the captain was not satisfied and felt that he was only doing half his work. The master wrote:

> The Bosun was sent to overhaul and make up the foresail which the sail maker reported as finished and found several places which had not been repaired and pointed these out to the sail maker who thereupon became very insolent (this was the third time he had said this sail was thoroughly repaired and each time on overhauling it was found not to be so) – I then went on deck and asked the sail maker why he did not repair the sail thoroughly and was met with insolence. I told him to hold his tongue and get on with his work properly but he continued to use insolence and made gestures of violence. I held him at arm's length although I was holding a baby in my arms at the time. He then struck me, also hitting the baby on the mouth at the same time causing it to bleed. I then struck the sail maker in self defence and walked away. He immediately seized a belaying pin and came after me and struck me on the head. I then had him put in irons and locked up in the after store room.

The sail-maker was then reported to have said to the steward 'that many a man would have taken his knife and ripped my bloody guts out and to the bosun he the sailmaker said he was sorry that he had not taken a knife and ripped me up afore said.' When the captain approached the sail-maker two days later and asked him about these threats 'he replied he was only sorry he had not had the presence to have taken a knife and not a belaying pin and ripped me up'.

Later on in the journey in June 1902 15 men had refused to work and this resulted in the pilot refusing to take the ship over the bar at Astoria. The situation was so bad that the sheriff and his men had to come on board and remove knives from the sailors and five sailors who still refused to work were put in irons.

A Hard and Dangerous Life

Life could be extremely hard for members of the crew. The frequent references to the cut in food allowances was the excuse that food was running short. In 1904 the log of the *Allerton* reported that 'the members of the crew have this day had the daily allowance of beef and bread reduced to ½lb per man per day. They were having as a substitute for the bread ½ pint of peas daily.' In March 1905 the crew were reduced to ¼lb of meat per man per day and this only lasted a few days before they were reduced to no beef at all but 'they are however receiving full and plenty of bread, also getting soup made of beans etc. every day.'

These conditions predictably caused tension between the crew. The master of the *Fulwood* on a journey to Falmouth in 1904 wrote 'it has been reported to me that Peter Couhlin, Bosun, was going forward at about 6am when Kay Philstrom attacked him and laid him out on the fore-hatch.' Mr Parry who was the chief mate hearing his cries for help, ran forward and as soon as Philstrom saw him released his hold on the bosun: 'there you are, mister, you can't do nothing to me as you didn't see me strike him. I am well posted in the English law so I am not afraid.' The log goes on: 'The bosun lodged a complaint to me, his face bears marks of being very much ill-used.'

It could be a dangerous life as well, and there were frequent deaths reported. For instance the second mate, Mr Shooter, on the *Allerton* in December 1902 'was returning on board after having been ashore when close to the ship's gangway he slipped and fell through the wharf into the water. He was picked up as quickly as

The *Fulwood*. Tensions could run high in the difficult atmosphere on board ship.

possible and every means taken to restore life.' He had apparently struck some crossbeams and supports of the wharf. Later on in the journey the master himself, Captain Toye, died at the age of 58 from locomotor ataxy and gastritis which he had suffered the whole of the passage, and from July 1903 to 8 September when he died he was occasionally delirious, and for three days before his death he went into a coma, only being relieved by brief intervals of consciousness, from which he never recovered. Later in the voyage one of the able seamen by the name of Tate 'who was attending to the gear during the operation of settling the main topgallant sail had his thigh broken by the breaking and the yard coming down on the lifts.' The *Gitana* on her voyage from Cardiff October 1884 to Valparaiso and back to Hamburg arriving in October 1885, had several unfortunate incidents. Peter Tewes who was the sail-maker died in port on the west coast of South America through falling down the hold. Likewise, William Storey was discharged at Valparaiso and died in hospital from injuries received by a fall from aloft. Two able seamen were drowned at sea on different occasions: John Brown aged 23 and Oscar Richter aged 19.

Occasionally the brief and happier event of a birth on board ship is recorded. For instance on 7 April 1902 Mary Grace Jackson was born on the *Halewood* to Mrs Jackson who was the stewardess on her husband's ship.

The *Gitana* Incident

The reaction of the crew does not always seem to have been justified. Take the case of the *Gitana*, recorded in the *Journal of Commerce* on 1 April 1893 in Liverpool. (The original has been broken into paragraphs.)

> One of the most flagrant and uncalled for cases of insubordination ever reported on ship board has just occurred on the Liverpool ship *Gitana* which left the Mersey on Tuesday March 21st outward bound. The vessel carried a crew of eighteen hands all told and two days after leaving this port she missed her course and touched the ground on the Malahide Sands near Dublin. A tug was telegraphed for but before any assistance had arrived the vessel was lifted off by the tide and floated safely into deep water. Early on the following morning the ship arrived at Kingstown in order to be thoroughly examined and a competent diver was then sent down to inspect the skin of the vessel.
>
> The diver's report was as follows: 'I examined the bottom of the barque *Gitana* from bow to stern both sides and could find nothing wrong. On her starboard side her bilge shows traces of having rubbed on sand but nothing more.' In addition to this both Lloyd's Surveyors and the Board of Trade Surveyors at Kingstown personally inspected the ship and found nothing to object to, and in spite of these recommendations nine of the crew refused to proceed to sea unless the vessel was brought back to Liverpool and there unloaded drydocked and resurveyed. It ought to be mentioned too that before leaving the Mersey on this trip the *Gitana* had been surveyed by Lloyd's and passed a number two survey, officials personally complimenting the owners on the excellent condition of the vessel and remarking that there were very few of her strong type of construction now sailing.
>
> These, in brief, are the facts up to the time of the men's refusal to sail and we hold that not only did Messrs Leyland do the right thing in insisting upon the vessel going to sea but that, under the circumstances, no other possible course was open to them, either as guardians of the cargo or as men of business. Anyone acquainted in the slightest degree with shipping matters knows that such cases are a daily if not hourly occurrence, and if all the vessels that graze the ground were turned back to their port of departure, in spite

This photograph of some of the crew of the *Leyland Brothers* is noteworthy for the inclusion of Ralph, R W Leyland's son, seated in the middle of the front row. His father believed in training when young and so he was sent away on Leyland ships at the early age of 11.
SOUTH STREET SEAPORT MUSEUM

of the results of close examination, ship owning as a business would cease to exist.

To resume the story. The men having refused to work were given in charge and marched to jail, and afterwards came before the Kingstown magistrates. On Tuesday last by order of the last named official, the insubordinates were put on board again by the police, the magistrate evidently imagining that the day or two spent in jail would have effectively cooled the ardour of the foolish seamen. At the trial which led up to this proceeding the Board of Trade Surveyor stated in court that he was personally so well satisfied with the seaworthiness of the ship that he would be quite willing to sail in her himself. It was natural to suppose that after this evidence the men would have readily done their duty but on the morning following their return to the vessel the solicitor of the Dublin branch of the Sailors Union sent a letter on board and after this precious communication was unfortunately allowed to reach the men they refused to take the ship to sea, and insisted on going on shore with their baggage.

There were only two courses open to the officers, either to let the men go or prevent them by force and very luckily for all concerned the first course was adopted. The telegram was dispatched to the owners and on Wednesday evening nine men were sent from Liverpool and we are informed by the owners that the vessel left Kingstown for Valparaiso, fully manned, on Thursday evening's tide. Ultimately, we believe, the insubordinate men came on to Liverpool and are now doubtless waiting to ship again, obtain another advance note and once more earn another month's wages for three days' work. This matter of the month's advance is certainly one which seems to have affected the action of the *Gitana* malcontents and the effect of the case upon the owners should be to make them resolutely refuse advances of pay to all except those who they can fully trust. The owners of the ship are absolutely helpless unless they summons the men for desertion, the loss of several hundreds of pounds in hard cash as well as the delay to the vessel, it is absolutely impossible to make good. In showing the strength of the *Gitana* it will be remembered that she was ashore for some five months five or six years ago, in the North Sea, and was successfully floated without any but the most trifling damage to her hull. Instead of reading this lesson aright, the men foolishly urged that the fact the vessel had been ashore added another reason for her alleged unseaworthiness; but it is evident that the severe test to which the ship had been put and the full confidence placed in her by the various surveyors, had proved quite clearly that she was a sound and taut craft.

The difficulties of ship-owners seem to be increasing on every hand and as far as the labour question is concerned such conduct as we have above described renders the problem still more complicated and disheartening. It has been suggested that with a view to put a stop to cases of this kind the men's discharges should all be kept in the custody of the Captain, and there may be something in the idea; but it seems to us that if the insubordinate half of the *Gitana's* crew had not received a month's advance we should not have heard of any doubts of the vessel's seaworthiness.

In the *Shipping Gazette Weekly Summary*, it was pointed out that 'sufficient good seamen were picked out from amongst dozens who offered their services' to sail in the *Gitana* and this was largely due to the company 'who have the highest reputation for the safety of their ships and their considerate treatment of sailors and crews'. The problems of ship management could be enormous.

Captain Thomas Wilcox held concerts on board the ship *Grassendale* when she was at Liverpool in 1886 and this is an example of the concert programme.

CHAPTER EIGHT

Voyages, Cargoes and Wrecks

When a sailor signed on, the articles of agreement specified that men should serve until they returned to the same neighbourhood, even though this was not always observed. This generally meant sailing from and returning to Europe and the voyage might be anywhere between 60° south latitude and 75° north for a period of three years. In the late nineteenth century and early twentieth century voyages often consisted of an outward passage to a Chilean port with case fuel and the hope of a nitrate cargo on return to Europe. However, there might be one or more passages up to San Francisco for grain or across to Newcastle for coal to take back to Chile. Good passages frequently consisted of some luck, and good judgement. The vessels were often driven hard by their masters who took advantage of the winds and wind changes to put their ships in the best positions. The objective was to seek the best and shortest passage in terms of winds and weather. The Leyland ships, like other vessels, had their share of fast and slow passages.

The *Leyland Brothers* – a Long Passage

In the *Journal of Commerce* for 1901 there was an article on the *Leyland Brothers*. It read:

> The immense growth of steam in the mercantile service and the corresponding diminution of sail has robbed the nautical world of many interesting topics of discussion in the way of voyages, either remarkable for speed or for slowness. A case has just come to hand which revives both points.

It then goes on to record the passage from San Francisco to Sydney, a total distance of 6600 miles, which the ship covered in 46 days – a remarkable voyage. However, in 1906 she sailed from Antwerp at the beginning of April and did not arrive in San Francisco until 4 November, taking 213 days for a voyage. On the earlier voyage she had very favourable winds; the delay in the latter voyage was due entirely to adverse weather particularly on beating round Cape Horn. Some years later an apprentice in the ship on that voyage, Gerald Buckle, wrote an article about this journey. He wrote: 'Every detail of this voyage was impressed on my memory at the time by sheer hardship, and by the fact that I had joined the ship as an apprentice only three days before the voyage commenced.' On this voyage they were several months overdue and posted lost. There seem to have been few events up to Rio de Janeiro. However off the River Plate they were caught by a terrific squall during which the gooseneck of the main lower topsail yard was carried away; this heavy iron yard was left hanging and supported only by the topsail sheets. However, some hands went aloft and were able to lash it to the mast but the wind increased in force and blew a steady half gale. Shortly after, the master felt it was better for the yard to be cut loose and allowed to go overboard, and a man was sent aloft to cut it away, but he had a blackout and cut the fall above the hand by which he was holding on. Both the yard and the seaman went overboard but fortunately they were able to pass him a line from the stern. With the loss of the yard the master decided to head for Montevideo to obtain a replacement but they encountered adverse headwinds. For 17 days they attempted to draw nearer but eventually abandoned the idea of entering Montevideo and set a course for the Horn. The ship could of course have put into the Falkland Islands for repairs but this was not considered necessary. It was ten weeks before they cleared the Horn and in that time they encountered very bad weather, being driven off course both south and east and within the Antarctic Circle. They were in this area for six weeks and several of the crew suffered from frostbite but fortunately the weather improved.

The ship was enveloped in ice for more than eight days, and scarcely any part of the vessel could be seen. 'Not a brace or halliard would work, and the sails – frozen stiff – were billowed out as if drawing to a seven knot breeze.' After some weeks they sighted Cape Horn to leeward and later when off Valparaiso they encountered a tidal wave of fair proportions. Mr Buckle believed that this was about the time of the San Francisco earthquake. Although the ship had left behind the worst of the weather the crew were beginning to feel the effects of

One side of the harbour at Newcastle, New South Wales in about 1900 during the coal strike. On the other side of the harbour there were as many ships waiting for cargoes.
NATIONAL MARITIME MUSEUM

what they had been through. The coloured steward who fell ill, later contracted tuberculosis and died. A little while later they ran short of water, and although there was plenty of food, including salt beef, this too had to be rationed since they were limited to one quart of water per man per day for everything, including the issue of lime juice.

Later still in the voyage they ran short of oil, tobacco and matches and resorted to sailing without sidelights in order to save oil. Almost every member of the crew fell ill with scurvy or beriberi, and some also suffered from an eye complaint caused by the eggs of some fly being deposited on the underside surface of the eyelid.

The strain put upon both the crew and the captain was enormous. There were a number of fights among the members of the crew for almost no reason, and Mr Buckle recalled that the captain's black hair turned almost white during the seven months at sea. Sadly all was not over for the crew, for when within three days sailing of 'Frisco, they met headwinds and spent the next eight weeks beating towards and away from the port. They sighted several ships including an American schooner *Mindora* who was able to send some food across to the *Leyland Brothers* and this brought about a marked change in the

Ships waiting for guano cargo, near the Chincha Islands of Peru.
MERSEYSIDE MARITIME MUSEUM

condition of a number of the crew. On 4 November they reached the Golden Gate and encountered the gunboat *Princeton* which had been sent out by the United States Government to search for them even though they were capable of going to San Francisco under their own sail. Mr Buckle concluded his article by writing:

> In fairness to her Captains, officers and crew it should be noted here that very shortly after this terrible voyage she all but made a record passage to Australia, missing doing so by a mere two or three days, despite being becalmed on the line for well over a fortnight.

A Voyage on the *Allerton*

Other ships had unfortunate experiences. Matthew Murray who was an able seaman joined the *Allerton* at Barry Dock in 1898 and later wrote an account of his journey in this vessel. The *Allerton* made an uneventful passage from Barry Dock to Hong Kong in 144 days with only one stretch of bad weather in which Mr Murray was uncertain as to whether they would survive. He wrote:

> during that night, although I was not religiously inclined, I prayed that if I was to be drowned it would at least be in the hours of daylight. With the coming of dawn I felt relieved and inwardly concluded that a ship which could survive the buffeting the *Allerton* had taken would come safely through any storm.

It took three weeks to discharge and then they took on ballast for Astoria, which they reached after a passage of 57 days. They soon moved to Portland and loaded a new cargo. Here one of the able seamen, John Whittle, who boasted of never having made a round voyage in the same ship went ashore. By May 1900 they were ready to proceed to sea and Murray took stock of the number of able seamen left on board ship, which was now eight. Together with the others he realised how short-handed they were, but he had also heard that the captain had refused to replace the deserters since he was not prepared to meet the demands of the Grant brothers, at that time in control of the supply of seamen in Portland. After an hour's towing they arrived at Astoria. Here the captain tried to obtain more crew for his vessel but being unsuccessful he asked the second mate, Mr Lynn, to inform the crew of the situation and ask them to discuss amongst themselves the possibility of taking the ship home or to San Francisco, where they might obtain a full crew. After much discussion Murray was chosen as the spokesman and he presented such strong terms that the master refused to discuss them. However the outcome was that they agreed to take the *Allerton* to San Francisco and that their pay during the passage would be at the rate of £2 per month in addition to their original wage of £3 per month for which they had signed on at the commencement of the voyage. They had told the captain that with so few seamen they thought it would be best to go to San Francisco. Murray also insisted on a written agreement and eventually this was drawn up by the second mate and duplicated and signed by the captain, Mr Lynn, and Murray on behalf of the crew. Murray insisted that this was put in the official log book and this was done.

A short while later Murray, who was at the wheel, had misgivings that perhaps they were not going to San Francisco after all, but were in fact heading down the Pacific towards Cape Horn. He realised that they should have been able to see the coastline if they had been going down to San Francisco since they would be sailing roughly parallel with it. However, he stopped worrying about this when the captain, who was in his fifties, appeared from the companionway. While the sails were being set, the captain took the wheel. As the day passed, he and the rest of the crew accepted the situation.

The next part of the journey proved to be uneventful and they experienced quite good weather going round Cape Horn. On reaching the Trades two events occurred. First they sighted the Ascension Islands, also passed on their previous voyage to Hong Kong, and then the four-masted barque, *Pinmore*, which they had met earlier in the Columbia River towing to Portland, came past them at about one knot faster under full sail. They passed several more ships on the way to the Doldrums. During their time in the ports of the north latitude, it had been announced that their ration of routee (a substance made from a cob of bread) was to be cancelled. However, the main event for Murray on this stage of the passage was the loss of a loaf that had been baked for the captain and mates. The loaf disappeared and the captain was determined to find the thief. In the discussions that followed between the seamen it was decided that Dennis the pig who was a villainous animal had taken it. Apparently he had been particularly successful at acquiring unlimited supplies of good cargo from number one hold including pieces of rope and old canvas, which augmented his own comfort. On many occasions too he had been through the galley unmolested by the Chinese cook. However, in the evening as they helped themselves to biscuits, they found to their astonishment the loaf cut into four pieces and put within the broken parts of what was left of their daily ration of biscuit. They were so amazed by this sudden appearance of good fortune that they laughed and fully enjoyed their meal.

The next morning another loaf disappeared from the galley and the captain was soon on the scene to hear from the Chinese cook of its disappearance. He offered a pound of tobacco to the person who could help him in locating the loaf or establishing guilt. That evening and early the next day it was discovered that Dennis the pig was in a poor condition having eaten something which disagreed with him.

A while later the Fastnet Light was sighted and towards nightfall the Queenstown pilot boarded the vessel and informed them that they had orders to proceed to Sunderland. Near the *Allerton* was the *Argos* which had left Astoria the same day. They had seen nothing of each other during the passage of 135 days. However, the passage was not quite completed for in the North Sea they ran into bad weather and lost the foresail, fore lower topsail, and two main topsails. It was a miserable time and the mate was severely injured and remained in his room for the rest of the voyage. Later when the gale had subsided they signalled to a barque that was close by for food and a boat was sent for provisions, which included potatoes, beef, a bag of rusks and some tea and sugar. Two days later they sighted the Roker Light and at daylight the following morning they were in view of Sunderland and they completed their voyage in 154 days from Astoria.

In this article, Murray gives some interesting descriptions of food on board and clearly there was a shortage of provisions. He described biscuits as :

> eight to the pound, bearing the triple hallmark of a firm now defunct. They were hard as flint, but could be prised in two by exerting a little pressure with the point of a knife. When their insides were explored, little tufts of a web-like texture could be found. Inside that web was a maggot which we knocked on the deck before starting to chew the biscuits which were dirty white in colour and suggested a composition of bone and pea meal, and a bill sticker's paste to make all adhere while baking was being done.

He refers to the doling out of lime juice as feast day:

> in that it gave us all a drink with a bit of taste in it, and something with which one could, if so inclined, make crackerhash. The preparation of this brand of hash consisted of smashing biscuits in a canvas bag. When the desired state of fineness of what was left of one's pound of pantiles was attained, it was mixed with a little lime juice and some fat from our allowance of salt beef. The preparation was done in the watch below and taken to the galley to be heated by the cook. Strange as it may seem, the concoction was palatable and was looked upon as dainty for the evening meal. It must also have been sustaining because all of us without exception, showed our culinary skill on this sweetmeat.

Later on he wrote: 'Time was passing rapidly and we were all in good heart, notwithstanding our empty stomachs.' The original tea and coffee had finished, their place was taken by another variety:

> this was wheat which had been roasted in a frying pan and ground in a small handbowl. It was not too bad to taste and it must also have had some nutritive value as we all preferred it to the original brand and were fighting fit.

Training of Seamen

In a meeting of the Liverpool Ship Owners Association in 1891 some anxiety was shown at the loss of seamanhip in the British sailor. Leyland contributed to this debate by commenting on the training of boys as sailors. His speech was recorded in a local newspaper as follows:

> His firm had tried to experiment in their vessels by means of apprentices, boys from training vessels, and boys taken directly from the streets. He did not care much for those

A number of deep sea square-rigged ships in San Francisco Bay wait their turn to dock.
NATIONAL MARITIME MUSEUM

whom they had taken as apprentices but the boys they had had from training ships had been really good and were turning out as excellent sailors. Many of those from the streets, he was sorry to say, had not turned out so well but they had adopted a principle which he thought was a good one and which he should like to see more generally adopted by shipowners. They heard of certain good boys who desired to go to sea. They had not money to buy an outfit and his firm took from three to four boys on almost every vessel now at 1s. od per month and gave them a small outfit. If at the end of the first month they were found to be good lads their payment was increased and by and by they attained ordinary seamen's wages. If they could recruit boys from the streets and give them this training they would benefit infinitely by their services and also benefit the mercantile marine of the country.

One such boy was 17-year-old Richard Dale who joined the *Toxteth* in the South West India Dock in London on 13 December 1894. He recorded his first voyage in the sailing ship by writing a daily journal. They took a general cargo to Sydney and then travelled from Newcastle to San Francisco with 3800 tons of coal and from there home to Antwerp in 1896. The journal consists of a collection of notes written each day on the position and speed of the ship and the nature of winds. It gives some insight into life on board ship as seen by a boy who shared a cabin with three others of similar age. On several occasions he was homesick. For instance on one occasion he wrote: 'Never felt so homesick in my life as I have felt today thinking about Christmas. I hope we shan't sail tomorrow being Christmas.' On another occasion he fell asleep on the hatch with pleasant dreams about home and then he felt disappointed when he woke up to find it was only a dream. His duties in the first mate's watch consisted of trimming the lamps, collecting coal for the cook, coiling and splicing wire as well as washing and painting different parts of the ship.

Once again there are a number of impressions of food on board which on the whole seems to have been extremely good. They started to run short of food 125 days out from San Francisco to Antwerp and Dale reported that butter and marmalade were all finished, and that they now had to exist on 'biscuits and salt junk' even though there was a little over 1000 miles to go. A week later the sugar allowances were cut by half because they had virtually run out and he reported 'we are running short of everything.' However the next day they killed their last pig and he enjoyed fresh pork.

He gives a good insight into the activities on board ship and he records the occasions they played draughts, or danced and waltzed with a melodion playing. In June 1895 during their passage from Newcastle to San Francisco he reported that there were six sharks around the ship.

> We had one fast for two minutes but he broke the hook at last and got away with part of the hook in his mouth. We did not catch any although we tried many times. The ship is surrounded with sharks now at present and also barracuda. I think they look magnificent in the water.

However, while fishing on another occasion they caught three within half an hour and they severed the backbones and jaws from them. They made walking sticks from backbones, and jaws became ornaments which they cured properly. They also played a number of games of football between the two different watches. The captain used to play as well and when he kicked the ball over the side on one occasion he announced that everyone should have a glass of grog from the steward and Dale thought 'it was not bad of the skipper'. On another occasion the captain, Dale and two others went swimming since the captain said there were no sharks in the area. However within half an hour a large shark was found swimming round the ship.

He also had some fun on shore and he recorded these details while at Port Costa in August 1895.

> I thoroughly enjoyed myself with the apprentices of the *Garnet Hill*, they were a decent jolly lot of boys. We used to visit all the fruit ranches and got more fruit than we could possibly eat. Sometimes we would have a concert on board the *Garnet Hill* on the half deck and I have seen as many as thirty of us boys inside there together, some on bunks, some on chests and each one had to take part in the entertainment. So we used to have a good programme each evening and I think we all used to enjoy ourselves.

Dale had a certain pride in his ship and he recorded the journeys of other rival ships. On their passage to Sydney they signalled in the Tropics the *Buckhurst* which arrived from Gloucester in 92½ days whereas the *Toxteth* took 94 days. Apparently in Newcastle the captain of the *Toxteth* had made an arrangement with the captain of the four-masted barque *Fingal* to leave at the same time but the captain of the *Fingal* had deceived them and had left 24 hours before them. Dale wrote: 'I think the captain of *Fingle* [sic] very mean to act as he did and I should like to see us pass him and we would like to show him the flag.' In this passage to San Francisco he recorded that six of the seven ships which left a week before them had not arrived yet – 'We have beaten the lot.' On another occasion he speaks highly of the ship when he wrote: 'Everybody speaks well about the ship going about for she went about like a yacht'.

Another person who went to sea at an early age in the Leyland vessels was R W Leyland's son, Ralph Leyland, who in 1903 at the age of only 17 joined the office staff in Liverpool. He had a fairly practical knowledge of life afloat having been on several voyages at an early age and this knowledge proved to be invaluable in enabling him to assist in the practical management of the sailing ships, particularly in connection with food and stores. He also had a first hand knowledge of what the ships were really like, and what the crews had to stand up to on these long voyages. He wrote many years later (in an article for *Sea Breezes*, vol 14, July-Dec 1952):

The busy South West India docks in London in the late 1880s. Richard Dale who wrote a record of his voyage as a boy aboard *Toxteth*, started his journey here.
NATIONAL MARITIME MUSEUM

After I had been in the office for a year or so, I was promoted to the position of Stores Supply Officer. Having watched with no little concern the blue pencil being wielded with a heavy hand by the previous stores officer on the Captain's and Chief Officer's and Steward's stores lists, I thought I would try to make the change and thereafter as long as I held that position, I never cut down on one single item for which they had indented. I knew very well that the reasonable items asked for were absolutely required, both to keep the ship efficiently run and safe at sea and the whole crew properly fed and happy. We always used to try and put on board something in excess of the Board of Trade scale of food. After all, conditions at sea in sail, say off the Horn, are very different to what they are in any other job in the world. A happy ship is a great asset to a ship owner and I wonder how many realise this. It means that everyone works together to get the best out of her under all conditions. It means a pride in the ship and in the old days, for instance, when going into port, or even coming up channel, members of the crew were not keen on passing a line to a tug if it could be helped, the attitude being 'we will show them'. This of course meant saving the cost of a tug. Another instance, say on the West Coast of South America, all cargo had to be worked in and out of the ship by the ship's own crew, using hand winches, because port facilities were bad and ships usually had to lie out at anchor in the roads. This loading and discharging, all by hand, was a dreadful job, but if the men were well fed and treated in a humane fashion, it was astonishing how they would stick to the ship instead of deserting and work hard and cheerfully and so get the ship turned round quickly – thus saving much time and money for the owners. It must be admitted that some owners and some ships, did get bad names. Sometimes it was the owners' fault, sometimes the captains', sometimes both were to blame, but in my opinion it was possible to have really happy ships.

With regard to the under-manning and lack of provisions on the ship *Allerton* mentioned earlier, Ralph Leyland wrote: 'I do not think that often happened with Leyland ships.' However, conditions on board ship in the early years of this century were very different to those in their heyday in the late 1880s and early 1890s.

Disasters at Sea

On some occasions ships disappeared and were never heard of again. The first Leyland ship to go missing was the *Grassendale*. In the Municipal Elections in Liverpool of 1892 one of the candidates made a reference to

The *Toxteth* under sail. Richard Dale wrote in his diary: 'Everybody speaks well about the ship going about for she went about like a yacht.' NATIONAL MARITIME MUSEUM

Leyland's ships as coffin ships and Leyland's reply to this accusation was reported in the local papers as follows:

> When the remark was made as to coffin ships, we suppose the speaker meant any ship that might be sent to sea and never afterwards be heard of. His brother and himself started their first ship in 1875 and during a period of nearly seventeen years that had elapsed, he was happy to tell them that they had only lost one ship with a crew and that ship was almost a new vessel, and was commanded by the Commodore Captain of their fleet. It was one of those mysteries of the deep seas that will never be unfolded.

She was a fairly new ship having made two or three previous voyages and on this occasion left New York for Shanghai with 72,500 cases of petroleum on 17 May 1884, commanded by Captain Richardson who had with him his wife and children and a crew of 29. She was reported all right off Rio de Janeiro on 30 August but in October, near the Straits of Sunda, some vessels passed through a quantity of floating cases of petroleum, whose hallmarks corresponded with those of the *Grassendale* cargo and nothing more had been heard of her. In the inquiry held at St George's Hall in Liverpool in May 1885, there was some question as to the amount of ballast on board and whether it was 100 tons or 140 tons. But it was added that at the time the vessel was launched with masts and yards standing without ballast she stood securely during a strong breeze. The court felt that she was properly and efficiently manned even though she had left New York with one man less making 29 hands all told.

The *Woolton* left Newcastle, New South Wales, on 14 June 1893 under Captain G R Johnston, loaded with coal and tallow for Valparaiso. She loaded 2807 tons of Moors End coal and 180 tons of tallow but she too disappeared. The investigation held at Newcastle said that she was 'fully and properly equipped, not overladen, and manned by a crew of 28 all told'. On leaving port, she was 'in every way thoroughly seaworthy in every respect.'

The *Toxteth* was one of several sailing vessels to go missing in 1908 around Cape Horn. The Italian barque *Cognati* limped into Montevideo in 1908 and reported that there was a lot of wreckage and a number of boats adrift in the ice; at this time too, it was reported in *Lloyd's List* that there were a number of vessels on the overdue list including the American *Arthur Sewall* and *Bangalore*, the British *Falklandbank*, *Carnedd Llewellyn* and *Toxteth*, and the German *Adolf Obrig*. None of these was ever heard of again. The *Toxteth* together with the *Falklandbank* left Port Talbot with a cargo of coal for South America 24 hours ahead of the *Birmark* and nothing was heard of those two again. Many years later, Ralph Leyland wrote of this voyage:

> I went from the office to Antwerp with the Captain and acted as his first mate on the run from Antwerp to Port Talbot, where she loaded. I very much wanted to continue the voyage in her but my father would not let me go. She sailed about a week later and from that day to this nothing more has been heard of her. It can only be presumed she foundered off the Horn as there was a lot of ice reported that year.

Several vessels were abandoned at sea on fire. The first of the fleet to be destroyed in this way was the *British India*. A Board of Trade inquiry was held at Liverpool in March 1894 in order to investigate the cause of the abandonment of the *British India* off Madeira on 19 January 1894, about 30 miles north west of Madeira, while on a voyage from Leith to Rio de Janeiro with a cargo of coal supplied by the Lothian Coal Company Ltd. The vessel was laid up for some time at Leith in 1893 but in November it started to load coal from the Battle Colliery belonging to the Marquis of Lothian which was sent to the vessel in instalments during November. This was a high class fuel almost exclusively used for export and there were no known cases of spontaneous combustion. This was not a full cargo, only about 1776 tons of coal, and the ship consisted of virtually one hold with three hatchways.

The Board of Trade's Mr Paxton said:

> During the loading a Board of Trade surveyor visited her and suggested to the then Master (Mr Whiteside) and to Mr Winter (a member of the firm Messrs Leyland) that test tubes should be fitted in the cargo, for the purpose of letting down thermometers for testing the heat. Both Mr Winter and the captain thought such tubes quite unnecessary for what they described as a short voyage to Rio de Janeiro. The

A view of Sydney in 1890. Richard Dale visited the port in 1895. He wrote: 'We arrived at Sydney on a Sunday and I thought that it was a treat to see the green grass and the trees and also to hear the birds singing. Sydney is a magnificent harbour both for safety and scenery. During our stay in Sydney I visited several people from my native town in St Ives, Cornwall, England so I was quite at home in that port.'
NATIONAL MARITIME MUSEUM

November 24

LOSS OF THE "OTTERSPOOL."

Finding and order of a Naval Court, held at Valparaiso, on the 21st day of November, 1900, to investigate the circumstances attending the loss of the British ship *Otterspool*, of Liverpool, No, 91,173, at or near Caldera on or about November 4, 1900.

The *Otterspool* was a vessel ship rigged of 1,711 tons registered tonnage, official Number 91,173, built at Jarrow in the county of Durham in 1885 and belonging to the Port of Liverpool.

It appears from the evidence given before this court that she sailed from Newcastle-on-Tyne on August 10th last bound for Iquique with a cargo of coals and a crew of 22 hands all told.

On Friday night, November 2nd, a tarry smell was noticed proceeding from the forehatch and about 10 p.m. the same night smoke was observed coming out of the ventilators forward. The third mate, Mr. Carvell, went down the forehatch which had smoke in it but he found no trace of fire. The ship was at this time in Lat. 30°26" S. and Long. 72°9" W. about fifty miles off the land at Coquimbo. The master ordered everything to be battened down and this was done. All the ventilators were covered. Holes were cut in the deck round the main hatch and the pump was kept at work pouring water into the hold until the ship arrived at Caldera. Water was also drawn by hand and poured down the holes cut in the deck. The first explosion took place about 2 o'clock on Saturday morning and for some time the explosions succeeded one another at intervals of about half an hour; subsequently the intervals lengthened considerably, but the explosions were more violent. At each explosion the fore hatches were lifted and partly blown off, and the main hatch was also lifted. At some of the later explosions a blue flame came out of the forehatches and went as high as the foreyard.

The weather was fine with a steady breeze. After each explosion the crew replaced and battened down the hatches, until at noon on Saturday, November 3rd, the, fore hatches were blown right over the fore yard. A new sail was then lashed over the forehatch with a heavy davit on top. This sail remained in its place until after the ship was anchored at Caldera, when it was blown up and as it came down caught and hung on the fore top gallant yard. After the first explosion on Saturday morning, November 3rd, the temperature in the hold rose very rapidly and the master decided to make the first available Port. The wind was light southerly and west. Sighted land at daylight November 3rd to the southward of Carrizal. The ship entered the Port of Caldera in charge of the Pilot and, when she has anchored, at the request of the master, the British Vice-Consul and the masters of the various vessels in the Port came on board and after a lengthy inspection were unanimous in advising the master to move the ship into shallow water and endeavour to scuttle her. Mechanics from the shore came off promptly and worked till dark trying to cut a hole on each side of the conflagration. The vessel rose so rapidly that the holes were soon above waterline and not much water entered by them. There were at Caldera no appliances for putting out or controlling the fire. The plates got too hot to work at, and the explosions threw the mechanics into the water, and the masts were expected to fall, so that after dark the mechanics refused on any terms to continue working. The deck begining to buckle up the crew left the vessel by orders of the master about 4 p.m. on Sunday afternoon, November 4th. Shortly after the crew left the ship she was a mass of flames. The Court having regard to the circumstances above stated finds as follows:—

That the fire was due to spontaneous ignition of the coal cargo:

That the hatches were properly ventilated during the voyage.

That everything was done that could be done to extinguish the fire and save the ship.

The Court desires to place on record its high opinion of the coolness, bravery and devotion to duty of the master, officers and crew, and considers that the conduct of the master is specially worthy of commendation. Richard A. Buck, acting chief mate, and John Carvell, 3rd mate, in the opinion of this Court set a fine example to the crew and deserve the highest praise. The expenses of this Court, fixed at £18 17s. 2d., are approved.

Dated at the British Consulate General in Valparaiso this 21st day of November, 1900.

(Sd.) Berry Cusack-Smith, K.C.M.G.

Her Majesty's Consul General for Chili,
President of Naval Court.

(Sd.) E. J. Fritz. (Sd.) H. C. Brown,
(Members.)

vessel left dock under the command of Captain Whiteside on 4 December and was taken to Leith Roads, where she was brought to anchor, and where she remained until the 10th or 11th of December. On December 7 Mr Winter went on board and discharged the master and two officers as Mr Winter said: 'because they were neglecting their duties, and were guilty of drunkenness.' However, no complaints seemed to be made to the Board of Trade and the master himself declared that he was discharged because he had not taken the vessel to sea sooner. The master also stated that the weather was unfavourable and the officers said that no reasons were given for discharging them. Mr Roberts was appointed master and on the 11th the vessel left on her voyage with a crew of 18 hands all told.

On 16 January 1894 there was a strong smell of gas at the main hatchway plus some heat. However on 19 January at 2.40am smoke was found to be coming from the number one ventilator and all hands were called on deck. Water was poured down the ventilator and one of the fire hatches was opened and had to be quickly replaced due to a thick cloud of smoke. The master had a hole cut in the deck near the windlass and water was poured down there for about half an hour before the men were driven away by the smoke. Another hole was also cut near the forehatch down which water was also poured. They also threw some coal overboard in order to try to get near the fire. However, within a few hours the deck was on fire and shortly after there was an explosion. The crew took to the boats and stood by but at 9.30am the foremast caught alight and at 10.30am the mainmast and the ship was all ablaze. Two tugs came from the island but the vessel sank shortly after. In the judgment of the court they found that there was insufficient evidence for spontaneous combustion of the cannel coal, a reaction which had never previously been recorded, However, this was possible. They felt that the owners were justified in disposing with any means of testing the temperature of the coal bearing in mind the history of the cargoes of cannel coal. However point 11 in the judgment says: 'Neither the master nor the first or second mate was to blame in regard to any of the above matters. The Court is of the opinion that the owners should have provided more efficient means of extinguishing the fire'.

Loss of the *Otterspool*

The loss of the *Otterspool* was not dissimilar. On 10 August 1900 she sailed from Newcastle-on-Tyne bound for Iquique with a cargo of coal, and with a crew of 22 hands. A couple of days before they arrived at Caldera in early November they observed smoke coming out of the forward ventilators. The third mate, Mr Carvell, went down the hatch but could find no trace of fire, nevertheless the master decided to batten down all the ventilators. Holes were cut in the deck around the main

The *Otterspool* was destroyed by fire in 1900.
COURTESY J H REID

SALE OF SHIP.

By authorization of Captain John H Reid, and with the knowledge and consent of H. B. M. Consul General and of the Agents of the London Salvage Association, the undersigned will sell by auction at N.º Calle Blanco on Monday, 10th instant, 2 P. M., the Britis Ship

"OTTERSPOOL"

now lying at anchor in the port of Caldera, in the condition in which she now exists, together with the cargo on board, anchords, chains, boats, etc.

The sale will be made in three lots:

First. The hull as it stands, including three anchors and about 180 fathoms of chain.

Secondly. The cargo of coal originally 2800 tons of West Hartley.

Thirdly. Two boats in excellent condition, one 23 feet and the other 25 feet long, one anchor, and about 60 fathoms of chain, oars, sails, paint and canvas, as per list to be seen at the office of the undersigned.

For further particulars apply to Messrs. Duncan Fox & Co. the consignees, or to

GEORGE GARLAND,
(Auctioneer).

83 87

Remate de buque.

El lunes 10 del corriente á las 2 P. M., rematará el que suscribe en su almacén calle Blanco número 189, de orden del capitán John H. Reid y con anuencia del Sr. Cónsul General de S. M. B. y de los agentes de la Asociación de Salvadores de Londres, la barca británica

"OTTERSPOOL"

actualmente fondeada en el puerto de Caldera y en el estado en que se encuentre, junto con el cargamento existente á bordo, anclas, cadenas, botes, etc.

La venta se hará en tres lotes:

1.º El casco como se encuentre, incluyendo 3 anclas y m/m 180 brazadas de cadena.

2.º El cargamento de carbón West Hartley, originalmente de 2,800 toneladas.

3.º 2 botes en buen estado, 1 de 23 pies y el otro de 25 pies de largo; 1 ancla y m/m 60 brazadas de cadena, remos, velas, pintura y lona, según lista que podrá verse en la oficina del que suscribe.

Por demás pormenores ocurran á los Srs. Duncan Fox y Ca., sus consignatarios, ó á

JORGE GARLAND,
martillero público

87

hatch and the pump was kept at work pouring water into the hold until the ship arrived at Caldera. However, on Saturday 4 November some explosions started and succeeded one another at half hourly intervals. These were of sufficient violence to dislodge the hatches and on each occasion the crew battened them down again. The master was advised to move the ship into shallow water and endeavour to scuttle her. Mechanics came to try to cut a hole on each side of the fire. However this proved to be insufficient as the vessel rose, and it was discovered that there were no appliances for putting out or controlling fires at Caldera. On the Sunday afternoon the crew left the ship when she was a mass of flames and the mechanics had been unable to do anything further. The court found that the fire had been due to spontaneous ignition of the coal cargo, and that they believed that everything had been done to extinguish the fire and that the hatches were properly ventilated during the voyage. On this occasion the master and the officers of the vessel came in for special mention.

> The Court desires to place on record its high opinion of the coolness, bravery and devotion to duty of the master, officers and crew, and considers the conduct of the master (Captain Reid) especially worthy of commendation.

In October 1900 the *Roby* was abandoned off Montevideo gutted by fire. The ship had been bound for Valparaiso from Liverpool under the command of Captain Jones. The master, mate and eleven seamen were picked up by the Brazilian barquentine *Alnia* and the second mate and fourteen men were picked up by the French steamer *Santa Fe* on her way from Buenos Aires to Le Havre.

Stranding and Loss of the *Aigburth*

The master of the ship *Otterspool* who came in for commendation when the vessel caught fire was Captain John Reid; when he returned to Liverpool he was given the command of the ship *Aigburth*. He was less successful on this voyage, for in November 1901 he stranded the vessel on the South Arklow Bank and he was suspended for three months. In 1904 she was wrecked on an unknown reef at Rooke Island, New Guinea, on a voyage from Newcastle, New South Wales to Java, still under his command. In the inquiry that followed it was found that she was on the port tack and shallow water was found on her port bow and right ahead. She was sailing at about 4 knots. The master tried to back off with sails and finding it useless he clewed them up and tried to use kedge anchors to keep her head round. For three days the master and crew tried to get her off the Coral Reef, but on the fourth day she started to take in water at a rate of about 6 inches an hour. With 9ft 6in of water in the hold, they abandoned ship and the crew were distributed between two lifeboats and two smaller boats, one of which was a new open boat acquired on their most recent

Advertisements for the auction of what remained of the *Otterspool*. COURTESY J H REID

The *Falklandbank* was one of the largest vessels that went missing at about the same time as the *Toxteth*, around Cape Horn in 1908. Built for Andrew Weir & Co, she left Port Talbot with the *Toxteth*. Both were carrying cargoes of coal and neither were heard of again.
NATIONAL MARITIME MUSEUM

visit home. After nine days the master and the men in the open boat arrived at Frederick Williams Haven. Here the master chartered a small steamer and later he went to Herbertshore and interviewed the governor about the possibility of a man of war helping to search for the missing boats. During this time the first mate and the sail-maker each in one of the smaller boats reached safety but the second mate and seven men were still missing at the time of the inquiry.

About a week before sailing the master had received a telegram from the owners telling him not to go through Torres Straits. In the cross examination the master was questioned as to what was meant by the telegram and whether the owners in fact meant him to go round south of Australia but he felt that was not what the telegram meant and he was within his instructions to go north with the south-east trades to Java. He was questioned at some length as to whether he would have gone through Torres Straits if he had not received the cable from the owners.

The inspector and surveyor in the Department of Navigation, Mr Alexander Sangster, who inspected the ship in Sydney, was also called to give evidence. He had inspected the ship on 21 April and found that the necessary lamps were in good order and that the ship had two boats in excess of requirements. The lifeboats were well fitted with all the necessary appliances. The starboard side had an extra boat which was old but good and fitted with all the necessary appliances. All he insisted on was that some lifelines were put on davit heads and this was done while he was there. He found all the boats in good order and he stated that to his mind the ship appeared to be well-fitted and in order throughout. Finally the master was re-called and asked if he put down the accident to not enough wind and a misleading current, and that he had expected a variable wind and course in steadying direction.

In the judgment the court decided that John Henry Reid had made an error of judgement in keeping his ship on a course too much to the north and west after he had found his position earlier. The force of the current which was considered to be stronger than anticipated put the ship north-west by north while the course was west-north-west. The court did not punish him for his mistakes feeling that he had already suffered sufficiently, and concluded by expressing hope that the other boat would turn up.

This was the official version of the wreck of the *Aigburth* but the story that Captain Reid told of his journey in the lifeboats after they had left the ship is even more interesting. There are two accounts of the experiences of the captain and his crew, both of which were printed in Liverpool newspapers. One was a report given by a seaman named Thomas Ellis, who with others was captured by cannibal natives. He reported that they had been fattened, and five of them set aside to be eaten. However, a neighbouring tribe which had captured the master of the vessel and two others, attacked the cannibals and rescued the prisoners. When rescued, Ellis and his companions were bound close by a huge fire, through which a crude grid-iron had been fixed.

The account of the captain which was reported in a Liverpool newspaper sounded just at improbable. He reported that when they landed at Frederick Williams Land the natives were very wild and assumed a threatening attitude towards the crew. He said:

> They came down to the beach in large numbers, looked at himself and also at the crew, touching them and feeling their

A modern Ulysses deriding Polyphemus.

arms and limbs to find out what sort of condition they were in. The situation was terrible while it lasted but they all kept very cool. 'I', said Captain Reid, 'fortunately had with me a gun, some caps, powder and shot. I kept eyeing them intently, watching every movement. Then I kept putting something into the gun from time to time manipulating it in such a way that the savages soon came to the conclusion that I meant serious business. When they saw what was going on they began to sneak gradually away from us, eventually they cleared away'.

He added that the savages were in a dreadful condition and that they were absolutely naked, the only ornament they possessed being a bone stuck through their nostrils, giving them 'a most appalling appearance to a stranger'. Captain Reid finished by saying that he was 'exceedingly thankful that he and the crew had escaped with their lives from such tremendous dangers.'

Ordeal of the *Garston*'s Crew

However, possibly the worst experience was for a number of sailors who were in the *Garston* when she was wrecked off Starbuck Island in 1889. The ship had been on a passage from Newcastle, New South Wales to San Francisco and the crew took several weeks to sail to Wallis Island where they were rescued by the schooner *Olive*. The following story was told by one of the unfortunate seamen on this voyage.

On 13 May 1889, the full rigged ship *Garston* of Liverpool left Table Bay for San Francisco; 34 days later she cleared the southern point of the Australian Continent and set a course north-east across the wide Pacific to pass 20 days later still, the westernmost outlie of the Cook group of islands on the edge of the South East Trades, a longitude of 160 degrees West. When the Trades set in strong after passing these islands, the course was altered to north with a little east to pass lonely Starbuck Island at a distance of fifty miles. On 17 July no sights of the sun were to be obtained but 'dead reckoning' placed the ship some 45 miles east of Starbuck so the course was maintained. At 9 o'clock on the same evening, however, the ship struck a detached reef which turned out to be three miles only east of Starbuck. An unperceived current had sent the ship 40 miles to the south west and the 33 hours that had elapsed since her position had been ascertained at noon the previous day.

The sound of tumbling surf had been heard some minutes before the ship struck but the officer of the watch thought the noise was due to a shoal of leaping fish, such as had been seen and heard on several occasions during the day and the warning passed unheeded. The night was dark and nothing was seen until the ship was right on top of the breakers and by that time nothing could be done to extricate her. She struck heavily and was at once washed by heavy seas and commenced to break up. When the sea entered the hull of the ship through the cracked bottom plates, the area inside

An amusing drawing of Captain Reid in which he is depicted as the hero, holding back the oncoming savages. COURTESY J H REID

compressed beyond what the hatches could sustain, and the latter were blown sky high with a roar, the ship was immediately filled by the seas that washed over her, yet the crew, working under extreme difficulties, were able to launch the three boats and get away safely from the wreck.

The two lifeboats were well provisioned, to the credit of the captain in a day when such was not the rule, but the gig had neither provisions nor equipment other than as much of the former as a last minute raid on the steward's pantry provided; and three oars and a compass. But the fact occasioned no alarm to the nine men which included the captain and second officer, who had been the last to leave the ship, who found themselves in a tiny boat, for orders had already been given that the boats would make at daybreak for the island, then dimly discernible, where a landing would be made and plans set as to how best to make for safety.

For some hours the boats lay in easy distance of each other, the lifeboat showing lighted lanterns, but some time before dawn, the trades came away strong with driving rain and they were separated. When daylight broke, neither lifeboats nor islands were to be seen from the gig; which had been set further to the south west by the current that had wrecked the ship, and now, unequipped, it was impossible for her to get to windward, against the current.

A council of war was held and stock taken of the provisions, which consisted of half of a beaker of brackish water, about 10lb of biscuit and as many of meat, in reputed pound tins, and these the captain took charge of – to sit on them in the stern seat as he navigated the boat. Beyond the poor compass, there was not a single instrument of navigation and the lives of all in the boat depended upon the captain's knowledge of that part of the desolate ocean, a sea of wide spaces. He decided duly to rig the boat with an oar for mast and the men's clothing made into sails, in an endeavour to return diagonally across the track of ships to the island they had passed in the ship ten days before. The decision was a heroic one. There was no alternative except to accept death by inaction and starvation and such was not for this crew of brave men.

For rations each man received a large spoonful of water morning and evening, while the nine shared between them at noon each day three quarters of a pound of meat (about one and a third ounces per man) and two biscuits weighing half a pound. It was estimated that the islands may be reached from 12 to 15 days.

The Trades were light and each and every day a burning sun shone down upon the castaways and the sky of burnished brass unmarked only by the white packed cumuli of the trades such as usually prevailed in this region. From the second day all suffered the agonised torment of thirst and starvation.

The boat with her human freight was loaded down right to the gunwale strake, and when at night the winds came away fresh, the top of every little sea tumbled inboard and the men had incessantly to bale out with their boots, there being no baler or anything else that could be used as such in the boat. Sleep was possible only in snatches, the men's bodies lying in the few inches that washed over the bottom boards to every little roll, and after the sixth day every man had to bear the torment of salt water sores which covered the whole of their bodies, when even the slightest movement was torture, owing to swollen joints due to the ever-lasting cramped position. Meanwhile the boat, with her ill-fitting baggy sails was unable to stand up to the wind. She went to leeward like a crab, till by the tenth day it was seen that no hope whatever remained of reaching the Cook Islands, so course was altered to the westward, and the gig bore away before the wind in an effort to make either the Friendly Islands or Samoa, or failing these by passing midway between them, latitude being unobtainable, the Fijis.

On this day the water gave out and the position of the distressed castaways, who until now had borne their privations with great courage, weakened though they were both physically and mentally by their sufferings, desperate and seemingly hopeless. But happily this did not obtain for long. There came a downpour of heavy tropical rain, which not only gave every man his fill but enabled a half beaker to be saved by wringing out the sails. The water saved, in this fashion, was intensely brackish, for the sails had long been permeated with salt from the sprays that had continuously drenched them, but it was drinkable, their burnt swollen tongues and parched throats like acid for a time.

On the fourteenth day the biscuit gave out and the men were left with but four tins of meat and the water, which they had been able to replenish on three occasions. The captain's pith helmet was eaten on the fifteenth day and on the day following, all the boots that remained were cut into pieces and shared out for chewing: they lasted about three days. By this time the men were reduced to skin and bone, and their open sores burnt agonisingly in the heat of the sun's rays coming directly from overhead at noon, and the bite of the salt sprays which almost incessantly swept over the boat. Of clothing there were only shreds left, every piece above a few inches square had gone to repairing the crazy sails so the men's emaciated bodies were left without protection from either the scorching heat of the day or the bitter cold of the nights. Their vitality rapidly diminished.

On the twentieth day when the meat ration had been further reduced and there were but two tins left, members of the crew begged the captain to then serve out all that remained, and afterwards when their limit of strength and fortitude had been reached, they would draw lots among themselves, to see which man should be sacrificed, that his comrades might live. The captain, who as well as being a superb seaman was evidently a man of strong character, was able to persuade them, largely by saying that even at the moment he was expecting to raise the mountain peaks of Samoa above the horizon, to carry on for another couple of days, then had the position not changed for the better, he would doubtless agree to the course. The peaks of the Samoan Group never materialised. They had been passed at too great a distance off, or under cover of darkness, but the

The crew of the *Aigburth* are examined by cannibals.
COURTESY J H REID

captain said now that an island may heave in sight at any moment, there were many such to leeward off Samoa, though here he was either too optimistic or he spoke in guile for such were now fewer and further between than before. This was on the morning of the twenty-second day, and three of the men were obviously at their last extremity, laying on the bottom boards of the boat without movement for hours; even the captain's brave heart must have begun to fail. The next day at most must inevitably witness a climax to the sufferings that were being borne by body and mind alike through starvation and exposure. Over-strained nature was at its last gasp. However it was not to be strained much further, for at sunset on this day the loom of distant land was seen straight ahead, and at daybreak on the twenty-third morning since leaving the wreck the boat sailed inside the reef of Vea (Wallis Island, some 200 miles to the west of Samoa).

There were three trading stations on the island and the Europeans in charge took the castaways to nurse them back to health and strength, a long process. Three months later the men received a passage to Auckland in a trading schooner, to learn on arrival that their shipmates had long been rescued, while making for the Fanning Island, the cable station some 630 miles north of Starbuck, by steamer bound for California which had, unknown at the time, passed within 20 miles of the gig two days before. The gig in the 23 days sailed 2000 miles, an epic voyage, demonstrating once again that while life exists is there hope on the face of the old ocean.

Another mammoth journey was achieved by a bottle sent from the ship *Allerton*. Probably the longest bottle drifts are in the Southern Ocean and in 1893 when the ship was south of the Falklands she sent one. Three years later it was found on the shores of the Great Australian Bight having travelled 8500 miles!

CHAPTER NINE

The *Ditton*, *Speke* and *Liverpool*

From December 1887, no new ships were started by Oswald, Mordaunt & Co at Southampton but eight were launched before the takeover of the yard by the Southampton Naval Works in 1889. Some time in this year Oswald moved to Milford Haven and set up a new company called T R Oswald & Co. Although Oswald's days as a prolific shipbuilder were largely over, amongst the ships he built at Milford Haven were the two largest three-masted square rig ships ever built, the *Ditton* and *Speke* for R W Leyland & Co, as well as two other square-riggers, the *Windermere* and *Lyderhorn*, both launched in 1892. Oswald may well have moved to Milford Haven with the knowledge that although R W Leyland would not go into business with him he would, however, put orders for three-masted sailing ships through him and this may well have helped in the backing of his new venture.

Leyland ordered the *Ditton* and *Speke* from Oswald some time in 1889 and in March 1890 there was communication from Oswald that he could possibly sell number 259 (later the *Speke*). Leyland was quite keen on the idea and asked in a letter whether this was possible and at what price. However, nothing came of this venture and they proceeded with the ships and the payment by Leyland to Oswald for their construction. The payment of the half framing instalment probably came in November when Captain Enright had come down from Liverpool to Milford Haven to give his certificate for the ship, the *Speke*. The *Speke* was launched on 11 March 1891 and the *Ditton* was launched shortly after on 20 July 1891. By the end of November of the same year Thomas Oswald had run into difficulties and was approaching Leyland over a business proposition which Leyland was both unwilling and unable to accept.

These two ships, of which the *Ditton* was fractionally the larger – about one inch greater all round than the *Speke* – were tremendous vessels. They were 310ft long and with three masts this left a large unfilled space between the masts. They were not fast ships even though they were fairly lofty with main skysails over a single topgallant. Their main yards were 106ft long and like other ships in the Leyland fleet at this period they had their accommodation amidships, with a separate forecastle for each watch of ten able seamen. As with other ships in the Leyland fleet, seamen complained of the lower yards being so large in circumference that they had difficulty in reaching over to furl or reef the sails. The *Ditton*, whose deadweight capacity was 4500 tons on a draught of 24ft, was a popular ship with seamen despite her huge spars. In 1904 when the desertion of ships' crews on the Pacific coast was extremely high, the *Ditton* distinguished herself at San Francisco by losing only one man by desertion. This record beat that of any other British sailing ship in that port for that year.

The *Ditton*'s Career

According to Basil Lubbock the *Ditton*'s first master was Captain Henry Stap who for a number of years commanded the *Great Britain*, the only successful auxiliary ever built. The *Ditton*'s first voyage was to Sydney, New South Wales, where she was the cause of a great deal of interest among the shipping community. On her second voyage she went to San Francisco and on her third she sailed for Melbourne via Rio de Janeiro.

The *Ditton* will possibly be best remembered for her visit to Newcastle, New South Wales, during her voyage which started in October 1901 from Liverpool. William Davis took over as master of the ship on this voyage and there is an entry in the log for 4 April 1902 which reads as follows:

> At 7.30pm on the night of the 4th inst, when coming into port, the ship collided with the ship *Port Crawford* carrying her foremast and other damage and our bowsprit and gear attached to it. Previous to our ship, the *Ditton*, passing the Nobbys the pilot ordered the flying jib to be loosed which was done by James Hobbs AB. Shortly after the pilot ordered the flying jib to be made fast again as it would not be wanted. Hobbs being on the boom and making the sail fast when the collision occurred. As soon as possible after this disaster, mustered all hands and found Hobbs missing. Took lights and searched all over the ship but, could not find him.

> Several boats were pulling around the ship, looking for him, but they were unable to pick him up. Next morning, Peter Johnson, night watchman, saw the body of Hobbs lying on the bowsprit, crushed to pieces with his head hanging on one side and his body on the other side. Covered the body over until the police authority viewed the body and took it onshore to the morgue.

This somewhat brief description fails to reveal the facts of this case. The *Ditton* was picked up by the tug *Champion*, about 24 miles south of Newcastle. This tug was said to be the most up-to-date tug in the southern hemisphere but there were no tugs in Australia fitted to shorten a hawser when towing. The *Ditton* was making about 5 knots and the tow line was 100–120 fathoms. Leslie Caskey, the pilot, boarded the *Ditton* from the pilot steamer *Ajax* at 6.30pm, two miles east of Nobbys, the vessel having been in tow for some hours.

Shortly before dark, a fleet of vessels appeared, all wanting to enter port that night and two of them, the *Ditton* included, were successful. There is some question as to the timing of the accident – 6.45pm or 7.30pm – but it was dark and at this time a squall swept over the city. The pilot, on boarding the vessel, immediately tried to get her to moorings in the North Harbour of Yankee Bay, and in order to do this it was necessary to keep good way on the vessels rounding Stockton Point. It was presumed that the intention of the pilot was to round to under the stern of the vessels *Port Crawford* and *Peebleshire*, which were lying loaded ready for sea at the North Harbour buoys and due to sail the next day. The *Port Crawford* was under the influence of the flood tide with her port side to the Stockton shore. The *Ditton* refused to answer her helm, and sagging over against it, she drifted down on the *Port Crawford* – a collision was inevitable in the pouring rain and the fierce squall. The anchor was let go but the momentum was so great that it struck her just on the

One of the four main vessels built by T R Oswald at his new yard was the *Lyderhorn*. Launched in 1892 she was a steel four-masted barque built for De Wolf & Co. Apparently she had a long and remarkable journey from Liverpool to Vancouver. She arrived at Pernambuco with most of her crew in irons – they had become drunk from imbibing the cargo of liquor in her hold. Her replacement crew were not much better – they mutineered off Cape Horn.
NATIONAL MARITIME MUSEUM

The *Ditton* at anchor. She was built at T R Oswald's yard in Milford Haven in 1891. She had a carrying capacity of 4500 tons and a mainyard 106ft in length.
NATIONAL MARITIME MUSEUM

SCHIEDAM
LYDERHORN, LIVERPOOL.

The graceful and towering presence of the *Ditton* with most of her sails set. Note the large space between her masts.
NATIONAL MARITIME MUSEUM

sidelight screen. The *Ditton*'s bowsprit drove into the port rigging of the *Port Crawford* with a tremendous sound of ripping and grinding of iron, and the *Port Crawford*'s gear came tumbling down on the *Ditton*'s forecastle and smashing her bowspirt like a carrot, as one local carpenter commented. The *Port Crawford* crashed into the *Peebleshire*. The shock of the impact on the *Port Crawford* tore her away from her buoy but Mr Jones, the mate who was standing on the deck of the vessel, at great personal risk was able to let go her anchor to prevent her from drifting away.

The *Ditton* and the *Port Crawford* were thus locked together and although the *Ditton*'s stern swung round, the mass of wreckage forward kept her head fast to the *Port Crawford*. Captain Newton who was the deputy superintendent of navigation said nothing could be done to moor the *Ditton* till daylight because the number of vessels that had entered the bay the previous two days had blocked the channels. There were 60 ships in port at the time. Almost immediately after the crash, the crew of the *Port Crawford* were panic stricken and thought their vessel was sinking, abandoned the ship, going ashore by boat. Their officers remained on board and the crew subsequently returned.

The only casualty – it was surprising that there were no more – was James Hobbs AB who was making fast the flying jib when the collision occurred. The master of the *Ditton* realised, soon after the accident, that Hobbs was missing and three sailors, Samuels, Hicky and Menzies, searched in vain for him. However, he was found the next morning crushed by the *Port Crawford*'s gear, face down, about 12 feet out on the remains of the bowsprit. His body was horribly mutilated and gashed – it took two hours hard work with tackle etc for the crew and the police to remove him. He was a 23-year-old Liverpudlian man, who had been with the *Ditton* four years and he was about to sit his second mate's certificate. In the subsequent inquest, the verdict was given as an accidental death caused by the falling gear of the *Port Crawford*.

In the morning it was found that there was little damage to the *Ditton* but that the *Port Crawford* needed a replacement for her foremast which had been carried away just above the forerail about four feet from the deck. The lower yards fell across the foredeck, while the lighter spars and tangled mass of rigging fell on the forehatch. Many of the spars of the *Port Crawford* were splintered and battered beyond further use.

In the inquiry Mr Jones, mate of the *Port Crawford* said: 'When she struck us we had bright lights fore and aft,

This photograph was taken the morning after the collision between the *Ditton*, *Port Crawford* and *Peebleshire*. It can be clearly seen how the massive *Ditton* rammed these two ships which were loaded and ready to leave port.
NATIONAL MARITIME MUSEUM

which must have been plainly visible.' It was apparent that the anchor gear of the *Ditton* was defective and the safety pin in the starboard cathead was rusted. They concluded that the collision was due to failing to let go either port or starboard anchor of the *Ditton* when ordered to by the pilot and the omission of a second tug on so big a ship on so squally a night – a grave error.

Stanley Bracewell who was aboard the *Peebleshire* later said:

> She [the *Ditton*] let go her starboard anchor and came pretty near putting it down the *Port Crawford*'s main hatch; about the only good it did was to act as a spring, and I think that saved the *Port Crawford*'s plates to some extent. The *Peebleshire* fared a little better, as she only carried away her port royal and topgallant backstays and forelift and sundry blocks which came tumbling down on top of the half deck.

Things were not much better when she had loaded a cargo of coal. The log for 3 July 1902 reads:

> At 4.30pm the ship hove out from Number Six coal crane, government pilot in charge. At 5.15pm it collided with the German ship *Anemone* and British barque *Sardhana*, doing considerable damage to both vessels. Our own damage slight.

Apparently in the early evening, the *Ditton* which had been loading coal under the Number Six crane till nightfall, was shifted out as there was no more coal for her. She was towed out from the Carrington Dyke to anchorage in the stream by the tugs *Enterprise* and *Irresistable*, under the pilot, W H Beale. It was about the same time as the previous collision, the top of high water and the wind a light north-easter. While the *Ditton* was proceeding she swung round in response to wind and tide and the end of her bowsprit caught the fore lift and backstays on the ship *Anemone*, carrying them away and swinging her foreyard around into the *Sardhana* which brought down the *Sardhana*'s fore topgallant mast and topmast. The *Sardhana* was an iron barque of 1146 gross tons built in 1885 at Port Glasgow by Russell & Co and owned by Andrew Weir & Co. She had loaded 1763 tons of coal for Caldera. The *Anemone* was a fairly new German ship, formerly called the *Macullum Moore*, of 1469 tons. Under Captain Angarty she had loaded 1970 tons for Acapulco.

On 11 July the *Ditton* was arrested by Captain Spain, Deputy Marshal of the Admiralty Court, upon a writ issued by Captain Flugge of Hamburg, the owner of the

A close-up of the *Ditton*'s bowsprit, taken from the *Port Crawford*. In the collision one unfortunate seaman James Hobbs who was on the bowsprit of the *Ditton* was killed. His mutilated body was not found until the next morning, entangled in the debris of spars and rigging.
NATIONAL MARITIME MUSEUM

Despite the change in her appearance, including the dismantling of her foretopmast, the form of the *Ditton* (left) is discernible. This photograph was taken in July 1914 in Montevideo. By this date she had been renamed *Nordfarer* and sailed under the Norwegian flag of Carl Bech of Tvedestrand.
NORSK SJØFARTSMUSEUM

The *Port Crawford* at anchor. She was a three-masted ship, built in 1883 and owned by Crawford and Rowat.
NATIONAL MARITIME MUSEUM

The *Nordfarer* was sold to the Christiansands Shipping Co Ltd in 1917 and this distant photograph shows her wearing World War I neutrality markings, bearing her new name *Bragdo*.
NATIONAL MARITIME MUSEUM

On 2 November 1921 *Ditton*, now named *Bragdo*, was wrecked at Boobjerg on a voyage from Liverpool to Norway. Her unfortunate end attracted considerable attention. She is reputed to have been refloated in 1922, condemned and broken up.
NORSK SJØFARTSMUSEUM

Anemone, to cover the cost of the rigging. This was the start of much legal work initiated in order to receive compensation for damage done by the *Ditton*. Later, it transpired that the pilot had asked for the first mate of the *Ditton* to let go the port anchor under her forefoot but the mate and sailors ran off the forecastle head. When he was asked by the pilot why he had not let go the port anchor, Mr Masson, the mate, had answered that he was not staying there to get killed. The pilot was blamed for adopting an improper course and the inquiry referred to the danger of letting the *Ditton* be handled by the tide in a narrow channel. She was an awkward ship.

Although only one sailor deserted the ship in 1904 while in San Francisco, the atmosphere aboard in August 1905 while in Acapulco deteriorated. The master in particular was troubled by his crew becoming involved in drunken brawls and demands for liberty ashore etc. He was physically assaulted on more than one occasion in his own cabin, together with his wife, who apparently completed the voyage. Various seamen were locked up in jail whilst the vessel was in this port from June to September 1905. Shortly after leaving Acapulco in early September 1905 two able seamen who had signed articles at Newcastle in February died on board. Both men were old to be at sea and although Thomas Matthews had signed his age on the articles of agreement as 65 years he later admitted to being 73 years old. Similarly James Crowley signed on as 63 although he said later he was 'about 68'.

These were by no means the only deaths on board the *Ditton* in the early years of this century nor the only adventures. For instance on 13 September 1904 the ship was stranded while on a passage from Newcastle, New South Wales, to San Francisco. According to Basil Lubbock, Captain Davis had run into foggy weather on 8 September 1904 and the ship went ashore on the night of the 13th. However she was refloated without much difficulty and continued her successful career.

The *Ditton* was sold in 1911 by J H Welsford & Co to a Norwegian company, C Bech & Co, and renamed *Nordfarer*. Later she was to be owned by three different Norwegian companies, one of whom changed her name to *Bragdo*. In 1921 she discharged in Liverpool for the last time, and it was on her way back to her home port in Norway that she was wrecked at Boobjerg on 2 November.

The *Speke*

The *Ditton*'s sistership the *Speke* also had an adventurous career. After her launching in 1891, the *Speke* was under the command of Captain Gyllencreutz who had been master of the *Allerton* from 1887. The previous year, James Gyllencreutz was mentioned in the *Shipping Gazette Weekly Summary* when he was master of the *Allerton*, after a seaman named Beeny was charged with wounding him. Apparently Beeny had taken on board a bottle of whisky and when in Barry Roads he came on deck drunk with a bottle in his hand. The mate took the bottle from him and the prisoner drew his sheath knife. The captain interfered and the prisoner struck him in the back and for some time the captain was in a serious condition. When he had recovered he was appointed master of the *Speke*. Towards the end of the century Captain Stott took over as master of the vessel and a journey under his command is described elsewhere.

William Barton Tilston was mate of the *Speke* for three years under the command of Captain Stott. He was then appointed master of the *Wavertree* in February 1904 and sailed her from Newcastle to San Francisco where he arrived on 14 July. Here Albert Brew took over the ship and sailed to Sydney, but Tilston went from Los Angeles in command of the *Speke*, crossing the Pacific to Newcastle, New South Wales and loading back to Peru. From here the ship, still under Captain Tilston, returned to Australia in ballast and, calling off Sydney Heads, received orders for Melbourne.

During the night of Wednesday 21 February, while on a port tack beating down the coast, Captain Tilston instead of continuing on his course for Port Phillip when inside the radius of the Cape Shank Light mistook this light for the light on Split Point and kept his ship so far to the eastward that he set a dangerous course. On the Thursday morning the ship was close inshore and heading for the rocks on the southern side of Phillip Island. Apparently the ship refused to wear round and bear up, and everyone on board realised the seriousness of the position. As she was in ballast, her great height above the water offered a resistance to the wind and sea which counteracted the effects of sails and rudder. Even if she had worn round on this dangerous course it is doubtful if she would have avoided the perils of the coastline. Captain Tilston in trying to avoid disaster let go the anchors but one of the chains parted and the other anchor dragged. One crew member was reported as saying 'From midday we knew it was all up with us. The only question was, whether we would go ashore on a bad spot or not.' The *Speke* then drifted into Kitty Miller's Bay onto the rocks near the eastern beach. The sea and surf were terrific, and directly the ship struck in but a few fathoms of water the whole ship was swept from stem to stern. The captain gave orders for the lifeboats to be launched and the starboard one was put over the port side with four men in her. Unfortunately she capsized and one of the men, Frank Henderson, was drowned. One shipmate was quoted as saying:

> Poor Henderson I can see him now. He struggled in the water like a man who could not swim. Only his face and wildly beating arms were visible, and we were powerless to help him. He was still for about ten seconds, then a huge wave broke over him.

The port boat was swung from the davits and the cook, a stout, elderly man referred to as the doctor, was placed in it. When they saw what had happened to the first boat the cook was hurriedly brought back on board. The first mate Mr Williams was concerned about the possible loss of two panama hats which he had bought in South America. To the amusement of some of the crew he appeared on deck with his two hats tightly clasped in his hands. In the rush of succeeding events the hats were unfortunately lost but one was washed onto the shore the following morning and was restored to its owner.

The only animals on board were a pair of cats which they forgot in the excitement of the hour. There was also a parrot which flew to land when the vessel struck the reef. For some remarkable reason the bird returned to the ship and perched on the counter, where the sea engulfed it and it was drowned.

A stunning portrait of the *Speke*, *Ditton*'s sistership.
NATIONAL MARITIME MUSEUM

During the confusion the crew were able to land a lifeline on the shore which was not far away and most of them were able to come down this lifeline to the shore. This required only a few fathoms of line but the vessel was on her side and manoeuvring from the deck to the rock, with the sea labouring heavily in the breakers, proved a most difficult operation. For one moment the line would be clear of the seas and the next most of it would be submerged. However, it was along this line that safety lay for the exhausted men. One man was caught in the swelling seas when he lost his hold due to exhaustion and if it had not been for the gallantry of a seaman called Herman he would have drowned. Mr Cook the second mate was also prominent in the rescue work; when all but two hands had been landed from the ship Herman went back to rescue the cook. During the confusion and the shouting from the shore the man on deck thought that the order was to slacken the line and both the doctor and Herman were let down into the sea. However both reached shore eventually.

The *Speke* had two apprentices, Rawlins and Poyntz, one of whom tried to save the portrait of his mother, placing it in a bag which went out in the ill-fated starboard lifeboat. Although the bag was not seen again the photograph was picked up ashore the following morning. The other apprentice lost his jacket which contained a pocket book. By an extraordinary coincidence, the jacket was lost but the book was discovered floating near the shore.

The crew on this voyage consisted of Captain Tilston who had been at sea 30 years and whose experience was confined solely to sailing vessels. Afterwards he referred to the seaworthiness and general construction of the ship in terms of the highest admiration, believing that a captain could not wish for a better vessel. The *Speke* was certainly a noble ship of graceful lines and towering masts. After the *Ditton*, she was the second largest three-masted ship, and carried a greater sail area than any other vessel of the same class in the world. The first mate was Mr Williams and the second mate was Mr Cook, both of whom were previously mentioned, together with 19 hands and two deck boys. The body of Frank Henderson was never recovered.

One Australian newspaper briefly recorded that several of the men on board the *Speke* had complained to a journalist not about the management of the ship, or the

Speke's premature end came in February 1906 when she was sailing in ballast, down the coast from Sydney Head to Melbourne. Captain William Tilston steered the ship on a course which was too close in shore and she was wrecked on the southern side of Phillip Island.
NATIONAL MARITIME MUSEUM

The *France* was launched in September 1890 at Henderson's yard. She was a five-masted barque and her enormous size is a reflection not only of the competition of sailing vessels with steamers but also the rivalry that existed between sailing ship companies. She had a massive sail area of 49,000 sq ft and a deadweight capacity of nearly 6200 tons.
NATIONAL MARITIME MUSEUM

matters which were responsible for the disaster, but rather about the conduct on board immediately prior to their flight from the ship. Whatever these complaints were they are unrecorded for they were contradicted by the master, officers and apprentices.

The owners were sent a telegram soon after the wreck occurred and a notice of the wreck appeared in the *Shipping Gazette Weekly Summary* on 2 March 1906. A telegram from Melbourne on 28 February recorded that some of the spars had come down, that the masts were moving under the strain, and the hull was broken in two. It recorded 'that it is expected that the rest of the hull will soon break up.' The rest of the crew of 20 in the charge of the mate Mr Williams were taken to Melbourne where it was noted that the greater part of the town turned out to see them. It was reported that a number of men were suffering from shock and exposure and they were sent to hospital. In the inquiry that followed in Melbourne on 7, 8 and 9 May 1906 a charge of misconduct was brought against the captain alleging that he had navigated the *Speke* recklessly and carelessly causing her to be wrecked. It recorded that he had mistaken the Cape Shank Light for the light on Split Point and so had steered a dangerous course. The judgment was that it was a gross act of misconduct and that his certificate of competency be suspended for a year. It might be argued that when travelling from Malendo he had loaded too little ballast for the size of the ship.

The *Liverpool*

Of all the private letters of R W Leyland some of the most interesting concerned the building of the four-masted, full-rigged ship *Liverpool*. There are 18 letters from R W Leyland to Russell & Co, Port Glasgow who built the vessel and launched her on 22 January 1889. Some time in about the middle of 1887 Leyland had discussions with Russell & Co about the possibility of building a new ship for his fleet. This was to be a special ship. He wrote:

> We have done nothing yet regarding the new big ship. We don't think we shall go into the special ship but are keeping a large one prominently before us. We want in round figures a vessel to register about 3500 tons – two decks, one engine – five masts – details to be arranged. Price £25,000.

The inclusion of an engine is interesting and shows that Leyland was forward thinking, but in the end he did not build a ship with an engine until his first steamer was launched in 1894.

Early in 1888 Leyland contracted with Russell to build the *Liverpool* for £23,300. In July of the same year he wrote to them asking whether they might repeat the *Liverpool* contract for a second *Liverpool* with delivery in June 1889. Leyland wanted this information to be strictly confidential, because there was tremendous rivalry between fleets at this time. Russell & Co however were not prepared to repeat the *Liverpool* contract since they reported that they would lose money on the building of

A formal oil painting of Leyland's flagship, the *Liverpool*. Leyland's solution to the competition of steamers was to build even larger sailing vessels. She was built in 1889 for the jute trade and she had a carrying capacity of 6000 tons. When she was launched she caused quite a stir in the shipping world as she was the largest sailing ship under the Red Ensign and the largest merchantman in the world until A D Bordes built the *France*, 18 months later. Leyland would have built the first five-masted ship if he could have agreed a price with Russell & Co of Port Glasgow.
MERSEYSIDE MARITIME MUSEUM

the *Liverpool* which was in their yard at this time. Leyland offered to increase his rate to £24,000 for a duplicate vessel and accept an April 1889 delivery if it would suit them. He was not over impressed with the rate of progress on the *Liverpool*, feeling that the company might well be occupied until April 1889 producing the ship.

Leyland was not to be put off and in August 1888 he wrote them a further letter suggesting a new contract for a vessel of 3430 tons minimum register for £25,900 less 1 per cent commission to Leyland. This ship was to carry a deadweight tonnage proportionate to the *Liverpool* register and he inquired what dimensions Russell would suggest. He said: 'We should require five masts in this ship – deck fully sheathed – quarter stanchions etc.' This letter clearly shows that Leyland wanted to build the first five-masted sailing ship. She would have been full-rigged and some two years earlier than the *France*. However, Russell & Co wrote back saying that they were not eager for new work at this stage as prices were increasing, and Leyland was sorry that he had been unable to do business with them before the rise in prices took place. Leyland wrote:

> We shall not follow the prices however. We have plenty of tonnage to work on now and can afford to become sellers instead of buyers when the price is a little further advanced. If you like next week to make us an offer of a similar contract to the *Liverpool* and nearer our ideas of price, we shall be glad to hear from you.

In their payment for the *Liverpool*, which was launched early in January 1889, they decided to remunerate £10,000 'which will leave an amount of £6650 to run for one year and £6650 to run for two years if required, but we hope to square off the whole affair by the end of the first voyage.' For this financial facility they offered 37/64ths

The *Peter Rickmers* was 400 gross registered tons smaller than the *Liverpool* but also built by Russell & Co. She was constructed of steel throughout and is seen here ashore on Long Island in May 1908.
NATIONAL MARITIME MUSEUM

shares in the ship as security for the balance. In the memo for the contract of this ship Leyland wrote: 'It is understood that as any portion of the bills is paid off as pro rata, surrender is to be made to R W Leyland & Co of the shares and insurance.' The final payment to Russell & Co was actually in May 1890 when they formed a separate account at the Bank of Liverpool to pay off their debt. When built, the *Liverpool* was the largest sailing ship under the Red Ensign at the beginning of the 1890s. Leyland had built her for the jute trade. Naturally the launching of this vessel in 1889 caused quite a stir in shipping circles. Her registered tonnage was 3330 with a deadweight tonnage of nearly 6000 tons on dimensions of 333.2ft × 47.9ft × 26.5ft depth of hold. She had two iron decks with web frames and steel beams. Many people considered that this giant was quite useless economically and also unwieldy. On this latter point they were probably justified, but Leyland's answer to the competition of steamers was to build larger ships. She was built to carry 26,000 bales of jute but on one occasion she carried a record cargo of 27,016 bales.

The *Liverpool* may not have been the most up to date vessel and ships such as the *Peter Rickmers*, built in the same year at the yard of Russell & Co but 400 tons smaller, were more modern as they were constructed of steel throughout. However, the *Liverpool* caused tremendous comment wherever she went. For instance, in Melbourne at the very end of 1890 on 13 December an article in one newspaper commented on the full cargo of timber that the ship had brought from Frederickstadt. It read:

> The quantity under hatches is represented by 1671 standard which means over 2 million superficial feet. No cargo equal to this extent has ever been brought here by a sailing vessel. The nearest approach to it is that of the steamship *Suffolk*, at present discharging at the South Wharf, which arrived with close on 2 million feet on board. The Scandinavian vessels which used to bring their 300 or 400 standard are out of the running altogether with these immense shipments. The *Liverpool* on her first visit here some 18 months ago when she was a brand new ship, had the distinction of being the largest sailing merchantman afloat. Her tonnage has been exceeded in one instance since then but she is still the biggest ship which has ever visited these waters. On her initial visit the noble appearance of the vessel compelled attention and on

Officers of the *Liverpool*, about 1898.
COURTESY J H REID

The peaceful but tragic end of the *Liverpool* came in 1902 when she drifted in dense fog onto the rocks of the Channel Island of Alderney with all sails set.

rounding to in the bay yesterday she looked as imposing as ever.

In March 1891 in an article on R W Leyland the *Liverpool Fairplay* commented on the ship *Liverpool* and her size when they wrote: 'The *Liverpool* was then the largest sailing vessel afloat, and remained the largest until quite recently, when a French firm, with a desire to eclipse Leyland's boat, launched the *France*.' The *France*, a five-masted barque, was launched from D & W Henderson's yard at Partick, Glasgow on 2 September 1890; her gross tonnage was 3784, registered length 361ft and deadweight tonnage 6200 tons. According to Basil Lubbock (*The Last of the Windjammers* Vol II):

> The *France* was built for A D Bordes, and was fitted for the handling of nitrate cargoes. In order to ensure quick loading and discharging she was given four steam winches to each hatch, and on one occasion she discharged 5000 tons of coal and loaded 5500 tons of nitrate at Iquique in 11 days. . . . Her windlass was worked by steam, her braces were of wire and all her standing rigging was set up by screws instead of deadeyes and lanyards.

She was rigged as a five-masted barque and she had a cellular double bottom with a capacity for 2000 tons of water ballast. She had two steel decks and only the usual collision bulkhead forward. Her sail spread was 49,000 square feet with masts only 160 feet high. One magazine commented on this as not being 'excessive but the appearance of her aloft is heavy decidedly and it is open to question whether the spars on these large modern ships might not be lighter than it is usual to make them.' The article also referred to this ship as being in time a crank vessel: 'as many of these heavily rigged ships have proved themselves to be. Double topsail and topgallant yards on four masts are a heavy weight to be carrying about aloft in a strong seaway.'

There was certainly great rivalry between shipping companies at this stage and the shipbuilders Russell & Co considered that they were doing even better when they built the *Maria Rickmers* at Port Glasgow in 1891. Most of these larger vessels were spanned amidships by a bridge deck and this was known as the Liverpool house. It consisted of a raised deck built about half-way between stem and stern and carried right across the full beam of the vessel, so that the only way from the after part of the main deck to the fore part was over the top of the house by means of ladders and handrails. Its sides, flush with the sides of the ship, were pierced by scuttles or portholes. This gave added comfort to the deckhands and petty officers. During a breeze of wind the weather scuttles had to be kept closed. Underneath were the saloon, quarters for the master, officers and seamen, as well as the galley, sail lockers, store rooms and undercover access to fresh water. It also provided an area for a day hospital.

This structure was unknown in clipper ships or the majority of vessels built in the 1880s. Accommodation for the crew was provided under the topgallant forecastle or in a deckhouse (as in the Leyland ships). The deckhouse was built of iron and timber and was situated on the

In November 1902, her hull smashed, the *Liverpool* started to break up and within a short time all that remained was her memory, a few girders and some concrete blocks.

upper deck just behind the foremast and in front of the main hatch.

It has been claimed that the *Liverpool* was the first ship to have this structure but this is untrue because the Leyland vessel, *Toxteth*, built in 1887, had a Liverpool house. However the *Liverpool* may possibly have given the name to this type of structure. Probably the earliest vessel to have a Liverpool house was the four-masted ship *Muncaster Castle* built in 1882 by W H Potter & Sons of Liverpool. In the case of the *Liverpool* this bridge deck was 52ft in length and it provided accommodation for ten officers and apprentices, as well as the thirty seamen. There were one or two spare cabins for passengers.

Ships with the Liverpool house became known as three island ships and the creation of a bridge deck was said to help prevent many open deck accidents. Certainly the Germans used the Liverpool house effectively; it saved lives and probably helped make for better passages in the early years of this century. It never became popular in British or American ships.

Liverpool's Maiden Voyage

Early in 1889 the *Liverpool* was sent to London to load a cargo for Melbourne and under Captain Thomas Calder she sailed on her maiden voyage from London on 9 March with one cabin and ten steerage passengers. She made her departure from the Start on 13 March arriving at Melbourne on 9 June, 88 days out. On this, her maiden voyage, there was a problem with the vessel leaking. Leyland wrote a letter to Russell & Co on 11 June 1889 which read:

> We have a telegram this morning from Melbourne as follows: 'Liverpool arrived Sunday am. The ship leaks

considerably.' We were glad to hear of the arrival but the latter portion of message is very serious. What can be cause of leak? It may be that some rivet holes have not been filled in with rivets – or it may be that some are slack and/or that caulking and riveting are not rusted up. But whatever it may be it is a serious statement (by wire) that ship leaks considerably and something must be done in Melbourne before the ship leaves the port. We think ship ought to go into dry dock but wish to have your sanction before giving order. Of course in a case of this sort where new ship on her first voyage leaks badly – we naturally look to the builders to make her right and this we formally notify to you and we have to say that we shall have to claim on you for all and every loss or damage that we may sustain or have sustained, in consequence of leak. We do not know whether there may be claim or claims on cargo account, in consequence of damage by salt water. Meanwhile we await your suggestions and/or instructions by wire or letter.

Whilst on her maiden voyage Thomas Oswald had written to Leyland from Southampton making various points about the ship *Liverpool* with particular reference to her build. Leyland wrote in return that he 'must candidly admit that the appearance of the ship is inferior to your build. She is however very strongly built and we think will prove a good merchantman.'

From Melbourne she went to Calcutta and then to Dundee, from which port she went to Frederickstadt for her outward cargo. Her cargo from Calcutta to Dundee was an enormous one of close on 26,000 bales of jute and then at Frederickstadt she picked up a full cargo of timber for Melbourne. In February and March 1891 she was loading wheat, wool and horns in Melbourne and she loaded 5045 bales of wool, 29 cows, 29,353 bags of wheat, and 3112 bags of flour besides bark, leather and tanning. She brought this cargo to the South West India Dock in London and arrived there 96 days after leaving Melbourne on 29 June 1891. According to Basil Lubbock the *Liverpool* was undoubtedly very powerful in strong

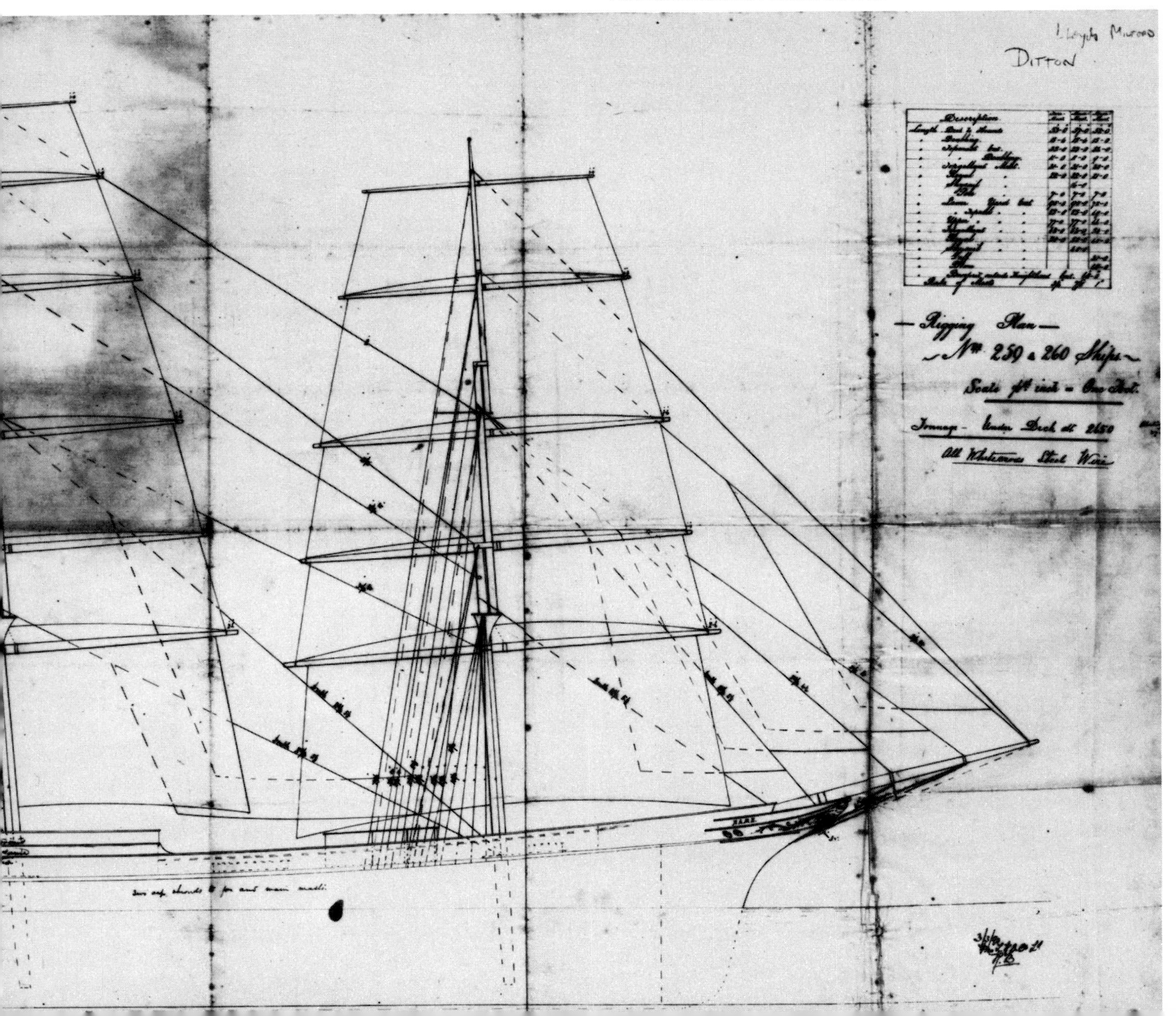

Sail plan of the *Ditton*.
NATIONAL MARITIME MUSEUM

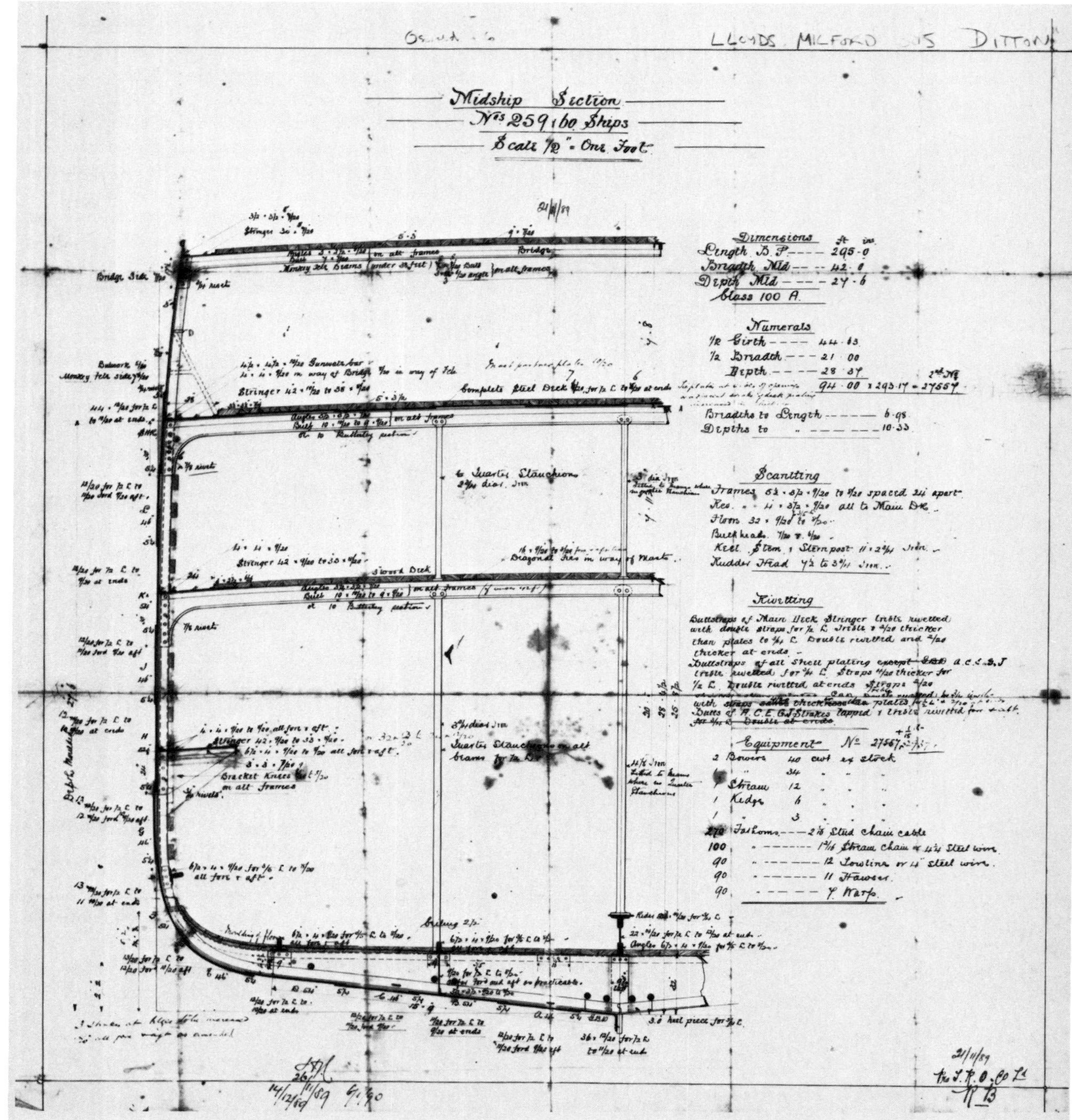

Midship section of the *Ditton*.
NATIONAL MARITIME MUSEUM

winds and probably her best passage was made in 1894 when she went from Liverpool to Calcutta in 83 days. In 1899 she made another good run up the Indian Ocean arriving in Hooghly on 27 August 92 days out.

The *Liverpool* sailed reasonably well but was very heavy on her crew and apt to be wet; on one voyage the second mate and the whole of the starboard watch with the exception of the wheel and look-out was lost overboard and this was not discovered until 8 bells.

After Captain Calder, Captain Whiting took command of the *Liverpool* and Tom Lewis, who was second mate in the voyage of 1897/1898 Liverpool to Calcutta carrying salt, and from Calcutta to Boulogne carrying jute, wrote of his experiences on this voyage some years later. He recalled that Captain Whiting was about 74 years of age and that this was his last voyage. He was relieved by Captain Owen Lewis, and Tom Lewis made the voyage with Captain Lewis from Middlesbrough to Calcutta and back to Dundee in 1898/1899. Tom Lewis recalled:

> Outward, running the easting down July 5th 1898, we got caught in a west north west hurricane and had a general smash-up, losing all our accommodation, stores, lifeboats, etc., but our spars we saved. However, with one broken compass we reached Calcutta (no charts or chronometers or instruments) six weeks after. She cost a few thousand pounds in Calcutta for refit. On our return to England, Lloyd's, the underwriters, made a presentation to the master, Captain Lewis, of £100 gold mounted purse and testimonial. The owners Messrs R W Leyland & Co gave the mate and me a gold watch each suitably inscribed for meritous services on the voyage.
>
> On the same voyage homeward, while in the Atlantic north of Azores, the sudden shift of wind caught us and we lost fore and main topgallant masts, mizzen topmast and topgallant mast. The jigger stood, however, and we reached Dundee safely. We worked by her for a while dismantling her. When a gang of riggers came from Liverpool I was glad to get home and try steam.

On another occasion in March 1893 there was an action in the High Court of Justice Admiralty Division brought for salvage services against the *Liverpool*. It appeared that the tug *Stormcock* had taken the *Liverpool* with the pilot on board at Bally Cotton Light under agreement to tow to Liverpool and dock there for £55. However, the keel scraped against mud/sandstone and grounded, but the defence of R W Leyland & Co who were the managing owners, maintained that she was towed round without difficulty even though the plaintiffs had claimed that the 15in manilla hawser was rendered useless. The *Liverpool* grounded on the foreshore of the river at a point 100ft from the dock wall almost at the entrance to Harrington Dock. However, with the help of the tug *Agnes Seed* on the port quarter, the *Liverpool* which was inward bound from San Francisco with general cargo was moved round and into dock. The defence upheld that 'the tug maintained no services outside the scope of the towage agreement for the nature of salvage services.'

Loss of the *Liverpool*

On 23 February 1902 the *Liverpool* left Antwerp bound for San Francisco with a crew of 35 hands and about 6000 tons of general cargo which included 1800 tons of girders, 700 tons of coke and a quantity of marble. She also carried supplies of tinned sardines, soap, candles, liqueurs, canned and preserved fruits, silks, olive oil and wine. At 1 o'clock the next morning the captain, Owen Lewis, discharged the pilot and with Beachy Head just in sight he took a bearing. He left Beachy Head under full sail making 4–4½ knots with a wind south-south-east and at 8.00pm was able to take a bearing off Harfleur Light. He then kept her off to the west and estimated his distance from Harfleur at about 18 miles, for it was clear then. At midnight he took another bearing and the wind was going down but he lost sight of the light at 1.00am on 25 February with fog coming down. He held the ship on a westerly course until 4.00am when he kept the vessel off a point to keep her off the west coast. He took soundings at 6.00am and found rock at 40 fathoms and then at 8.00am at 36 fathoms so he altered another point to west-north-west. The weather was apparently very thick and he could not see the fore end of the ship. At noon he gave orders to take soundings but the look-out man sung out that there were breakers ahead. He altered the helm but the vessel refused to answer and she drifted ashore on the coast of Alderney at a point called Les Homeaux Florains which is a small offshore fortification.

Two men who had been working in a quarry nearby, John Godfray and George Sharpe, rowed their boat out to the stranded vessel and climbed on board. The men found confusion on board and the captain was surprised by his position believing the ship to be near Casquets Lighthouse which was 10 miles away. There was six feet of water in the forward hold and a hole in her bottom. The crew left the ship with her canvas still set and by early afternoon hundreds of curious islanders had gathered on the scene to see the wreck. At low water it was found possible to clamber over the rocks to the ship and many islanders did so, helping the master to salvage the cargo. The islanders took advantage of this opportunity and for many days the people from the Channel Islands took part in the salvage work.

Among the archives in Alderney's museum is an eight-page news-sheet entitled the *Alderney Button Burster* which was published in 1902 and sold at 3d in aid of the Guernsey Cottage Hospital. In this was written:

> From a shipping intelligence point of view by far the most important event of the past year, was the arrival of the *Liverpool*. Some say she was consigned to Alderney by providence itself with a special purpose of raising the spirits of the inhabitants. Gloom and dullness of a long Alderney winter may well excite the compassion of the powers above, so there is much to be said for this view. Others think that the *Liverpool* came to Alderney for the purpose of being photographed.
>
> What ho she bumps! was the comment of the crew as the vessel arrived in port. She struck the island with her port side.
>
> An irreligious rumour has it that providence had nothing to do with it. It is said that the *Liverpool* was outward bound from Antwerp to San Francisco. In that case there is no mystery in her striking the island with her port side. We saw her crew and cannot think why they should go further out of their course than was absolutely necessary. But in point of fact, she must have been bound for Alderney, otherwise she would never have arrived and stayed here.
>
> One of the crew is reported (probably falsely) to have said that he thought Alderney was the Isle of Wight. Now why should a vessel outward bound from Antwerp strike the Isle

of Wight with her port side? Clearly the man must have had port on the brain.

The fish in Alderney waters must have been credited with exceptional intelligence. For days they had free access to cases of one star, two star, and three star brandy. They chose the last named and ignored the other two. Thus showing a high degree of selective acumen. Are teetotallers as a rule (fish are generally teetotallers) such excellent connoisseurs of brandy?

Since the *Liverpool*'s arrival many inhabitants have bought no soap. They used *Liverpool* soap eleven months ago. Since then they have used no other.

The remains of the ship were sold to a Guernsey syndicate for £250 but salvage was obviously out of the question, for after a short time the vessel began to break up and by November 1902 she began to disappear from view. Some of her cargo was taken to Guernsey by the steamer *Pioneer* and some of her fittings were stored on that island in a farm called Les Pelleys. About £8000 was realised from the sale of this cargo but a far greater sum could have been obtained had not the islanders in Alderney enjoyed plundering the vessel.

However, certain remains of the *Liverpool* still exist in Guernsey. A flight of stairs in the town hospital is paved with slabs of her marble and the safe is still preserved on the island. There is also a house adorned by curious flowerpot decorations which came from the ship, and in Sark's little harbour there is a chain cable which once belonged to the great ship. In the High Street on Alderney there are ceiling beams made from wood of the ship *Liverpool* and on the Godfray's Farm there is a shed door made from wood of the deck house of the *Liverpool*.

While the ship was still visible a number of excursions were arranged to view her and there was little attempt made to prevent many visitors to Alderney climbing out to the ship in search of souvenirs. Almost at the scene of where the *Liverpool* was stranded there now stands the Mannez Lighthouse which was built in 1910, and if that had been built only a few years earlier no doubt the *Liverpool* would have continued on her journey to San Francisco.

On 2 and 3 May 1902 there was an inquiry into the loss of the *Liverpool* held in Liverpool. Captain Owen Lewis had been employed as a master on Leyland ships for fifteen years and Henry Arthur Summerfield, his first mate since May 1897, reported that he had always found the master most careful. Details were also given concerning the four compasses on board and all were found to be in good order and sufficient for safe navigation. It was agreed that the casualty had been caused by the vessel being too far south of her presumed position and thus getting within the influence of Alderney Race, which would be running with great velocity on that date, at the height of Springs. The master was criticised for failing to check the speed of the vessel by patent or hand log and for failing to take into account the dangerous indraft which is known to exist in this part of the Channel. So ended a great sailing ship and one can but agree with Commander Leyland when he wrote: 'The *Liverpool* had a most curious and really very peaceful end.'

Riversdale's figurehead now restored, is proudly displayed outside the office of the Island, Tug and Barge Company in Victoria BC.

Part Four

The Legacy

The *Riversdale* as a working barge.

CHAPTER TEN

The Fate of the Ships

During the management of R W Leyland & Co a number of ships were lost at sea, wrecked or burnt, resulting in total loss. As well as these disasters, several were sold. Of the older vessels, the *San Luis* was sold in 1889 to H Bauer, Rostock, Germany and renamed *Hulda*, before disappearing from Lloyd's Register in 1894. The *Twilight* was sold to the Marine Association Company, Port Talbot in 1895 and probably hulked for she was out of the register in 1898. The *Thomas Hamlin* was detained at Cork in 1893 by the Board of Trade; she was sold through C W Kellock & Co for £625 to George MacLearie, a shipbroker in Port Glasgow. The *King Cenric* was sold in 1889 to Bruusgaard, Kjosterud & Co, Drammen, Norway, and continued her long career till she was wrecked in Mossel Bay in 1903.

Other ships, built specifically for the company, were sold during the management of R W Leyland & Co. The *Grassendale* (II) was sold to G Granlund, Raumo, Finland, in June 1900 for £10,000 and renamed *Imperator Alexander II*. She changed ownership twice more before being sold to S Loftman, Stockholm, Sweden, in 1919 and renamed *Ernst*. She was lost in the Hertha Flack minefield in April 1920. The *Cressington* was at Barry unloading in November 1899 and appears to have been sold in January 1900 to Edmund and William Roberts, Liverpool for £11,000. In 1903 she was sold to Repetto Bros, Genoa, Italy, who sold her in 1913 to Norwegians who renamed her *Songvand*. She was sunk by a submarine on 4 June 1917 off the Scilly Isles on a passage from Cardiff to Santon.

The steamers of the fleet continued to sail under the Welsford management for a few years before they in their turn were sold. The remaining sailing ships were valued and sold since they were unable to operate them profitably. The *Allerton* was berthed at Cammell Laird & Co's dock at Tranmere in March 1910 when C W Kellock & Co tried to sell her. During heavy weather the vessel broke adrift in the dock and sustained considerable damage. After repairs she was sold later in the year, through agents acting for the Chilian Government, for £2600 and was converted subsequently to a hulk at Valparaiso. About the same time, the *Halewood* was sold for £3175 to A J Grefstad, Christiansand, Norway. Later she was resold and her name changed to *Songvig*; and she was in the same fleet as the *Cressington*, under the ownership of S O Stray, Christiansand. She was lost on the Skerries on 14 February 1920. The *Fulwood* also served under the Norwegian flag, having been sold to P Bogen, Sandefjord, Norway: she went missing with all hands in 1919.

The dramatic wreck of the *King Cenric* seen here in Mossel Bay, South Africa in 1903. Leyland had sold her some years previously to a Norwegian company.
NORSK SJØFARTSMUSEUM

The *Leyland Brothers* was sold for £6000 in May 1912 to a Portuguese company, who renamed her *Empreza Nacional*. She had made her last voyage under J H Welsford & Co from Australia to Hull, with a cargo of wheat. After the First World War she was converted to a coal hulk. In 1941, it was decided to convert her into a motor cargo ship in Lisbon for the Angola service, under the name *Nacala*, since Portuguese maritime communication was hit by the shortage of ships. Progress in the conversion was slow as there was a general shortage of materials. Her old clipper stem was replaced by a straight one and additional bulkheads were fitted at either end of the midships engine room, giving two large holds. The original topgallant forecastle and poop were

The *Riversdale* in tow of the SS *Griffio* with most of her rigging now removed.
NATIONAL MARITIME MUSEUM

The *Riversdale*, with very little left of her, lying as a breakwater at Royston BC in 1971.

The *Leyland Brothers* as a coal hulk after the First World War.

The *Riversdale*, renamed *Crown Zellerbach No 3*, with her figurehead gone, working on the Fraser river in 1959.

retained, the former as a store only, but the latter, after being squared up to the deck, was fitted with the engineer officers' cabins on the port side and the engineers' mess and petty officers' cabins on the starboard. A new midship house was also added, having on the main deck five two-berth passenger cabins, the quarters of the junior officers and apprentices, the dining saloon and dispensary. Above it were the quarters for the captain, senior officers and wireless operators. She sailed on her

Riversdale's wheel on display at the Maritime Museum in San Francisco.

The *Leyland Brothers* almost unrecognizable as a motor cargo ship named *Nacala*.
COURTESY HAROLD HUYCKE

maiden voyage in the summer of 1944 but in the spring of 1967 her long career came to an end when she was scrapped in Portugal.

The *Riversdale*, the last sailing vessel to be built for the Leyland Line, was sold for £4150 in 1910 to Schluyter & Mack of Hamburg, Germany, and renamed *Harvesthude*. She spent the First World War at San Rosalia, Mexico, watched by British cruisers. In 1921 she was bought by the Dollar Line but was laid up in San Francisco for two years until she was sold in 1924 to James Griffiths & Sons, reduced to a barge and renamed *Riversdale*. Finally she joined the Crown Zellerbach Corporation as CZ No 3 being towed to Royston some years later. Today her figurehead is on display in the museum garden beside the office of the Island Tug and Barge Company in Victoria. The young lady in riding habit stares sightlessly skyward, recalling the day she tasted salt spray, fog and hail on *Riversdale*'s bow. It had been stored for 16 years until the president of the company, H B Elworthy, had it restored and positioned near the land-locked restaurant ship *Princess Mary*. As for the *Riversdale*, she broke into three parts and lies as a breakwater in Royston.

So of the many Leyland ships are there any survivors? In an article written in 1956 on these square riggers, the

The *Riversdale* and the *William T Lewis* as barges dry docked together.

same question was asked. (S J Oakshott 'Southampton and the Last of the Windjammers', the *Echo*, Southampton 27 August 1956.)

And that brings us to the final question: Are there any of these big Southampton-built square riggers afloat today? The answer is that there may be. If so they would probably be found in some out of the way backwater, their masts and yards gone, doing duty as hulks, with only their shape revealing the fact that they had once sailed the blue seas in all their glory.

And that is precisely how the *Wavertree* was found by Karl Kortum of the San Francisco Maritime museum in February 1966.

CHAPTER ELEVEN

The *Wavertree*

In May 1885, R W Leyland & Company entered a contract for the building of a ship to be called *Toxteth*, but she was sold prior to completion and named *Southgate*. In 1888 Leyland purchased her and renamed her *Wavertree*. In his private letters there are a number of details regarding the arrangements made between the two companies for the construction of this ship.

Delivery Refused

Leyland enabled Oswald, Mordaunt & Company to build ships and received a 1 per cent commission if the vessel was sold prior to completion. Thus, the launching date for the *Wavertree* was not supposed to be before 10 April 1886 and there were several interim payments, namely at half plating, full plating, launching and completion. For various reasons, probably because of financial problems and shrinking profit margins, with the possibility of the liquidation of assets at Oswald, Mordaunt & Company, the builders launched the ship earlier than they should have done. She was launched on 10 December 1885 and the builders hoped to obtain their launching payment from R W Leyland & Company. It is apparent that the shipowners knew nothing about the launching of their ship until several days after it had occured and they were not at all pleased. In fact, this was a major reason for selling her prior to completion, for she was dated an 1885 ship and yet her career was not to start till the next year.

In August 1885, as work progressed on the future *Wavertree*, Leyland agreed with Oswald, Mordaunt & Company that they could have an option to sell the ship named *Toxteth* prior to 31 December 1885 and that if a sale resulted then the shipowners would receive a 1 per cent commission on the sale. In addition the costs of their marine superintendent, Captain Semple, down at Woolston and visits by the company representative, Captain Enright, were to be paid by Oswald, Mordaunt & Co. Any bills maturing before the sale of the ship were to be transferred to another ship or taken up by Oswald, Mordaunt & Co.

By the middle of October 1885 there was the prospect of a purchaser for the *Toxteth* for about £24,500 and in December Leyland made a payment on the *Fulwood* keeping a bill open for six months. Leyland revealed that neither the final payment on the *Fulwood* nor bills on the *Toxteth* would have been due if the builder had carried out their contract. Leyland believed that they had been very supportive, allowing the builders to carry on building, so in December when they were asked to pay charges on their outstanding bills at 6 per cent interest whereas the bank rate was only 4 per cent they refused to pay. Leyland wrote asking if there was any problem concerning the bills and whether they were having any difficulties at Southampton.

They were not and the *Toxteth* had been launched a few days prior to this letter. An account of her launch from the *Hampshire Independent*, 19 December 1885 follows:

> On Thursday 10 December there was successfully launched from the Shipbuilding and Engineering Works of Messrs. Oswald Mordaunt & Co at Southampton a handsomely modelled iron sailing ship of 2150 tons net register, and of the following dimensions – length, extreme, about 280ft; breadth 40ft 6in; depth of hold 24ft 8in. The vessel is built in excess of Lloyd's highest class. She is full rigged and fitted with skysail on mainmast. Ample accommodation is provided in full poop for captain and officers, whilst petty officers and crew are berthed in large iron deckhouse amidships. She is fitted with Harfield's patent combined capstan – windlass for working anchors and chains. She has been built under the superintendence of Captain Charles Semple, nautical assessor of Liverpool. On the vessel leaving the ways she was christened by Miss Zina Methven of Woolston.

(Zina Methven was the daughter of James Methven, principal of a local private school called Woolston College).

By launching earlier than arranged, Leyland assumed that the builders had taken up bills due previous to the 10 April launching date, in the hope of selling the ship to the

A formal portrait of the *Wavertree* taken by T H Wilton's Elite Studio about 1900. She is at anchor off Telegraph Hill, San Francisco, with a full cargo of grain, ready to begin her long voyage south to Cape Horn and home to England. Her sails are bent and her anchor hove short against the flood tide coming through the Golden Gate.
SOUTH STREET SEAPORT MUSEUM

first potential buyer, Messrs Briggs. Therefore R W Leyland & Co were not prepared to meet the bills and G R Leyland wrote 'Should you not succeed in disposing of this vessel you cannot expect us to take her for an April 1886 launching contract when she was launched in 1885.'

However by the very end of the year any chance of a sale had disappeared and Leyland was furious, pointing out that they had enabled the shipbuilders to continue building in the hope of a sale before the end of the year. Oswald, Mordaunt & Co obviously wished to saddle the company with a vessel dated 1885 and not due before April 1886 although the agreement was that the launching should only take place in December if the vessel was to be sold.

Leyland wrote to them:

> We will be frank and tell you that at whatever cost to ourselves we are not disposed to tamely submit to such treatment. We have always treated you honourably and fairly – we have done all we can this year to spread the good name of your ships but your letter is a blow to our confidence that we shall not easily recover from.

Fortunately for both parties, the ship was sold to Chadwick & Pritchard in January 1886 and by a memo dated 21 January 1886, they agreed that:

> the present *Toxteth* now built and lying in Southampton is to be considered as taken off the hands of R W Leyland & Co (not to be tendered on 10 April contract). The bills for above ship maturing 10 April and previously to be covered by Oswald, Mordaunt & Co.

Sold to New Owners

The new owners, Samuel Rigby Chadwick and John Pritchard of 28 Brunswick Street, Liverpool were registered as joint owners on 18 February 1886 in Liverpool. A few days later they registered the transfer of $^{38}/_{64}$ths shares to Roderick Mackay of 3 Lothbury, London who had obviously lent them money for the purchase of the ship. Mackay transferred these shares into the joint names of himself, William David Lloyd and Henry William Lowe. They were in partnership as ship and insurance brokers and their office was at 7 East India Avenue, Leadenhall Street, London. Early in the same month the ship was registered as a company.

In November 1887 Chadwick and Pritchard sold their interest in the ship to Thomas Ridley Oswald (of Oswald, Mordaunt & Co) who registered the transfer of the ownership of the whole vessel immediately to Lloyd, Mackay & Lowe.

In the three years prior to Leyland purchasing her in June 1888, the ship *Southgate* made two voyages. The first was from Cardiff to Singapore with coal and then to Dundee with jute, arriving on 22 April 1887. Her second was from Middlesbrough on 8 June for Negapatinam, India where she arrived on 5 September. Having picked up a cargo of jute at Chittagong she sailed for Dundee where she arrived on 10 June 1888 under Captain James Toozes.

The contract for the cargo of coal from Cardiff in 1886 on her first voyage is recorded in the office books of the shipbrokers who conducted the agreement – C W Kellock & Company of Liverpool. It is dated 8 February 1886 and reads: 'Messrs Chadwick and Pritchard agree charter with Mr Alfred Holt of Liverpool chartered to go to Cardiff for coals and to leave Southampton on or before 28 February 1886.' The freight price (ie, carrying rate) was 17s 6d per ton and she was 'to be loaded within 12 working days after being in a loading berth. Cargo to be unloaded at average rate of not less than 80 tons per day. Not to sail from Cardiff before 6 March 1886.'

After her arrival in Dundee at the end of her second voyage carrying jute in June 1888, the ship was advertised for sale through C W Kellock & Co. An advertisement appeared in the Liverpool shipping papers listing her class, her rig and her dimensions. It recorded her inward cargo of 3320 tons/16,600 bales of jute and ballast of 260 tons, remarking that she 'is one of the finest merchant ships afloat.'

Purchased by Leyland Brothers

Ralph Watts Leyland and George Richardson Leyland purchased her for £15,750 on 21 June 1888 with a down payment of 10 per cent and the rest of the money to be paid within 30 days. She was surveyed at Dundee and the sale registered on 29 June 1888 in Liverpool. Captain

A beautiful small sketch of the *Wavertree* at sea. She could set over 31,000 sq ft of sail and the top of her mainmast was 140ft above the deck.

Toozes resumed command of the vessel under the new management and on 20 July 1888 the ship's name was changed to *Wavertree*. So started her 21-year career under the flag of R W Leyland & Co who had originally contracted to build her and had now brought her into their fleet at a bargain price.

The *Wavertree* was registered as a limited liability company in October 1888. Between them the Leyland brothers kept 25 £100 shares and the rest were sold to relations, friends and business contacts. By the end of July, virtually all the shares had been sold. In a letter to a shareholder, R W Leyland wrote:

> When I told you on Wednesday that *Wavertree* was closed I told you correctly – but since then Mr R Irving who originally took £2000 worth of shares – keeping £1000 open for a few days, has sent word he will only retain the £1000 for the present so it gives us ten shares to dispose of. Would you like five? If so I would advise you to take them as they are very cheap and ship is well placed sistership to *Fulwood*. Vessel sailed for Port Pirie 21 July so is well placed on her voyage.

On this, her first voyage under the Leyland flag, she arrived in Port Pirie and Captain Toozes reported her passage. Apparently at 4.10pm on 30 August a Swedish AB named Ingwald Solam who was assisting in bending the mainsail fell overboard. A newspaper commented:

> The lifebuoy was thrown over, and the copper punt launched. The ship was rounded to, and the starboard boat off the forehouse launched. She filled with water, and the port lifeboat was then leased away with a crew consisting of

(a) On 19 November 1907, the *Wavertree* dragged her anchors and ran aground on Desdemona Sands at the mouth of the Columbia river. She was en route to Portland from Tocopilla, Chile.
BINFORD AND MORT

Officers of the *Wavertree* at San Francisco, January 1904. The figure in the centre of the back row is Captain W B Tilston. To his right is Albert Brew, the mate, who later became master. On the captain's left, W J Shipton, his second mate. The three apprentices sit in the front row.
SOUTH STREET SEAPORT MUSEUM

(b) She shipped a considerable amount of water because of broken plates but eventually tugs succeeded in moving her off and she was towed to Young's Bay for repairs. There is some doubt as to the authenticity of the events and indeed of this picture.
BINFORD AND MORT

the second mate, the boatswain and four ABs. In the meantime the man got into the punt, where the second mate found him, and he was hauled aboard not much worse for his mishap.

A little later, on 10 October:

A Chilian AB was seen to jump overboard after throwing into the water a heavy wooden grating. Nothing was afterwards seen of the man, who was stated by his watch to be mad. All hands were called on deck and when everything was ready to search for the man in the boat the crew refused to proceed saying it was not safe to risk their lives in a high sea for the sake of a madman, who had coils of heavy wire round his body.

Apparently during her visit to Port Pirie the *Wavertree* caused a great deal of comment. She then sailed for the UK with the largest cargo of wheat ever dispatched in a sailing ship, at that time, namely 28,748 bags, equal to 122,900 bushels.

In June 1892, still under the command of Captain Toozes, there was a fire on board the *Wavertree* when she was in Sydney, Australia. It started on the starboard side of the lower hold. She carried a general cargo which was thought to be worth £58,000 and initial telegrams suggested that most of it had been destroyed. As she was discharged it was found that there was less evidence of damage. A large block of rails and tanks which were stowed in the vicinity of the fire probably prevented it from spreading. The estimate for the repairs to the vessel was £2200 exclusive of unexposed defects. From 1895 to 1897 the *Wavertree* was the subject of a prolonged legal battle, concerning this fire in Sydney in 1892.

The case went from the Supreme Court in New South Wales to the Judicial Committee of the Privy Council. The managing owners of the *Wavertree* brought a case against J R Love of Sydney, one of the 200 consignees of the cargo, who then appealed against the decision of the Supreme Court of New South Wales. It was an extremely complex matter but it concerned:

> the question whether or not, under the average bond entered into in consequence of a general average act which occured at Sydney, the consignees (resident in Sydney) were bound to furnish an average adjuster in Liverpool particulars of their claims for the purpose of the general average being adjusted in Liverpool.

Judgment was given for the shipowners. With regard

The *Wavertree* after her attempted voyage around Cape Horn – it proved to be her last. She was beaten back by hurricane winds, dismasted, and with water pouring into her, she made for shelter in the Falkland Islands. She is photographed in Port Stanley, more of a wreck than a ship.
SOUTH STREET SEAPORT MUSEUM

The deck of the dismasted *Wavertree*. Five of her crew were severely injured, including three with broken legs, as they battled with falling masts and spars, to bring the vessel under control to sail her downwind to the Falkland Islands.
SOUTH STREET SEAPORT MUSEUM

to this case, Leyland said in his speech to the general meeting of shareholders in June 1897:

> Some of you may have noticed a few days ago a report in the newspapers referring to one of our ships the *Wavertree* having received judgment in its favour, at the hands of the Privy Council, as against consignees in Sydney, New South Wales. This litigation has extended over some years. We fought the case through two colonial courts, and lost in each case, but we have finally succeeded in the Privy Council. The expenses have been borne entirely by underwriters, and do not fall upon the Company. The principle we have established is an important one for ship owners, and decided the point – namely, that a ship owner has the right of deciding where the general average statement in respect of the vessel he manages should be made up.

In 1894 the value of the *Wavertree*'s shares had dropped to £50 which would have given her a market value of just

Caulking the poop deck.
SOUTH STREET SEAPORT MUSEUM

under £8000. When, in 1896, there was the amalgamation of the different single ship companies into the Leyland Shipping Co Ltd she was valued at £10,750.

In 1899, Ralph Leyland, the eldest son of R W Leyland was entrusted in the care of Captain Bromley of the ship *Wavertree*. This was his second voyage, then aged thirteen, and the ship sailed from Hamburg to Calcutta carrying salt. He noted later:

> This was an unusual run, especially when the next passage was from Calcutta to Mauritius with coal, then to South America, after which the ship went on to Australia, thence West Coast of South America and home. She was quite a fast ship under favourable conditions, and I remember we used to log as much as 15 knots with a strong wind of, say, force 6–7 on the quarter.

This would seem to be a somewhat exaggerated figure.

Wavertree had been aground at Wittenberge, near Blankenese, after her voyage from Iquique. She was under the command of the commodore captain of the fleet, Captain James Bromley who took command of the steamer *Planet Mars* on her completion when he left the *Wavertree*.

Leyland sent various letters to Captain Bromley with instructions. Ralph Leyland was to travel to Hamburg with Mrs Bromley and their son who was entered in the articles of the ship as a boy at 1s od a month wages. Ralph had a separate berth and Captain Bromley was asked to 'insist on his studying this voyage. He will have some books with him – and he can pursue what he has already learned at school – if you oblige him to study two or three hours per day. I also want him to practice his music.' In another letter after details of books that Ralph would be taking had been listed he wrote:

I should like him to learn shorthand if your son will be good enough to assist him – also if the French sailmaker will talk to him in French every day for a short time. Spanish and German I think he will scarcely have time for as his writing and grammar should occupy a great part of his attention.

The *Wavertree* enters New York on 11 August 1970, escorted by several vessels and watched by many people, on her way to her new berth at South Street Seaport Museum.

SOUTH STREET SEAPORT MUSEUM

Building the top for the main lower mast.

The major operation of stepping the mainmast.

Leyland also made arrangements for his son in Calcutta. He wrote to the agents for the company there asking about a trip to Darjeeling 'to escape the possibility of fever on river. He has already been round the world and is fairly robust.' He returned with the ship to Antwerp on 4 July 1901 under Captain Peterson.

George Peterson, who was mate on the *Wavertree* was appointed master in March 1900. The ship was at Antwerp in September 1901 and back in Falmouth in August 1903. He seems to have been an unsuccessful master and in charge of an unhappy ship. In consequence he was relieved of his command in 1903 when he returned to England. Shortly after the return of the ship, a seaman named Way sued the company for wages due to him. Apparently this seaman had signed on in San Francisco on a voyage to Port Elizabeth and Bahia Blanca. On this voyage the food was found to be unsatisfactory and the men were dissatisfied. At Bahia Blanca the master offered to discharge the men if they wished, but this it was alleged, was due to the low rate of pay at this port which was £3 10s 0d. Nine men were discharged including Way. Peterson made out a wages account for him and deducted £23 for alleged damages in the galley. He then offered £20 in settlement, which was contrary to the Merchant Shipping Act, and Way refused this lower amount. He eventually accepted £25 but the money never came and the ship left port without him. A boarding house master offered him some money and took his kit as security. He then worked his passage home.

His counsel maintained that since he had not been properly discharged he was entitled to his wages right through to then but as the amount would have been more than £50 it was reduced to £49 10s, so as to come within the jurisdiction of the court. R W Leyland had given him personally £3 10s in Liverpool to help him.

In his defence Peterson said that Way was a deserter, had worked in a drinking saloon and had refused to rejoin the ship. He entered him in the log as a deserter but offered him £25 which he failed to pay because he did not have enough money. He maintained that they were all deserters, even if the mate gave evidence which suggested that they were not, and that he entered these additional payments as balance of wages due, rather than gratuities to deserters, and in fact as deserters they were not really entitled to any money. The defence abandoned their case on the evidence of the mate and were obliged to pay Way £49 10s. The company dismissed the captain from their employment.

Difficult Times

This visit to Falmouth and later to Newcastle, where she left with an outward cargo on 9 February 1904 bound for San Francisco, was the *Wavertree*'s last visit to European waters for nearly five years, before she was laid up at Ellesmere Port at the end of 1908. During this time, shipping suffered a depression with little workable home trade and low freights. It was difficult for the managers to maintain the vessel financially and from such a distance repairs to the ship were neglected as George Spiers' account reveals:

> During these long fine spells, there was plenty of work done. The light suit of sails were bent and I could see that much of the gear aboard was of poor quality and condition, and that although the ship was good to see when loaded, and at anchor with her beautiful sheer, painted ports, and all white masts and yards, yet the running gear was not in very good order.

She continued to have her share of disasters and misadventures. Although it is largely dismissed in Spiers' account, the *Wavertree* went aground on Desdemona Sands at the mouth of the Columbia River on 19 November 1907. She had been en route to Portland from Tocopilla, Chile when she dragged her anchors. She was there for a considerable time, before tugs succeeded in getting her off and escorting her to Young's Bay for repairs. Spiers seems to indicate that this stranding was short-lived which seems unlikely from the photographs that were taken. The owners were not told of this incident and the costs of the rescue were paid from the ship's disbursements and in consequence, Spiers' journey in the ship was an unhappy one.

With these low freights for sailing vessels Leyland in 1906 contemplated selling some of the sailing vessels and the *Wavertree* was valued at £6000. In January 1909 when the management of the fleet was taken over by J H Welsford & Company, the vessel was laid up at Ellesmere Port and valued at only £3500. She had been rammed by a steamer in 1908, and therefore missed her cargo. She lay at Ellesmere Port throughout 1909.

Wavertree Sold

On 31 March 1910 she was sold to Ernest Harry Neal, a merchant in Hertfordshire. He sold her on 11 May 1910 to J and A Brown for £2875. In C W Kellock's advertisement it stated that she had passed her special survey No 2 in 1908, when she was dry docked, painted and the rudder rebushed. This was the last work done on her before she was sold.

On 26 May 1910 under her new owner, the *Wavertree* set sail on what was to be her final voyage. She had obtained a cargo of coal from Cardiff for Valparaiso but the voyage was probably intended as a one way passage around Cape Horn to end up as a breakwater in Chile. However, this was never to be for she was beaten by Cape Horn and she had to return to Montevideo for repairs. She tried and failed again but was able to turn back to the Falkland Islands, 300 miles down wind with five of her crew severely injured and three with broken legs. She arrived off Port Stanley harbour on 7 December 1910. Captain Irving, aged 64 at this time, tried to bargain for a tow into harbour but without success. Eventually one side or the other gave way and she was towed into shelter on Christmas Eve by the tug *Samson*.

She had been dismasted by winds of hurricane force, and water had poured into her through ruptured decks. Her hull was as sound as ever but her rigging was rotten or poorly repaired. She was destined never to sail again. It would have been impossible to have her repaired in the Falkland Islands and anyway far too costly. On 30 April 1911 she was sold and towed to Punta Arenas. Here, in the Straits of Magellan, and in company with many other hulks which had not survived as square-rigged vessels, she lay for 37 years, being used to store and carry bales of wool from the sheep farms of the Menendez family.

In January 1948 she was towed to Buenos Aires by the Chilian steamer *Arica*, apparently to be broken up. However, reprieve came at the last minute and she was converted into a sand barge. Her hatches were greatly enlarged and sand bins built down below the tween deck to expose the interior structure of the ship. Her bowsprit, forecastle head and house and the remaining bulwarks were cut away.

She changed ownership again, but she was not entirely forgotten in maritime circles. For instance in the 3 May 1951 issue of *Shipbuilding and Shipping Record* Ian McLaren of Buenos Aires wrote a letter which was given the title 'Southampton Built Windjammer'. It referred to the *Wavertree* being in a shipyard in Buenos Aires and it read:

> Although I have been over this ship various times during the last 6 months, it was only recently that I came across the bronze builder's plate which has been unshipped by somebody and stowed in one of the aft cabins. This plate gave the name of the builders and also the fact that the

> number given to her by her builders was 231 and the year 1886. Her roving days are probably over now as she is being fitted out as a sand deposit hulk, with a large sand tank in her hold and two lines of dredging buckets driven through suitable gearings by diesel engines. I understand she will be moored in the River Plate.

This was followed by letters, published in the two subsequent issues, from Frank C Bowen and K C Barnaby over the numbering of the vessel. There was also a letter about this time from Captain Harry Daniel who was the Houlder Line Superintendent at Montevideo. Of all seafaring folk in South America in the area of Montevideo and Buenos Aires, he had the greatest knowledge of the whereabouts of the remaining sailing ships that had once gone round Cape Horn. In 1956, in a letter to Karl Kortum of the San Francisco Maritime Museum about the captains and men connected with the *Balclutha*, he had mentioned that there were 'some old sailing ship hulls still in service in the River Plate.' A year later in 1957, Captain Daniel had written an article for the Melbourne Annual *Dog Watch* entitled 'The Bay of Dead Ships'. In this he mentioned that the *Wavertree* had replaced the *County of Kinross* as a sand barge in the Parana River.

However it was not until 1966 that Karl Kortum was able to follow up further enquiries about the *Wavertree* and indeed by this stage he was uncertain whether she still existed. He went to the Falkland Islands to look at the *Great Britain* and found that she was salvagable. Then he returned to Montevideo and crossed the Rio de la Plata to Buenos Aires. Over the next few days he spoke to many people and travelled along the Riachuela. Few people could help or advise him over the question of whether a large sailing ship of the type he was looking for still existed inland in any backwater. He was almost at the end of his searches and thinking of abandoning his project when turning a bend in the river he saw the *Wavertree* for the first time: 'Black hulled, deep sheered, fore and mizzen lower masts still in place. Clamshell buckets were clanging in her hatches. She was in use, cared for, in a way alive. And big.' He had found the *Wavertree* and these exciting moments he has described elsewhere.

South Street Seaport

Meanwhile in New York the newly created South Street Seaport Museum was urgently looking for an

Logs arriving in New York to be used eventually as topmasts for the *Wavertree*.

The main deck during restoration showing her lower masts in place.

appropriate vessel that would symbolise the nineteenth century age of sail when South Street was known throughout the world as 'the street of ships'. The *Wavertree* had, in fact, visited New York once in 1895. On 25 November 1968 South Street Seaport was able to acquire the *Wavertree* for their museum. Peter Stanford who was the President of the Museum, Rudolf Shaefer, and in particular Jakob Isbrandtsen, Chairman of the Museum, were notable among those dedicated to saving the *Wavertree* and it was the latter's generous gift of the ship that enabled her to be brought to South Street once it had been established that she could be restored.

The *Wavertree* was dry docked for repairs to the hull to make her seaworthy at the Arsenal Naval, Buenos Aires. However it was not until 3 July 1970 that, the work having been completed, she was able to leave Argentina for New York in tow of the tug *Titan*. On 5 August she arrived at Staten Island, New York. Here attractive exhibits describing the Leyland fleet were fitted on her main deck. Six days later on 11 August, with a number of guests on board, she made the final six mile stretch of her triumphant journey to her berth at the South Street Seaport Museum. Between her fore and mizzen lower masts she was draped with bunting, fluttering in the morning sunlight. The two-masted schooner yacht *America* accompanied the *Wavertree* and she was joined by tugs, fireboats and helicopters. There were several ceremonies on her arrival, including an address by Mrs John V Lindsay, the wife of the mayor.

Many of the fittings of the *Wavertree*, both on deck and below, together with her rigging had long since disappeared. Oswald Brett, however, who was on board the vessel for her last six miles to South Street wrote a description of the saloon as he found it then. He said that the saloon is:

> Under the whaleback poop, reached by a long alleyway on the port side. Between this alleyway and the port side there are six cabins, little altered with the passage of time. Forward is the mate's, then a two-berth cabin for the 2nd and 3rd mate, the steward's room, pantry, and aft are two spares. On the other side of this alleyway, forward, is a narrow fore and aft mess room with a mizzen mast in the fore part. Under the side benches, alongside the table, in her lime juice days, were pigeon holes for the signal flags. Abaft this mess room, access to the poop is gained by a small, wooden, spiral companionway. Under the starboard side of the poop is a large store room. The saloon itself is in an excellent state of preservation when one considers that it has been in constant use since 1885, but now lacks chairs for the cabin table. The marble top sideboard and dresser are both fine pieces and one is still fitted with beautiful mirrors. The cabin skylight above imparted a soft, luminous, diffused light to

the saloon furniture evoking a mood of Victorian elegance to this apartment.

He went on to describe the bare wood settee that followed the curve of the counter which at one time had been upholstered with red plush cushions. He also mentioned the stanchion at the end of the cabin table that served as a stand for pikes to repel boarding pirates in Eastern waters, should she ever be attacked, for it should be remembered she was built for the jute trade. Under the rudder locker there was also a stand for swords.

Restoration

However, since the *Wavertree* arrived in New York she has had mixed fortunes and one could almost write a history of the last 15 years, in which many people have worked in order to return her to her former glory. Despite all, she has survived the many problems and still stands prominently berthed at the museum.

In the years until 1979 her poop deck was rebuilt, a steel deck constructed, and much of her standing rigging was raised. All this had required much painstaking work, for several years under the guidance and supervision of Richard Fewtrell. Fourteen tons of fittings from the later Leyland vessel, *Riversdale*, were given by Crown Zellerbach, amongst many other donations. There were also several discoveries, such as the *Wavertree*'s cutter which had been in Port Stanley since the ship arrived there in 1910. It was brought to New York in exchange for a diesel launch, *Captain Archie* which arrived in the Falklands in the summer of 1975.

At that time the poop deck was being dismantled and almost all the planking removed. The work required numerous drawings and photographs to record all the details. It was found that the many stringers and much of the shelf plating would have to be renewed in steel. At about the same time, work was started on the forestay, which was the beginning of the permanent standing rigging. They also salvaged many of the deck beams from the iron ship *Conemaugh*, as well as repairing the steering gear which had been damaged in the spring of 1973. By early in 1977, the poop deck was virtually completed. During the previous winter months, they had refitted the taffrail, and installed teak pillars at the break of the poop along with the necessary brass work and handrails.

After much discussion it was decided to try to get the *Wavertree* dry docked, so that the work could be done on sand blasting the hull, and repainting her bottom. Early in May 1978 the ship was towed to Bethlehem Steel Corporation's shipyard at Hoboken, New Jersey and the work was started. This was made possible by a substantial grant from the National Trust of Historic Preservation as well as a further sum from the W R Grace Foundation. This money allowed work to be carried on with the maintenance and rigging of the ship as well as obtaining the necessary gear to step the masts.

In the same year the historical significance of the *Wavertree* was officially recognised when she was listed in the Register of Historic Places. However in 1979, the money for the restoration of the *Wavertree* finally ran out, and she was closed completely to visitors.

But once again help came along, for in October 1980 the American Ship Trust decided to devote its energies to the restoration of the *Wavertree* and in November of the same year, the launching of the World Ship Trust in London greeted this decision favourably. At about the same time Prince Philip, President of England's

The *Wavertree* – starboard side.
SOUTH STREET SEAPORT MUSEUM

Wavertree in dry dock at Buenos Aires undergoing repairs before her journey to New York.
SOUTH STREET SEAPORT MUSEUM

The *Wavertree* converted to a sand barge.
SOUTH STREET SEAPORT MUSEUM

Maritime Trust, visited the ship and was most impressed with the work that was being done to restore her. The National Society's Ship Trust then called upon Jakob Isbrandtsen and Allen Rupley of W R Grace & Company to serve as co-chairmen of the Ship Trust Committee. The idea was to bring new life to the project and by working with volunteers and often with donated material to try and complete the restoration of the *Wavertree*.

In 1981 there were 10 weeks of extensive work on the upper deck of the *Wavertree* when 110ft of the deck was restored to its original configuration. Much of the work was done by the Bethlehem Steel Corporation shipyard at Hoboken, New Jersey. At the same time it was possible for Alexander Boyt at the shipyard to determine the size of the missing deckhouse by spotting the boundary bar of the house plating, and this showed that the house was 32ft long, and not 40ft as had been assumed for many years. Thereafter the location and the size of hatches was determined by finding the original rivet holes, where the original tie plates were located. Deck beams, formed to the ship's camber, were placed every 4ft from forward to aft of the ship. Originally the decks had been supported by a series of pillars along the centre line, but with the lower deck missing, the shipyard installed a system of girders. When funds are available the lower deck can be reconstructed, and the pillar support system can be re-introduced to the ship.

Bethlehem Steel made a gift of the administration work it did in connection with the yard work, McAllister Brothers towed her to and from Hoboken 'for free', and Georgia Pacific donated 67,000 board feet of yellow pine for the deck. Work done at the Hoboken yard included the installation and rigging of a new steel bowsprit, built for *Wavertree* on Long Island, and the restoration of the hatches to their original size. After the main deck had been re-planked, the ship's company started to rebuild the forward deckhouse which served as the living quarters of the seamen and petty officers. The replacement of missing rigging and spars, and the restoration and furnishing of the officers quarters would be done later.

So on 4 June 1983 the *Wavertree* was opened to the public once more, with the restoration incomplete but the ship's company in good spirits. The volunteers had worked every Saturday and on other occasions for some considerable time to produce these results. It is Isbrandtsen and the ship's company that deserve the

▲
After purchase by the South Street Seaport Museum, the *Wavertree* was towed to dry dock in Buenos Aires.
SOUTH STREET SEAPORT MUSEUM

Karl Kortum found *Wavertree* in a backwater of the Riachuela in 1966.
SOUTH STREET SEAPORT MUSEUM
▼

praise for all the recent work on the *Wavertree*. It is through Isbrandtsen and his no-nonsense attitude that the restoration of the *Wavertree* has finally got moving. It is his ability as both a manager and trader, keeping volunteers hard at work and donations coming into the project, which has kept the restoration going. Clearly the *Wavertree* means a great deal to all these people. It has an individual meaning to different people and no doubt each volunteer, in his or her way takes something out of it. The *Wavertree* has a noble and inspiring presence and it is difficult not to be moved by her.

The American Ship Trust has on several occasions put forward that the restoration of a ship is a major investment, in that restoring a ship involves finding out something of ourselves which is precious and needs to be learned by each new generation. Perhaps in this case it is the ability and imagination to conceive great voyages and to see them succeed. Certainly the *Wavertree* makes us aware of our great maritime past that existed before the advent of the engine-powered freighters and tankers that we now know so well. There were just natural forces behind these sailing vessels and the *Wavertree* remains a link between two eras, in that she was made of iron in imitation of the modern boats of her time but with wood boat technology. She is thus a product of our past and even in her restoration we can learn something of ourselves and something of the quality of life in the latter days of sail.

The *Wavertree*'s long boat found in the Falkland Islands (still in use) is now restored to her original place in the ship.

The ship's bell, inscribed with the *Wavertree*'s original name, *Southgate*.
SOUTH STREET SEAPORT MUSEUM

APPENDICES

APPENDIX I: SPECIFICATIONS OF LEYLAND SHIPS

Dimensions are given in feet and inches. Registered tonnage figures are given in the following order: gross tonnage/under deck tonnage/net tonnage.

Aigburth
Built 1882 by R Williamson & Son, Workington. Iron ship. Tonnage: 1838/1717/1798. Dimensions: 266.7 × 39.0 × 23.6. Wrecked Rook Island, New Guinea 2 August 1904 on voyage Newcastle NSW to Sourabaya.

Allerton
Built 1884 by Oswald, Mordaunt & Co, Southampton. Iron ship. Tonnage: 2080/1936/2028. Dimensions: 272.7 × 40.1 × 24.6. 1910 sold to Chile for £2600 and converted into a hulk in Valparaiso, Chile.

British India
Built 1864 by Laird Bros, Birkenhead. Iron ship. Tonnage: 1199/1136/1199. Dimensions: 207.2 × 35.2 × 22.2. Original name was *Sorabjee Jamsetjee Jeejeebhoy*, owned by J Parsons of Liverpool. 1867 sold to British Shipowners Company and renamed *British India*. 1881 bought by Leyland 2 March 1894 abandoned on fire off Madeira, on passage Leith to Rio de Janeiro.

Chile
Built 1856 by C Lungley, London. Iron barque. Tonnage: 777/746/739. Dimensions: 182.0 × 28.4 × 21.1. Originally a brig-rigged screw steamer built for Seymour & Co's South America run. 1859 engines removed; converted to a full-rigged ship. 1860–80 journeys to Australia and New Zealand. 1867 sold to Shaw, Savill & Co. 1877 converted to barque. 1880 bought by J F Gibb, London. 1881 bought by Leyland. 10 September 1892 destroyed by fire, two days after leaving Iquique, with the crew in open mutiny.

Cressington
Built 1883 by Oswald, Mordaunt & Co, Southampton. Iron ship. Tonnage: 2211/2058/2160. Dimensions: 289.5 × 40.4 × 24.5. 1900 sold to Edmund & William Roberts, Liverpool for £11,000. 1902 sold to Repetto Bros, Genoa, Italy for £9750. 1913 sold to S O Stray, Christiansand, Norway for £5650, renamed *Songvand*. 1916 sold for £21,000. 4 June 1917 sunk by submarine off Scilly Isles on passage Cardiff to Santon.

Ditton
Built 1891 by T R Oswald & Co, Milford Haven. Steel ship. Tonnage: 2901/2689/2850. Dimensions: 311.0 × 42.3 × 25.7. Main skysail yarder. Bridge amidships. 17 April 1902 triple collision with *Port Crawford* and *Peebleshire* at Newcastle NSW. 1911 sold to C Bech, Tvedestrand, Norway, renamed *Nordfarer*. 1917 sold to Christiansand Ship Co, Christiansand, Norway, renamed *Bragdo*. 2 November 1921 wrecked at Boobjerg on voyage Liverpool to Norway.

Doxford
Built 1868 by W Doxford & Sons, Sunderland. Iron barque. Tonnage: 709/668/682. Dimensions: 178.0 × 29.8 × 19.4. 1878 bought by Leyland. 1903 bought by Indische Handels Co, Batavia and renamed *Henriette Haasman*. 1909 stranded and removed from register. 1915 reappears as schooner barge owned by Texas Co of Port Arthur, named *Ida*. 1917 owned by Cuban Molasses Co, Havana as schooner barge *Panuco*, carrying molasses in bulk. Afloat 1925.

Fulwood
Built 1885 by Oswald, Mordaunt & Co, Southampton. Iron ship. Tonnage: 2170/2014/2118. Dimensions: 279.0 × 40.2 × 24.4. Sistership to *Wavertree*. 1910 sold to P Bogen, Sandefjord, Norway for £3000. Employed as a floating oil refinery, between UK and South Georgia. 1917 resold to Akt Glenesk, Sandefjord. 1919 went missing on a passage from Buenos Aires to Korsor.

Garston
Built 1883 by R Williamson & Son, Workington. Steel ship. Tonnage: 1852/1733/1812. Dimensions: 267.0 × 39.1 × 23.6. 1889 lost on Starbuck Island on passage Newcastle NSW to San Francisco.

Gitana
Built 1861 by N Cox, Chester. Iron ship. Tonnage: 1367/1331/1367. Dimensions: 220.5 × 36.0 × 24.9. Originally owned by Moore & Co, Liverpool. 1870 owned by E Bates & Sons. 1881 bought by Leyland. April 1896 abandoned off Cape Horn on passage Iquique to Hamburg in a dismasted sinking condition.

***Grassendale* (I)**
Built 1882 by R Williamson & Son, Workington. Tonnage: 1842/1720/1800. Dimensions: 266.5 × 39.1 × 23.6. First ship built by Williamson after moving from Harrington. 17 May 1884 left New York on a passage to Shanghai with petroleum and went missing.

***Grassendale* (II)**
Built 1885 by R Williamson & Son, Workington. Iron ship. Tonnage: 1860/1727/1819. Dimensions: 267.0 × 39.1 × 23.6. 1900 sold to G Granlund, of Raumo, Finland for £10,000, renamed *Imperator Alexander II*. 1907 sold to F Lehtinen, Raumo. 1917 owned by N Panelius, Raumo. 1919 sold to S Loftman, Stockholm, Sweden and renamed *Ernst*. April 1920 lost in Hertha Flack Minefield.

Halewood
Built 1885 by Oswald, Mordaunt & Co, Southampton. Iron ship. Tonnage: 2153/1998/2100. Dimensions: 274.3 × 40.1 × 24.9. 16 October 1902 in collision in San Francisco Bay when SS *Quito* of Greenock struck the hull of the ship abaft the main rigging port side causing damage to plates. 1910 sold to A J Grefstad, Christiansand, Norway for £3175. 1914 sold to S O Stray, Christiansand, Norway for £4400 and renamed *Songvig*. 14 February 1920 lost on Skerries; supposed struck a mine.

King Cenric
Built 1874 by J K Dunlop, St John, New Brunswick. Wood ship. Tonnage: 1519/1387/1490. Dimensions: 208.5 × 39.3 × 24.0. 1885 bought by Leyland. 1889 sold to Bruusgaard, Kjosterud & Co, Drammen, Norway. 1903 wrecked in Mossel Bay.

Leyland Brothers
Built 1886 by Oswald, Mordaunt & Co, Southampton. Iron ship. Tonnage: 2291/2143/2238. Dimensions: 284.0 × 40.0 × 24.2. 27 April 1908 to 26 June 1910 laid up at Portland (Oregon). 1912 sold to Portuguese for £6000 and renamed *Empreza Nacional*. Post First World War converted to hulk. 1941–44 converted to motor cargo ship, renamed *Nacala*. 1967 scrapped.

Liverpool
Built 1889 by Russell & Co, Port Glasgow. Iron four-masted ship. Tonnage: 3400/3224/3330. Dimensions: 333.2 × 47.9 × 26.5. 25 February 1902 wrecked off Alderney, Channel Islands, on voyage Antwerp to San Francisco.

Londos
Built 1860 by Richardson Duck & Co, Stockton on Tees. Steel screw steamer. Tonnage: 283/268/174. Dimensions: 159.2 × 22.7 × 9.8. 1888 owned by J M Mordaunt. 1889 sold to Leyland. 1890 sold to Osborn Wallis.

Nelson
Built 1862 by Hill, Glasgow. Iron ship. Tonnage: 1333/1176/1248. Dimensions: 214.4 × 36.2 × 22.9. Owned by Potter, Wilson & Son. 1864 bought by British Shipowners Co, Liverpool. 1880 bought by Leyland. 25 October 1895 abandoned in sinking condition off Schouwen.

Otterspool
Built 1884 by Palmers Co, Newcastle. Iron ship. Tonnage: 1850/1752/1798. Dimensions: 266.5 × 39.4 × 23.5. 5 November 1900 burnt at Caldera.

Planet Mars
Built 1900 by Northumberland SB Co Ltd, Newcastle. Steel screw steamer. Tonnage: 4320/4130/2820. Dimensions: 360.0 × 48.0 × 28.2. Engines by Wallsend Slipway Co Ltd, Newcastle. Under J H Welsford & Co renamed *Ikaria*. Out of Register 1916/17.

Planet Mercury
Built 1894 by Workman, Clark & Co, Belfast. Steel screw steamer. Tonnage: 3223/3035/2092. Dimensions: 335.0 × 43.7 × 18.4. Engines by Workman Clark & Co. Went missing February 1900.

Planet Neptune
Built 1901 by Napier & Miller Ltd, Glasgow. Steel screw steamer. Tonnage: 4322/4037/2821. Dimensions: 385.1 × 48.7 × 27.0. Engines by Dunsmuir & Jackson, Glasgow. Renamed *Ikala* by J H Welsford & Co; later sold to G Gavarone of Genoa, Italy and called *Sanzorzu*. Out of Register 1934/35.

***Planet Venus* (I)**
Built 1894 by W Hamilton & Co, Port Glasgow. Steel screw steamer. Tonnage: 3689/3459/2378. Dimensions: 350.7 × 43.1 × 19.0. Engines by D Rowan & Son, Glasgow. 1896/97 sold to J Holman & Sons and renamed *Birchtor*.

***Planet Venus* (II)**
Built 1900 by Napier & Miller, Glasgow. Steel screw steamer. Tonnage: 4329/4059/2820. Dimensions: 385.0 × 48.7 × 27.0. Engines by Dunsmuir & Jackson, Glasgow. Under J H Welsford & Co renamed *Ikalis*. Out of Register 1919/20.

Riversdale
Built 1894 by W Hamilton & Co, Port Glasgow. Steel ship. Tonnage: 2206/2065/2113. Dimensions: 275.8 × 41.9 × 24.2. 1910 sold to Schluyter & Mack, Hamburg; renamed *Harveshude*. Interned at Santa Rosalia throughout First World War and then run by Dollar Line. 1924 bought by Coastwise SS Co, Vancouver BC for a barge and renamed *Riversdale*. 1935 resold to Island Tug and Barge Co, Victoria BC. Later owned by Crown Zellerbach, before finally being used as a breakwater at Royston, Vancouver from 1961.

Roby
Built 1887 by Oswald, Mordaunt & Co, Southampton. Iron ship. Tonnage: 2293/2144/2239. Dimensions: 284.0 × 40.1 × 24.1. 1889 bought by Leyland (ex *Jubilee*) from T R Oswald. 1900 burnt at sea.

San Luis
Built 1864 by T Royden & Sons, Liverpool. Iron barque. Tonnage: 600/576/591. Dimensions: 171.2 × 27.8 × 17.7. 1879 bought from J M Gladstone. 1889 sold to H Bauer, Rostock, Germany; renamed *Hulda*.

Speke
Built 1891 by T R Oswald & Co, Milford Haven. Steel ship. Tonnage: 2875/2663/2824. Dimensions: 310.3 × 42.2 × 25.6. February 1906 on passage, Peru to Melbourne, in ballast, went ashore on Phillip Island, Victoria and became a total loss.

Thomas Hamlin
Built 1851 by Coutts & Parkinson, Newcastle. Iron barque. Tonnage: 732/671/688. Dimensions: 161.0 × 30.1 × 20.0. Owned by Hamlin & Co, Greenock and sold to P Webster, Scarborough. 1879 bought by Leyland. May 1893 sold to G MacLearie, Port Glasgow and broken up on the Clyde.

Toxteth
Built 1887 by Oswald, Mordaunt & Co, Southampton. Iron ship. Tonnage: 2595/2422/2526. Dimensions: 305.5 × 41.7 × 24.4. 1908 went missing on passage Port Talbot to Tocopilla.

Twilight
Built 1855 by R Napier & Sons, Glasgow. Iron barque. Tonnage: 631/607/631. Dimensions: 167.3 × 30.0 × 20.0. 1882 bought from E Bates & Sons. 1896 sold to Marine Association Co, Port Talbot; January 1897 broken up.

Wavertree
Built 1885 by Oswald, Mordaunt & Co, Southampton. Iron ship. Tonnage: 2170/2014/2118. Dimensions: 279.0 × 40.2 × 24.4. 1888 bought from Chadwick & Pritchard and named *Wavertree*. 1910 sold to J & A Brown. December 1910 put into Falkland Islands dismasted, on passage Cardiff to Valparaiso. 1911 onwards, used as a wool storage hulk at Punta Arenas, Chile. 1948 sand bins installed. 1968 acquired by South Street Seaport Museum.

Woolton
Built 1885 by Oswald, Mordaunt & Co, Southampton. Iron ship. Tonnage: 2152/1998/2101. Dimensions: 274.3 × 40.1 × 24.9. 14 June 1893 left Newcastle NSW for Valparaiso and went missing.

The second *Grassendale* built in 1885 by Oswald, Mordaunt & Co, was sold to Gabr Granlund & Co of Raumo, Finland, in 1900 and renamed *Imperator Alexander II* (seen here).
NATIONAL MARITIME MUSEUM

The *Fulwood* is seen here as an oil refinery vessel. She went missing with all hands in 1919, on a passage from Buenos Aires to Korsor.

George Campbell's reconstruction of *Wavertree*'s probable sail plan and rigging.
SOUTH STREET SEAPORT MUSEUM

APPENDIX II: CONTRACT FOR *RIVERSDALE*

It is agreed this first day of November 1893. between MESSIEURS WILLIAM HAMILTON AND COMPANY, Shipbuilders, Port Glasgow, and MESSIEURS R. W. LEYLAND AND COMPANY, Shipowners, Liverpool, that the latter purchase from the former (for a Company to be formed by Messrs R. W. Leyland and Company, to take over the vessel, and such Company to be named the Sailing Ship Riversdale Company, Limited) a Steel Sailing Ship now building by Messrs William Hamilton and Company, and Numbered 105. in their Books, and of the following particulars, 'Viz' – Registered dimensions about 276.8 × 42′ × 24.2. Gross Register tonnage about 2200. and to carry about 3800. tons total deadweight, including Stores, on Board of Trade freeboard in salt water.

The price to be paid by Messrs R. W. Leyland and Company for the said Ship, completed to the Specification signed by both parties as relative hereto, and according to the Plans approved by Mr R. W. Leyland yesterday, to be Seventeen thousand two hundred pounds, stg. (£17.200.)

Not less than Eight thousand pounds, stg. (£8000.) of this amount to be paid to Messrs William Hamilton and Company, in cash, on or before delivery of the vessel; but if more than this sum shall be taken up in the Company referred to, then such additional sum shall be paid to Messrs William Hamilton and Company, in cash, as above. Any balance (not more than Nine thousand two hundred pounds, stg.) remaining unpaid on delivery of the Vessel, shall be paid in Eight equal three monthly instalments from time of delivery or within two years in all from delivery.

For such balance Messrs R. W. Leyland and Company shall grant their acceptances to Messrs William Hamilton and Company; and as security for the due payment of such Bills – fully paid up Shares in the Company for the amount of such Bills, shall be handed to Messrs William Hamilton and Company by Messrs R. W. Leyland and Company. Messrs William Hamilton and Company to transfer back to Messrs R. W. Leyland and Company, or their order, as each instalment of deferred amount is paid, an amount of shares equal to such instalment until all is finally wiped off.

Such acceptances to be made payable in London, and cost of Bill Stamps and Interest at the rate of five per centum per annum on the amount of such acceptances from time to time shall be paid by Messrs R. W. Leyland and Company to Messrs William Hamilton and Company, in cash, in advance in each case as the Bills are drawn, as well as the cost of any transfer duty on the Shares; but should Messrs R. W. Leyland and Company pay any sum or sums on account of such Bills during their currency, Bills to a corresponding amount to be returned to them on such payments, together with rebate of interest at the rate of five per centum per annum – less the charges made by the Bank.

Approved policies of insurance on the Ship to cover any amount so due on Bills – to be handed to Messrs William Hamilton and Company and held by them until the Bills are paid off.

For each deadweight ton which the said Ship shall be proved to carry less than a total deadweight, including Stores, of 3775. tons, on Board of Trade freeboard in salt water, Messrs William Hamilton and Company, shall allow to Messrs R. W. Leyland and Company a pro rata reduction from the Contract price.

Messrs William Hamilton and Company bind themselves to the conditions of the foregoing contract up to the Eighteenth day of November next for the purpose of giving Messrs R. W. Leyland and Company an opportunity of floating the Company, it being agreed that if on or before that date the sum of Eight thousand pounds shall have been subscribed this Contract shall become of full force and effect on both parties; but should the aforesaid sum of Eight thousand pounds not be subscribed by the date before named then Messrs R. W. Leyland and Company to have the option of cancelling this Contract.

BIBLIOGRAPHY AND NOTES ON SOURCES

MANUSCRIPTS AND PLANS

Leyland Papers in Author's Collection

Vol 1 1880–1893 Private Letters
Vol 2 1894–1908 Private Letters
Vol 3 1884–1897 Upton Manor Letters
Vol 4 1895–1906 Mrs R W Leyland Trust
Vol 5 Miscellaneous Collection of Letters and Company Papers
Vol 6 Estate of R Leyland
Vol 7 1892 Diary

National Maritime Museum. Plans of Merchant Ships; Lubbock Collection; Lloyd's Register Survey Reports; E Bates & Co private letters; C W Kellock & Co collection.

Public Record Office. Ships' Official Logs; Files of Dissolved Companies

Private Collections. J H Reid; R M Cookson; A A Hurst

University of Glasgow. Robert Napier & Sons; Lithgows Ltd

South Street Seaport Museum, New York

SS *Great Britain* Project

Devon Record Office. R Dale's diary

NEWSPAPERS

Argus (Melbourne)
Birkenhead News
Hampshire Independent
Law Reports
Liverpool Courier
Liverpool Fairplay
Liverpool Daily Post
Liverpool Weekly Mercury
Lloyds Weekly Summary
New York Times
Shipping Gazette Weekly Summary
The Everton Journal
The Express
The Glasgow Herald
The Journal of Commerce
The Liverpool Review
The Liverpool Star
The Porcupine
Wallasey Guardian

PERIODICALS

The Mariner's Mirror (London, since 1912)
Sea Breezes (Liverpool, since 1919)
Sea History (New York)
South Street Reporter now called *Seaport* (New York)
Shipbuilding and Shipping Record (London)

BOOKS

BARNABY, K C, *A Hundred Years of Specialized Shipbuilding*

BEHREND, ARTHUR, *Portrait of a Family Firm. Bahr, Behrend & Co 1793–1945* (Liverpool 1970)

BRETTLE, ROBERT E, *The 'Cutty Sark', Her Designer and Builder, Hercules Linton* (Cambridge 1969)

BROWNE, R G M, *The Statute Law of Merchant Shipping 1821–1888* (London 1889)

CHANDLER, GEORGE, *Liverpool Shipping, A Short History* (London 1960)

DAVIES, PETER N, *Sir Alfred Jones Shipping Entrepreneur Par Excellence* (London 1978)

DOMVILLE FIFE, C W (edt), *Square Rigger Days* (London 1938)

FLETCHER, R A, *In the Days of the Tall Ships* (London 1928)

FORWOOD, SIR W B, *Reminiscences of a Liverpool Shipowner* (Liverpool 1920)

FOX SMITH, C, *Sailor Town Days* (London 1923)

HOLMES, JAMES W, *Voyaging* (London 1970)

LEYLAND, RALPH WATTS, *Round the World in 124 days* (Liverpool 1880)

LEYLAND, RALPH WATTS, *A Holiday in South Africa* (London 1882)

LLOYD'S REGISTER, *Lloyd's Register of British and Foreign Shipping* (London, annually since 1834)

LUBBOCK, BASIL, *The Last of the Windjammers* (Glasgow 1935, 2nd Ed, 2 Vols)

MATHIAS, P and PEARSALL, A W H, *A Survey of Historical Records* (Newton Abbot 1971)

MOYSE-BARTLETT, H, *From Sail to Steam* (London 1946)

NATIONAL MARITIME MUSEUM, *Problems of Ship Management and Operation 1870–1900* (Maritime Monographs and Reports No 5) (London 1972)

ORCHARD, B G, *Liverpool Exchange Portrait Gallery* (Liverpool 1884)

PAYNE, P L, *British Entrepreneurship in the Nineteenth Century* (London 1974)

PETRIE, SIR CHARLES, *The Victorians* (London 1960)

REGISTRAR GENERAL OF SHIPPING AND SEAMEN, *The Mercantile Navy List* (London, annually since before 1951)

RUSHTON, GERALD A, *Whistle up the Inlet* (Vancouver 1974)

SPIERS, A GEORGE, *The Wavertree; An Ocean Wanderer* (New York 1969)

VILLIERS, ALAN JOHN, *The Way of a Ship* (London 1954)

VILLIERS, ALAN JOHN, *The War with Cape Horn* (London 1971)

INDEX

Figures in italic refer to illustrations and their captions.

A

B

C

D

E

F

G

H

I

J

K

L

M

N

O

P

Q

R

S

T

U

V

W

Y

Z